65.00

D0 5

v 493
2005

Aging:
Lifestyles, Work,
and Money

Aging: Lifestyles, Work, and Money

Elizabeth Vierck and Kris Hodges

GREENWOOD PRESS
Westport, Connecticut • London

Library of Congress Cataloging-in-Publication Data

Vierck, Elizabeth, 1945–
    Aging : lifestyles, work, and money / Elizabeth Vierck and Kris Hodges.
        p. cm.
    Includes bibliographical references and index.
    ISBN 1–57356–548–2 (alk. paper)
    1. Older people—United States—Social conditions. 2. Older people—Employment—United States. 3. Older people—United States—Economic conditions. 4. Lifestyles—United States. I. Hodges, Kris. II. Title.
HQ1064.U5V493 2005
305.26′0973′021—dc22   2004053043

British Library Cataloguing in Publication Data is available.

Library of Congress Catalog Card Number: 2004053043
ISBN: 1–57356–548–2

First published in 2005

Greenwood Press, 88 Post Road West, Westport, CT 06881
An imprint of Greenwood Publishing Group, Inc.
www.greenwood.com

Printed in the United States of America

The paper used in this book complies with the Permanent Paper Standard issued by the National Information Standards Organization (Z39.48–1984).

10 9 8 7 6 5 4 3 2 1

To Craig
To Jeff, Ken, and Erik

Contents

List of Tables, Charts, and Figure   viii

Preface   xvi

Introductory Essay: The Typical Older American *by Elizabeth Vierck*   1

Lifestyles

CHAPTER 1   Marital Status, Living Arrangements, and Family Life   7

CHAPTER 2   Where the Elderly Live: Geographic Location and Mobility   15

CHAPTER 3   Transportation and Housing   32

CHAPTER 4   Community Life, Social Activity, and Leisure   55

CHAPTER 5   Crime and the Elderly   82

CHAPTER 6   Citizenship, Language, and Education   97

Work and Money

CHAPTER 7   Income and Poverty   113

CHAPTER 8   Finances—Assets, Savings, Debt, and Attitudes   133

CHAPTER 9   Consumer Spending   152

CHAPTER 10   Work and Retirement   180

CHAPTER 11   Social Security and Supplemental Security Income   201

APPENDIX A   World Records and Fascinating Facts   213

APPENDIX B   Resources in Aging Services, Gerontology, and Geriatrics   221

Glossary   266

Selected Bibliography and Useful Web Sites   287

Index   291

List of Tables, Charts, and Figures

CHAPTER 1 Marital Status, Living Arrangements, and Family Life

CHART 1.1 Marital Status of the Elderly: March 2002   *8*

CHART 1.2 Percent Widowed by Age and Sex: March 2002   *9*

CHART 1.3 Percent of Elderly Living in One- or Two-Person Households by Age: 2002   *11*

TABLE 1.1 Marital Status of the Population Aged 65+ by Age and Sex: March 2002   *9*

TABLE 1.2 Percent of Elderly Living Alone by Age and Sex: March 2002   *10*

TABLE 1.3 The Caregiving Relationships of Aged 60+ Whose Grandchildren Live with Them: 2000   *12*

CHAPTER 2 Where the Elderly Live: Geographic Location and Mobility

FIGURE 2.1 Percent of Population Aged 65+ by County or Equivalent Area   *18*

TABLE 2.1 The 65+ Population by State: 2000   *16*

TABLE 2.2 Counties Exceeding the U.S. Portion of Elderly, United States and Regions: 2000   *19*

TABLE 2.3 Top Ten Places with the Highest Portion of Elderly: 2000 (Places with Populations over 100,000)   *20*

TABLE 2.4 Places with the Lowest Portion of Elderly: 2000 (Places with Populations over 100,000)   *21*

TABLE 2.5 Percent of Elderly in the Ten Largest Cities: 2000   *21*

TABLE 2.6 General Mobility for the Elderly Population by Age and Sex: 1995 to 2000   *24*

TABLE 2.7 Inmigration, Outmigration, and Net Internal Migration, and Rate of Internal Migration (per 1,000) of the Elderly for the Population 65+ Years by Region, Division, State, and Age: 1995 to 2000   *25*

CHAPTER 3 Transportation and Housing

CHART 3.1 Percentage of Drivers by Health, Disability, Status, and Age, October 6, 1998, to January 8, 1999   *38*

CHART 3.2 Homeownership, by Age of the Household Reference Person: 2001   *41*

CHART 3.3 Mortgage Status among Homeowners, by Age of the Household Reference Person: 2001   *42*

CHART 3.4 Mortgage Status and Home Value by Income   *43*

CHART 3.5 Average Annual Expenditures for Home Improvements by Age: 1994 to 2001   *45*

CHART 3.6 Housing Cost Burdens of Very Low-Income Elderly   *47*

TABLE 3.1 Minutes and Miles Spent Driving Daily by Driver Age: 2001   *33*

TABLE 3.2 Automobile Attitudes of Those Owning a Vehicle, Percent Agreeing: 2002   *34*

TABLE 3.3 Passenger Vehicle Driver Deaths per 100,000 Licensed Drivers: 2002   *35*

TABLE 3.4 Percentage of Drivers Killed with Blood Alcohol Concentration (BAC) ≥0.08 by Age: 2002   *36*

TABLE 3.5 Pedestrian Deaths per 100,000 People by Older Age Group: 2002   *37*

TABLE 3.6 Mortgage Status and Home Market Value in Households with an Elderly Reference Person, by Region: 2000 to 2001   *43*

TABLE 3.7 Percent of 202 Housing Residents Having Difficulty Performing Various Activities, as Reported by Manager   *48*

CHAPTER 4 Community Life, Social Activity, and Leisure

CHART 4.1 Reported Voting and Registration among Age Groups: 2000   *57*

CHART 4.2 Club and Organization Membership, by Age and Sex: 2003   *58*

CHART 4.3 Volunteers by Median Annual Hours of Volunteer Activities: September 2002   *60*

CHART 4.4 Percent Participating in Particular Social Leisure Events in the Past 12 Months, by Age and Sex: 2003   *69*

CHART 4.5 Percent Participating in Particular Sport in the Past 12 Months, by Age and Sex: 2003   *73*

CHART 4.6 Percent Attending Particular Cultural Event in the Past 12 Months, by Age and Sex: 2003   *74*

CHART 4.7 Percent Playing Particular Game in the Past 12 Months, by Age and Sex: 2003   *75*

CHART 4.8 Percent Participating in Particular Hobby in the Past 12 Months, by Age and Sex: 2003   *76*

TABLE 4.1 Political and Community Involvement (Past Year), by Age: 2003   *56*

TABLE 4.2 Registration in Presidential Election Years by Age: November 1964 to 2000   *57*

TABLE 4.3 Percent of Elderly Volunteering by Age Group: September 2002   *59*

TABLE 4.4 Percent Volunteering by Age, Race, Ethnic Group, and Sex   *60*

TABLE 4.5 Hours Volunteers Work by Age   *61*

TABLE 4.6 Percent Distribution of Volunteers by Type of Organization: September 2002   *61*

TABLE 4.7 Past-Year Gambling Behavior, by Age: 2002   *64*

TABLE 4.8 Opinions about Computers and Technology, by Age: 2003   *64*

TABLE 4.9 Percent Having Various Type of Appliance, Electronic Product, or Service in Their Household: 2002   *65*

TABLE 4.10 Sources Used When Wanting to Communicate with Other People Verbally or in Writing, by Age: 2003   *66*

TABLE 4.11 Sources Used When Wanting to Be Informed on a Variety of Different Subjects: 2003   *66*

TABLE 4.12 Sections of Daily Newspaper Read, among Those Reading a Newspaper: 2003   *67*

TABLE 4.13 Sources Used When Wanting to Be Amused or Entertained, by Age: 2003   *67*

TABLE 4.14 Percent Viewing Particular Type of Television Show, by Age: 2003   *68*

TABLE 4.15 Restaurant Behavior and Attitudes: 2002   *70*

TABLE 4.16 Pet Ownership, by Age: 2003   *71*

TABLE 4.17 Men's Interest in Various Spectator Sports, Percent Interested: 2002   *72*

TABLE 4.18 Women's Interest in Various Spectator Sports, Percent Interested: 2002   *72*

TABLE 4.19 Past 12-Month Participation in Selected Vacation Activities: 2002   *77*

TABLE 4.20 Domestic and Foreign Travel Statistics, by Age: 2003   *78*

TABLE 4.21 Opinions about Travel (Agree Completely), by Age: 2002   *78*

TABLE 4.22 How Important Is Religion in Your Life?   *79*

TABLE 4.23 Religious Preference of Americans by Age Group   *80*

TABLE 4.24 Attendance at a Religious Institution   *80*

TABLE 4.25 Membership in Religious Institution   *80*

CHAPTER 5 Crime and the Elderly

CHART 5.1 Victimization Rates for Personal Crimes, Persons Aged 12 and Over: 2001   *84*

CHART 5.2 Percent Reporting Crimes to the Police, by Age: 2001   *87*

CHART 5.3 Items Stolen from Elderly Households, 1992–1997   *92*

TABLE 5.1 Personal Crime Victimization Rates for Persons Aged 12 and Over, by Types of Crime and Age of Victims: 2001   *84*

TABLE 5.2 Average Annual Rate (per 1,000) of Violent Crimes, by Age: 1999–2000 and 2001–2002   *85*

TABLE 5.3 Victimization Rates (per 1,000) of the Elderly, by Sex: 2001   *85*

TABLE 5.4 Victimization Rates (per 1,000) of the Elderly, by Race: 2001   *86*

TABLE 5.5 Property Crime Victimization Rates (per 1,000), by Age of Head of Household: 2001   *88*

TABLE 5.6 Purse Snatching and Pocket Picking: Place of Occurrence and Time of Day, by Age: 1992–1996   *89*

TABLE 5.7 Property Crime: Place of Occurrence and Time of Day, by Age: 1992–1997   *90*

TABLE 5.8 Average Annual Property Crime Rates per 1,000 Elderly-Headed Households: 1992–1997   *90*

TABLE 5.9 Sentenced Prisoners Aged 55+ under State and Federal Jurisdiction by Race, Hispanic Origin, and Age: 2002   *93*

CHAPTER 6 Citizenship, Language, and Education

CHART 6.1 World Region of Birth, by Age: March 2002   *99*

CHART 6.2 Educational Attainment of the Population, by Age and Sex: 2002   *102*

CHART 6.3 Earnings in 2001 by Educational Attainment of the Elderly, by Sex: March 2002   *104*

TABLE 6.1 Citizenship Status and Period of Entry, by Age: March 2002   *98*

TABLE 6.2 Language Spoken at Home and Ability to Speak English, by Age: 2000   *100*

TABLE 6.3 Percent Who Speak a Language Other Than English at Home for the Total U.S. and States, by Age: 2000   *101*

TABLE 6.4 Educational Attainment of the Population, by Age and Sex: 2002   *103*

TABLE 6.5 Educational Attainment of the Elderly, by Labor Force Status and Sex: March 2002   *104*

TABLE 6.6 Educational Attainment of the Elderly, by Nativity, Period of Entry, and Sex: March 2002   *105*

TABLE 6.7 Educational Attainment of the Elderly, by Metropolitan and Nonmetropolitan Residence and Sex: March 2002   *106*

TABLE 6.8 Educational Attainment of the Elderly, by Region and Sex: March 2002   *107*

TABLE 6.9 Percent of the Elderly Population with at Least a Bachelor's Degree for the Total U.S. and States, by Sex: 2000   *107*

CHAPTER 7 Income and Poverty

CHART 7.1 Percent of Elderly Aged Units with Income from Specified Source: 2000   *115*

CHART 7.2 Percent of Elderly Aged Units with Income from Specified Source: 1976–2000   *116*

CHART 7.3 Percent of Aggregate Income among Elderly Aged Units, by Source: 2000   *117*

CHART 7.4 Percent of Aggregate Income among Elderly Aged Units, by Source: 1976–2000   *118*

CHART 7.5 Percent of Aggregate Income among Elderly Aged Units, by Source and Age: 2000   *119*

CHART 7.6 Earnings Income among Elderly Aged Units, by Age: 2000   *121*

CHART 7.7 Median Income of Aged Units, by Age: 2000   *123*

CHART 7.8 Distribution of Income Received by Elderly Aged Units: 2000   *124*

CHART 7.9 Median Income of Aged Units, by Age and Marital Status: 2000   *125*

CHART 7.10 Median Income, by Age, Marital Status, and Race: 2000   *126*

CHART 7.11 Median Income of Elderly Nonmarried Persons, by Sex and Marital Status: 2000   *127*

CHART 7.12 Poverty Rates by Age: 1959 to 2002   *128*

TABLE 7.1 Relative Importance of Social Security Income for Elderly Aged Units among Those Receiving Social Security, by Age: 2000   *118*

TABLE 7.2 Percent of Elderly Aged Units Who Derive 100 Percent of Their Income from Social Security, by Race and Marital Status: 2000   *120*

TABLE 7.3 Relative Importance of Asset Income for Elderly Aged Units among Those Receiving Asset Income, by Age: 2000   *120*

TABLE 7.4 Relative Importance of Earnings Income for Elderly Aged Units among Those Receiving Earnings, by Age: 2000   *122*

TABLE 7.5 Relative Importance of Public Assistance Income for Elderly Aged Units among Those Receiving Public Assistance, by Age: 2000   *122*

TABLE 7.6 Percent Difference in Median Income and Ratio of Median Income among Aged Units, by Age and Marital Status: 2000   *125*

TABLE 7.7 Elderly Living in Poverty (100 Percent of Poverty Level), by Sex and Race: 2002   *129*

TABLE 7.8 Percent of Elderly Living in Poverty (100 Percent of Poverty Level), by Age and Race: 2002   *129*

TABLE 7.9 Percent of Elderly with Incomes below 125 Percent of the Poverty Level, by Sex and Race: 2002   *130*

TABLE 7.10 Percent of Elderly below 100 Percent of the Poverty Level, by Citizenship Status and Sex: March 2002   *130*

TABLE 7.11 Percent of Oldest-Old Living (Aged 85+) in Poverty (100 Percent of Povety Level), by Sex, Race, and Ethnic Background: 2002   *131*

TABLE 7.12 Percent of Oldest-Old Living with Incomes below 125 Percent of the Poverty Level by Sex: 2002   *131*

CHAPTER 8 Finances—Assets, Saving, Debt, and Attitudes

CHART 8.1 Median Family Net Worth (in Thousands of 2001 Dollars), by Age of Family Head: 1992, 1995, 1998, 2001   *134*

CHART 8.2 Percent of Elderly-Headed Families Holding Specific Type of Financial Asset, by Age of Family Head: 2001   *135*

CHART 8.3 Percent of Families Holding Transaction Accounts and Median Value of the Accounts (in Thousands of Dollars), by Age of Family Head: 2001   *136*

CHART 8.4 Percent of Families Holding Retirement Accounts and Median Value of the Accounts (in Thousands of Dollars), by Age of Family Head: 2001   *137*

CHART 8.5 Percent of Families Holding Cash-Value Insurance Policies and Median Value of the Accounts (in Thousands of Dollars), by Age of Family Head: 2001   *138*

CHART 8.6 Percent of Families Holding Certificates of Deposit and Median Value of the Accounts (in Thousands of Dollars), by Age of Family Head: 2001   *139*

CHART 8.7 Percent of Families Holding Stocks or Mutual Funds and Median Value of the Accounts (in Thousands of Dollars), by Age of Family Head: 2001   *140*

CHART 8.8 Percent of Elderly Families Holding Stock (Directly or Indirectly), Median Value of the Stock Holdings (in Thousands of 2001 Dollars), and Share of Assets Attributable to Stock Holdings, by Age of Family Head: 1992, 1995, 1998, 2001   *141*

CHART 8.9 Percent of Families Holding Bonds and Median Value of the Accounts (in Thousands of Dollars), by Age of Family Head: 2001   *142*

CHART 8.10 Percent of Families Owning Specific Type of Nonfinancial Asset, by Age of Family Head: 2001   *143*

CHART 8.11 Median Value of Specific Nonfinancial Asset (in Thousands of Dollars), by Age of Family Head: 2001   *144*

CHART 8.12 Percent of Families with Debt and the Median Value of the Debt, by Age of Family Head: 2001   *146*

CHART 8.13 Percent of Elderly-Headed Families Holding Specific Type of Debt, by Age of Family Head: 2001   *147*

TABLE 8.1 Banking Services Used in the Past 12 Months, by Age: 2003   *138*

TABLE 8.2 Self-Impressions of Level of Investment Knowledge among Those Expressing an Opinion: 2003   *147*

TABLE 8.3 Level of Competency with Various Financial Processes, by Age: 2003   *148*

TABLE 8.4 Selected Financial Concerns, by Age: 2003   *149*

TABLE 8.5 People Whom Household Members Turn to for Financial Advice, by Age: 2003   *149*

TABLE 8.6 Credit-Card Incidence and Reasons for Using or Not Using a Credit Card: 2002   *150*

CHAPTER 9 Consumer Spending

CHART 9.1 Aggregate Annual Expenditures (in Thousands of Dollars), by Age of Reference Person in Household: 2001   *154*

CHART 9.2 Average Annual Expenditures, by Age of Reference Person in Household: 2001   *155*

CHART 9.3 Share of Spending among Households with an Elderly Reference Person: 2001   *157*

CHART 9.4 Average Annual Housing Expenditures and Share of Total Expenditures, by Age of Reference Person in Household: 2001   *159*

CHART 9.5 Share of Housing Expenditures, by Age of the Household Reference Person: 2001   *160*

CHART 9.6 Homeownership, by Age of the Household Reference Person: 2001   *161*

CHART 9.7 Mortgage Status among Homeowners, by Age of the Household Reference Person: 2001   *161*

CHART 9.8 Mortgage Status and Home Market Value among Households with an Elderly Reference Person, by Income: 2000–2001   *162*

CHART 9.9 Average Annual Transportation Expenditures and Share of Total Expenditures, by Age of the Household Reference Person: 2001   *165*

CHART 9.10 Health Care Expenditures and Share of Total Expenditures, by Age of Reference Person in Household: 2001   *167*

CHART 9.11 Food at Home Expenditures and Share of Total Expenditures, by Age of the Household Reference Person: 2001   *170*

CHART 9.12 Food Away from Home Expenditures and Share of Total Expenditures, by Age of the Household Reference Person: 2001   *171*

CHART 9.13 Per Person per Household Food Expenditures in Households with an Elderly Reference Person, by Income: 2000–2001   *171*

CHART 9.14 Cash Contribution Expenditures and Share of Total Expenditures, by Age of the Household Reference Person: 2001   *172*

CHART 9.15 Cash Contribution Expenditures in Households with an Elderly Reference Person, by Income and Region: 2000–2001   *173*

CHART 9.16 Entertainment Expenditures, by Age of the Household Reference Person: 2001   *174*

CHART 9.17 Apparel and Services Expenditures, by Age of the Household Reference Person: 2001   *176*

CHART 9.18 Pension and Social Security Expenditures, by Age of the Household Reference Person: 2001   *177*

CHART 9.19 Life and Other Personal Insurance Expenditures, by Age of the Household Reference Person: 2001   *178*

TABLE 9.1 Household Size by Age of Reference Person: 2001   *153*

TABLE 9.2 Average Annual Expenditures and Average Household Size among Households with an Elderly Reference Person, by Region: 2000–2001   *156*

TABLE 9.3 Average Annual Expenditures and Average Household Size among Households with an Elderly Reference Person, by Income: 2000–2001   *156*

TABLE 9.4 Share of Housing Expenditures among Households with an Elderly Reference Person, by Region: 2000–2001   *159*

TABLE 9.5 Mortgage Status and Home Market Value in Households with an Elderly Reference Person, by Region: 2000–2001   *162*

TABLE 9.6 Share of Housing Expenditures in Households with an Elderly Reference Person, by Income: 2000–2001   *163*

TABLE 9.7 Share of Transportation Expenditures, by Age of the Household Reference Person: 2001   *165*

TABLE 9.8 Vehicle Ownership Characteristics, by Age of the Household Reference Person: 2001   *166*

TABLE 9.9 Share of Health Care Expenditures, by Age of the Household Reference Person: 2001   *168*

TABLE 9.10 Share of Health Care Expenditures among Households with an Elderly Reference Person, by Region: 2000–2001   *168*

TABLE 9.11 Share of Health Care Expenditures among Households with an Elderly Reference Person, by Income: 2000–2001   *169*

TABLE 9.12 Share of Food at Home Expenditures, by Age of the Household Reference Person: 2001   *170*

TABLE 9.13 Sources Used When Trying to Purchase Products: 2003   *175*

TABLE 9.14 Pension and Social Security Payments, Age, Household Size, and Work Force Statistics in Households with an Elderly Reference Person, by Income: 2000–2001 (Average Annual Income)   *177*

CHAPTER 10 Work and Retirement

CHART 10.1 Civilian Labor Force Participation Rates, by Age and Sex: 2002   *182*

CHART 10.2 Full-Time and Part-Time Working Status among Employed Persons, by Age and Sex: 2000   *183*

CHART 10.3 Labor Force Participation Rates among Those Aged 55 to 64 and the Elderly, by Sex: 1950–2002   *185*

CHART 10.4 Average Age of New Social Security Beneficiaries, by Sex: 1940–2002   *187*

CHART 10.5A Average Annual Change in Labor Force Participation Rate for Men, by Individual Age: 1970–1985 and 1985–2002   *188*

CHART 10.5B Average Annual Change in Labor Force Participation Rate for Women, by Individual Age: 1970–1985 and 1985–2002   *189*

TABLE 10.1 Labor Force Participation Rates among the Elderly, by Sex and Race: 2002   *183*

TABLE 10.2 Labor Force Participation Rates for Selected Cohorts, by Sex   *186*

TABLE 10.3 Percent of Full-Time Employees Covered by Pension Plans in Medium and Large Private Establishments: 1989, 1993, and 1997   *191*

TABLE 10.4 Economic Dependency Ratio, by Age: 1975–2000 and 2010 Projection   *193*

TABLE 10.5 Aspects Considered as Part of the "Good Life" and Achievement of Those Aspects, by Age (Ranked by Aspect for 65+ Years): 2003   *197*

TABLE 10.6 Aspects Considered as Part of the "Good Life"" and Achievement of Those Aspects by age (Ranked by Achievement for 65+ Years): 2003   *198*

CHAPTER 11 Social Security and Supplemental Security Income

CHART 11.1 Women Beneficiaries as a Percentage of Retired Workers and Disabled Workers: Selected Years   *205*

CHART 11.2 Women Aged 62 or Older, by Basis of Entitlement: Selected Years   *207*

CHART 11.3 Ratio of Covered Workers to Social Security Beneficiaries   *208*

CHART 11.4 Cumulative Income Less Cost Based on Present Taxes and Scheduled Benefits   *209*

CHART 11.5 Distribution of SSI Beneficiaries, by Basis for Eligibility and Age   *210*

CHART 11.6 Percentage of SSI Beneficiaries Aged 65 or Older: Selected Years   *210*

TABLE 11.1 Increase in Social Security Payments for Delayed Retirement Past Age 65   *203*

TABLE 11.2 Social Security Trust Fund Operations in Billions of Dollars   *204*

TABLE 11.3 Hypothetical Monthly Social Security Benefits   *206*

TABLE 11.4 Hypothetical Social Security Benefits, Average Monthly Benefits   *207*

Preface

Issues relating to age and aging are now dominant players in social policy in the United States and, indeed, the world. *Aging: Lifestyles, Work, and Money*, as well as its companion *Aging: Demographics, Health, and Health Services* (Greenwood Press, 2003), provide quick access to a wide range of facts about this phenomenon. This volume is designed to stand alone or to be used with its companion. It is intended for use by librarians, gerontologists, geriatricians, health policy analysts, researchers, information specialists, marketing professionals, journalists, students, and others doing research on aging.

Aging: Lifestyles, Work, and Money is not just a dry book of statistics. We have worked diligently to present the content in an easy-to-read and interesting format. We describe trends and offer insights to provide a cohesive framework for the vast amount of statistics now available on aging.

The book is designed for browsing and serendipitous discovery as well as to locate a specific piece of information. The text is exhaustive in its coverage of issues, highlighted by easy-to-follow headings, 83 charts, and 100 tables. Important definitions and key facts stand out from the text for easy access. Sources include government reports, private studies, and never-before-published statistics from NOP World and Mediamark Research. Sources for all statistics are cited throughout the publication.

Aging: Lifestyles, Work, and Money begins with an introductory essay by Elizabeth Vierck titled "'The Typical Older American.'" Another form of this essay first appeared in the *Factbook on Aging* (Vierck, 1991).

The text is divided into two major topical areas: (1) *Lifestyles,* which covers marital status, living arrangements, and family life; where the elderly live and geographic mobility; housing; transportation; volunteering and community life; social activities, travel, and leisure; crime; education, and native language; and (2) *Work and Money,* which covers income and poverty; finances; consumer spending; work and retirement; and Social Security. There is a general bibliography and list of helpful Web sites, as well as an appendix, "World Records and Fascinating Facts," at the end of the text.

This volume represents many thousands of hours of work over a two-year period, during which we reviewed more than 1,500 documents. The result of these efforts is a book that provides one definitive, comprehensive source of information about people aged 65 years and older.

TERMINOLOGY USED IN THIS BOOK

Unless otherwise stated, the data used in this book describe the elderly (senior population), defined as the group aged 65 years and older. Within the elderly population are three widely recognized age brackets:

- Young-old (65 to 74 years)
- Middle-old (75 to 84 years)
- Oldest-old (85 years and older)

Unfortunately, not all data sources match this standard. Throughout the book we identify the age categories used by data sources that differ from these. However, sometimes a source may refer to older people and not clearly define which age category that includes. This book primarily describes the elderly or senior (65+) population. Note that the "+" symbol as used in this book refers to all ages above a particular age. Thus, 65+ means 65 years of age and older.

VALUE PROVIDED BY THE AUTHORS

As writers and analysts, we have designed this book for optimum use by the reader. Throughout the volume we go beyond just reporting data to provide analytical support and insight. We have computed and present percent changes and ratios, and we provide data from other age groups to aid in making comparisons. At times, the data have been calculated to provide more user-friendly statistics.

We also have included many data sources and insights that have never before been published. For example, we provide a new view of consumer spending from the Consumer Expenditure Survey. We have also included proprietary attitudinal and behavioral data from NOP World and Mediamark Research to provide other perspectives on today's elderly.

We have attempted to provide the most up-to-date statistics available. Data are current as of November 2003. Even though some data sources are updated frequently and may have missed our deadline, much of the information provided here does not change substantially from year to year.

One of the benefits of today's information highway is the wide accessibility to data. Some government data sources are available on CD-ROM or as downloadable files from the Internet. When relevant, we have obtained such data and analyzed it. In other cases we culled information from the most recently available printed tables and reports.

We have taken the utmost care in reviewing and checking data numerous times. Occasionally, we have found erroneous material from data sources and have corrected these errors. We have also checked and rechecked our data and have tested for internal consistency and simple face validity (i.e., whether the data make sense). However, some inadvertent errors are possible. We urge all readers to be as vigilant as we have been, for we are not infallible. References are provided to allow users to delve into further detail.

We have also paid careful attention to interpret data properly. For clarity's sake, we use "increases with age" or "declines with age" to explain trends in which rates go up or down across age groups. For example, in Chapter 7 we mention that "median income drops substantially with age, with the median income of the youngest elderly, aged 65 to 69, twice that of their oldest counterparts, aged 85+." By using the term "with age," we do not imply that as individuals age their income will necessarily drop or that the same effect will occur with future generations. Rather, the progression reflects one static point in time. Only longitudinal analysis, which follows the same group of people through a given time period, can determine a true age effect.

It is our hope that *Aging: Lifestyles, Work, and Money* and its companion book, *Aging: Demographics, Health, and Health Services*, provide a definitive, comprehensive source of information about people aged 65 years and older and will enable the reader to locate relevant data quickly and easily.

ACKNOWLEDGMENTS

As with our first book, *Aging: Demographics, Health, and Health Services*, we again thank the NOP World (formerly RoperASW) and Mediamark Research organizations for the generous access to their data. More specifically, we thank Diane Crispell and Lancey Heyman for their substantial time and effort in that process.

We also thank Gary Burtless, Senior Fellow at the Brookings Institution, and Joe Quinn, Dean of the College of Arts and Sciences at Boston College, for their assistance with the Work and Retirement chapter.

Last, but not least, we again thank our family and friends for their patience through this long process.

Introductory Essay:
The Typical Older American

Elizabeth Vierck

Who is the typical elderly American? The answer is a sketch—leaving much of the texture and ambiance in the paint box and off the canvas. If we make the statement that the typical older family had a median income of $23,048 in 2000, for example, we overlook Corrine Gable, who, like 47 percent of black women on their own, lives in poverty; the Rotondos, who have spent their life savings for care for Mrs. Rotondo, who has Alzheimer's disease; and multimillionaire Albert Myers, who at age 75 started yet another business.

Taking all these factors into account, the following is an attempt to tie the vast number of statistics about the elderly into a portrait. It is based on the information presented in the Vierck and Hodges books *Aging: Demographics, Health, and Health Services* and *Aging: Lifestyles, Work and Money* and current statistics from other sources.

Please note: This essay pulls together facts based on proportions, averages, or medians. Therefore, it is not possible to draw a completely accurate portrait that would reflect a real person's life cycle. For example, our "typical" older American's husband lives to be 81 because the average life expectancy today for men at age 65 is 16 years. However, that also means that if he left the labor force at age 62, he would have worked for 44 years, not the 39 years that is the average number of years in the labor force.

THE TYPICAL OLDER AMERICAN

Let me introduce you to the typical older American. Because older women outnumber older men 3 to 2, she is a woman. We will call her Mrs. Shaw. Like 8 in 9 elders, she is non-Hispanic white.

Born in 1930, Mrs. Shaw is 74 years old. She lived through World War II, the Great Depression, the Cold War, and the tragedy of 9-11. When she was born only 1 out of 20 Americans was over age 65. Today elders represent 1 in 8 people in the United States, 1 in 4 voters, and the largest and most affluent group of prime-time television viewers. As part of the "mature market" they control over $1.6 trillion in spending power (www.theoldernetwork.com). Furthermore, 1 out of 3 federal budget dollars is spent on their behalf.

HOW THE SHAWS LIVE

Mrs. Shaw lives with her husband, who is 78, although the odds are 50-50 that she lives alone. They own a single-family detached home in California.

The couple does work around their house. Watching television occupies most of their leisure time. Mrs. Shaw volunteers. They belong to AARP, contribute to charity, and devote time to their religion. The Shaws own a car. They take a vacation every year.

Mrs. Shaw says that she would like her husband to help more around the house. He says, "I'd like more interesting meals and to have sex more often."

THE SHAWS' INCOME AND WHERE IT GOES

The Shaws both retired at age 62 and they receive $1,216 a month from Social Security. Their yearly income is about $25,000.

The couple is loyal to brand names, and they go out of their way to shop at stores that give good service. They feel that advertisers are obsessed with youth. Their age group is the fastest growing segment of the Web market. The Shaws are heavy users of repair, lawn care, and home improvement services. The couple's top five expenses are transportation, shelter, health care, food at home, and utilities. Health care costs take 10 to 14 percent of their income. They have started to distribute some of their assets to their children.

HABITS, HAPPINESS, AND HEALTH

The Shaws are not heavy drinkers and they do not smoke. Mr. Shaw is overweight. They do not get regular vigorous exercise. They regularly take vitamins.

Mr. and Mrs. Shaw eat less fatty food than their parents did when they were elders. They also eat more grains, tomatoes, deep-green vegetables, nuts, and fruit. However, their fat consumption is above recommended levels, and their intake of fiber and vitamin E does not meet nutritional guidelines. Curiously, they are not aware of these over-indulgences and deficits.

The Shaws report: "We are happy with our lives. We like our ages, and we feel younger than our years." They say their health is excellent. However, Mrs. Shaw has arthritis and her husband is showing signs of heart disease. They complain about their memories, but their performance on memory tests does not show a deficit. However, half of their friends and siblings over age 85 have Alzheimer's disease.

THE MEDICARE PUZZLE

Incredibly, through Medicare, in 1999 the Centers for Medicare and Medicaid Services spent $5,657 on the Shaws' health care. The Shaws spent another $2,430 out of their own pockets. The couple finds Medicare complicated and confusing. Mrs. Shaw says, "When we first went on Medicare we were surprised that it does not cover medications, nursing home services or home health care." Mrs. Shaw and her husband each spend $686 per year out of their own pockets for medications, and each takes more than two prescription drugs annually.

A TIME FOR CARE

During their retirement Mrs. Shaw or her husband will be admitted to a hospital for at least a short time. The odds are 2 out of 5 that one of them will spend some time in a nursing home.

As they age, the couple will receive help with daily activities such as bathing and housekeeping. Mrs. Shaw and her daughter will provide most of the assistance for Mr. Shaw, who laughs when he hears his doctors refer to this tender loving care as "informal care." He pictures "formal care" as doctors and nurses arriving at his front door in ball gowns and tuxedos.

After Mr. Shaw's death, their daughter and community programs will help Mrs. Shaw. Some of her needs will go unmet. Happily, when Mrs. Shaw looks back she will say, "My older years have been more secure and contented than my parents' were." The Shaws had 19 years together since Mr. Shaw retired, compared to the ten years their parents had. Mrs. Shaw will die at about age 84 from heart disease. Sadly, like her husband, she will die in a hospital and not at home.

OLDER AMERICANS ARE RICH IN DIVERSITY

Although the Shaws represent the typical older American, the older population is rich in diversity and growing richer. Race, Hispanic origin and age distribution reflect this fact. For example, in 2000 over 16 percent of persons 65+ were minorities, among whom 8 percent were African-Americans, over 2 percent were Asian or Pacific Islander, and the remainder were Hispanic, American Indian, Eskimos, and Aleuts. By 2030, twenty-five percent of persons 65+ are expected to be minorities. During this time the white population 65+ will increase by 81 percent, compared with 219 percent for older minorities.

As we entered the new century the older population was about evenly divided between people aged 65 to 74 and those aged 75+. By 2050, the 75+ population is expected to outnumber the 65 to 74 age group by 10 million. During this time the 85+ group will be the fastest growing age group. It is expected to increase fivefold to 19.3 million by 2050, at which time the Administration on Aging predicts there will be 1 million centenarians.

Lifestyles

CHAPTER 1

Marital Status, Living Arrangements, and Family Life*

Call it a clan, call it a network, call it a tribe, call it a family. Whatever you call it, whoever you are, you need one.

—Jane Howard, "Families"

The family is changing, not disappearing. We have to broaden our understanding of it, look for the new metaphors.

—Mary Catherine Bateson

This chapter covers the family status and living arrangements of the elderly. While more and more people aged 65 live alone, the marital status and living arrangements of this age group are diverse. For example, today 2.3 million people over age 60 have their grandchildren living with them and, of this group, over 1 million are their grandchildren's caregivers. Other highlights from the chapter include:

- Most elderly men are married and most elderly women are widowed.

- However, the percentage of elderly who are widows and widowers has decreased over the last five decades.

- The number of elderly living with relatives decreased dramatically in the last century.

- The number of elderly living alone increases with age. By age 85, three in 5 elderly women are living alone.

- Multigenerational families are more likely in areas of high immigration.

---

*Unless otherwise noted, the information in this chapter is from the U.S. Census Bureau, "March 2002 Current Population Survey." Available online at http://www.census.gov.

MARITAL STATUS

Most elderly men are married

In 2002, 75 percent of elderly men were married, compared to 42 percent of elderly women (see Chart 1.1 and Table 1.1.).

Most elderly women are widowed

Almost half of all elderly women in 2002 were widows (46 percent). There were over four times as many widows (8.9 million) as widowers (2.0 million) in the aged 65+ population.

The disparity between marriage and widowhood widens with age

By age 85, seventy-nine percent of women are widowed, compared with 34 percent of men (see Chart 1.2).

The percentage of elderly men and women who are widows and widowers has decreased over the last five decades

The percentage of men aged 60+ who are widowed declined steadily from 19 percent in 1950 to 1 percent in 1980 and has remained at this level.[1] The corresponding percentage of women who are widowed also declined, from 47 percent in 1950 to 39 percent in 2000. This happy phenomenon is, in part, the result of increased life expectancy for both men and women.

CHART 1.1
Marital Status of the Elderly: March 2002

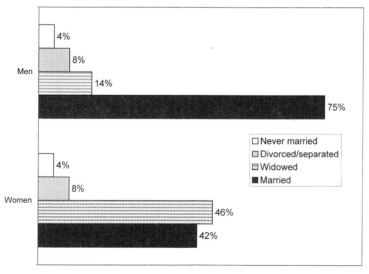

Source: Bureau of the Census. (2002). "Detailed Tables for Current Population Report, P20-547." Available online at www.census.gov.

TABLE 1.1
Marital Status of the Population Aged 65+ by Age and Sex: March 2002

	65 to 74 years		75 to 84 years		85+ years		65+ years	
	(000's)	%	(000's)	%	(000's)	%	(000's)	%
Total	**18,123**	**100.0**	**12,191**	**100.0**	**3,456**	**100.0**	**33,770**	**100.0**
Married	11,796	65.1	6,095	50.0	957	27.7	18,848	55.8
Widowed	3,724	20.6	4,913	40.3	2,237	64.7	10,874	32.2
Divorced	1,726	9.5	685	5.6	98	2.8	2,509	7.4
Separated	226	1.2	72	0.6	14	0.4	312	0.0
Never Married	650	3.6	426	3.5	150	4.3	1,226	3.6
Men	**8,245**	**100.0**	**4,898**	**100.0**	**1,093**	**100.0**	**14,236**	**100.0**
Married	6,451	78.3	3,528	72.0	651	59.6	10,630	74.6
Widowed	706	8.6	903	18.4	370	33.9	1,979	13.9
Divorced	672	8.1	243	5.0	33	3.0	948	6.6
Separated	112	1.4	28	0.6	5	0.5	145	1.0
Never Married	304	3.7	195	4.0	33	3.1	532	3.7
Women	**9,878**	**100.0**	**7,293**	**100.0**	**2,363**	**100.0**	**19,534**	**100.0**
Married	5,345	54.1	2,566	35.2	305	12.9	8,216	42.1
Widowed	3,018	30.6	4,010	55.0	1,867	79.0	8,895	45.5
Divorced	1,054	10.7	441	6.1	65	2.7	1,560	7.9
Separated	114	1.2	44	0.6	9	0.4	167	0.1
Never Married	347	3.5	231	3.2	117	4.9	695	3.6

Source: Bureau of the Census. (2002). "Detailed Tables for Current Population Report, P20-547." Available online at www.census.gov.

CHART 1.2
Percent Widowed by Age and Sex: March 2002

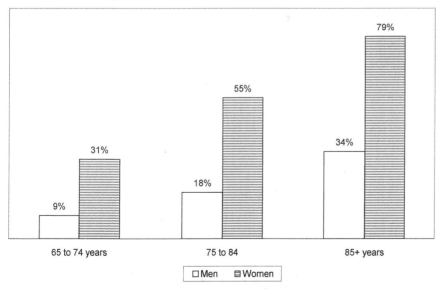

Source: Bureau of the Census. (2002). "Detailed Tables for Current Population Report, P20-547." Available online at www.census.gov.

■ The percentage of elderly who are married increased over the last 50 years

While the percentage of the elderly who are widowed has decreased, there has been a corresponding increase in the percentage who are married. Sixty-nine percent of men were married in 1950, compared to 79 percent in 1980.[2] This number decreased to 75 percent in 2000. The percentage of women aged 60+ who were married increased from 42 percent in 1950 to 46 percent in 2000.

■ The elderly have low rates of divorce and separation

Divorced and separated elderly people represented only 7 percent of all elderly in 2002.

■ The elderly are the least likely to have never married

In 2002 only 3.6 percent of the elderly had never married, compared to 29.6 percent of people age 15 to 64. The percentage never married was lowest for women aged 75 to 84 years (3.2 percent) and for men in the same age group (4 percent).[3]

LIVING ARRANGEMENTS

■ Over half of the elderly live with their spouse

Over half (55 percent) of the elderly who did not live in institutions lived with their spouse in 2000. This included approximately 10.1 million or 73 percent of elderly men, and 7.7 million or 41 percent of elderly women.[4] The proportion living with their spouse decreased with age, especially for women. Only 29 percent of women aged 75+ lived with a spouse in 2000.

■ About one-third of elderly people live alone

About 31 percent (10.5 million) of the elderly not living in institutions in 2002 lived alone (7.9 million women and 2.6 million men; see Table 1.2). They repre-

TABLE 1.2
Percent of Elderly Living Alone by Age and Sex: March 2002

	65 to 74 years	75 to 84 years	85+ years	65+ years
	%	%	%	%
Total	24	36	50	31
Men	15	20	31	18
Women	31	47	59	40

Source: Bureau of the Census. (2002). "Detailed Tables for Current Population Report, P20-547." Available online at www.census.gov.

CHART 1.3
Percent of Elderly Living in One- or Two-Person Households by Age: 2002

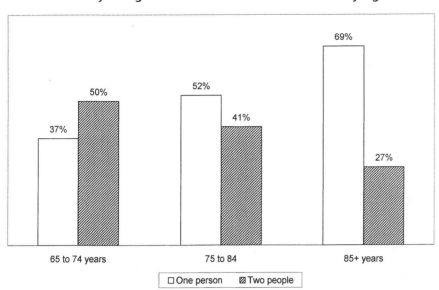

65 to 74 years   75 to 84   85+ years

☐ One person   ▨ Two people

Source: Bureau of the Census. (2002). "Detailed Tables for Current Population Report, P20-547." Available online at www.census.gov.

sented 40 percent of elderly women and 18 percent of elderly men. The proportion living alone increases with age. Among women aged 85+, 59 percent lived alone in 2002.

HOUSEHOLD SIZE

Household size decreases with age

The elderly have the smallest average household size of all age groups. Household size peaks during the years when householders are raising children. For example, in 2002 people age 35 to 39 had the highest average household size (3.29 people per household). In the same year average household size for people age 65 to 74 was 1.89 people per household. This number was 1.56 for people aged 75+.

With increasing age the elderly are more likely to live alone

The percentage of people living alone increases with age (see Chart 1.3). For example, slightly more than half of people age 75 to 84 live in single-person households, compared to well over two-thirds of people over age 85.

ELDERLY WIDOWS

■ **The percentage of elderly widows living alone increased dramatically over the last century**

Just 15 percent of widows aged 65+ lived alone in 1900, compared to 24 percent in 1950 and 69 percent in 2002.[5]

■ **Social Security benefits account for nearly two-thirds of the increase in elderly widows living alone**

The proportion of elderly widows living alone rose from 18 percent in 1940 to 62 percent in 1990, while the share living with adult children declined from 59 percent to 20 percent.[6] According to a recent study, increased Social Security benefits are the single most important factor causing the change in living arrangements, accounting for nearly two-thirds of the rise in the share of elderly widows living alone.

Changes in benefits from the means-tested Older Americans Act/Supplemental Security Income programs had a lesser impact on the decision to live alone but were a significant factor in explaining changes in the living arrangements of the poorest widows.

GRANDPARENT HOUSEHOLDS

■ **2.3 million people aged 60+ have their grandchildren living with them**

In 2000, 2.3 million people aged 60+ had grandchildren living with them (see Table 1.3), and 30 percent of them were responsible for the care of their grandchildren.

TABLE 1.3
The Caregiving Relationships of Grandparents Aged 60+ Whose Grandchildren Live with Them: 2000

	60+ Years		60-69 Years		70-79 Years		80+ Years	
	Number	%	Number	%	Number	%	Number	%
Grandparents living with grandchildren	2,317,199	100	1,378,378	100	733,440	100	205,381	100
Not caring for grandchildren	1,611,047	70	869,621	63	560,969	76	180,457	88
Caring for grandchildren	706,152	30	508,757	37	172,471	24	24,924	12

MULTIGENERATIONAL FAMILIES

■ The number of elderly living with relatives decreased dramatically in the last century

At the beginning of the 20th century, more than 70 percent of people aged 65+ lived with relatives.[7] By 1980, the percentage had dropped to 23 percent, and by 1998 to 20 percent.

■ Multigenerational families are more likely in areas of high immigration

Multigenerational families—households with more than two generations living together—have received a great deal of attention recently. Many such households include elderly family members. In 2000, there were 3.9 million multigenerational family households, making up 4 percent of all households. Hawaii had the highest percentage (8 percent). Two states exceeded 5 percent: California (6 percent) and Mississippi (5 percent). The state with the smallest percentage of multigenerational family households was North Dakota (1 percent). Puerto Rico also recorded a relatively high percentage of multigenerational family households (7 percent).

■ Homes in which children and grandchildren live with the householder make up the largest group of multigenerational living arrangements

Households with a householder and the householder's children and grandchildren are the largest group of multigenerational households, equaling 2.6 million households or 65 percent of such households in 2000.

■ Households in which the householder's parents and children live with them are the second most common multigenerational household

Those family households consisting of a householder, the householder's parents or parents-in-law, and the householder's children numbered 1.3 million households or one-third of all multigenerational families in 2000.

■ Four-generation family households are rare

There were 78,000 four-generation households in 2000, making up only 2 percent of all multigenerational family households.

NOTES

1. Bureau of the Census. (October 2003). "Marital Status: 2000." Available online at http://www.census.gov.
2. Ibid.
3. Administration on Aging. (2002). "A Profile of Older Americans: 2002." Available online at http://www.aoa.gov.

4. Suzanne M. Bianchi and Lynne M. Casper. (December 2000). "American Families." *Population Bulletin* Vol. 55, No. 4.

5. Kathleen McGarry and Robert F. Schoeni. (May 2000). "Social Security, Economic Growth, and the in Rise in Elderly Widows' Independence in the Twentieth Century." *Demography* Vol. 37, No. 2.

6. Bureau of the Census. (2003). "Grandparents Living with Grandchildren." Available online at http://www.census.gov.

7. Bianchi and Casper.

CHAPTER 2

Where the Elderly Live: Geographic Location and Mobility

Whether the opportunity is seized or not, moving to another geographic location to retire is usually reserved for people who are financially solvent.

—*Lewis R. Aiken,* Aging and Later Life

This chapter covers where the elderly live and their geographic mobility. Highlights include:

- The West and South had the highest growth in the elderly population between 1990 and 2000.

- People aged 65+ were much less mobile than those under the age of 65.

- The oldest-old were the most mobile of the elderly population.

- While the number of elderly grew, people aged 65+ represented a smaller *portion* of the nation's population in 2000 than in 1990.

- Six of the top 10 places with high concentrations of elderly are in Florida.

- The South Atlantic division is enjoying the largest migration gains of elderly.

WHERE THE ELDERLY LIVE*

Half of the elderly live in nine states

According to the 2000 Census, about half (52 percent) of the elderly live in nine states (see Table 2.1). California had 3.6 million elderly; Florida 2.8 million; New York 2.4 million; Texas 2.1 million; and Pennsylvania 1.9 million. Ohio, Illinois, Michigan, and New Jersey each had well over 1 million.

---

*Unless otherwise noted, the information on geographic location is adapted from the U.S. Census Bureau, "The 65 Years and Older Population." Available online at http://www.census.gov.

TABLE 2.1
The 65+ Population by State: 2000

	Number	Percent Age 65+	Percent Increase 1990-2000
Total United States	34,991,753	12	12
California	3,595,658	11	15
Florida	2,807,597	18	19
New York	2,448,352	13	4
Texas	2,072,532	10	21
Pennsylvania	1,919,165	16	5
Ohio	1,507,757	13	7
Illinois	1,500,025	12	4
Michigan	1,219,018	12	10
New Jersey	1,113,136	13	8
North Carolina	969,048	12	21
Massachusetts	860,162	14	5
Virginia	792,333	11	19
Georgia	785,275	10	20
Missouri	755,379	14	5
Tennessee	703,311	12	14
Wisconsin	702,553	13	8
Arizona	667,839	13	40
Washington	662,148	11	15
Maryland	599,307	11	16
Minnesota	594,266	12	9
Alabama	579,798	13	11
Louisiana	516,929	12	10
Kentucky	504,793	13	8
South Carolina	485,333	12	22
Connecticut	470,183	14	5
Oklahoma	455,950	13	8
Oregon	438,177	13	12
Iowa	436,213	15	2
Colorado	416,073	10	26
Arkansas	374,019	14	7
Kansas	356,229	13	4
Mississippi	343,523	12	7
West Virginia	276,895	15	3
Nebraska	232,195	14	4
Nevada	218,929	11	72
New Mexico	212,225	12	30
Utah	190,222	9	27
Maine	183,402	14	12
Hawaii	160,601	13	29
Rhode Island	152,402	15	1
New Hampshire	147,970	12	18
Idaho	145,916	11	20
Montana	120,949	13	14
South Dakota	108,131	14	6

TABLE 2.1   (Continued)

	Number	Percent Age 65+	Percent Increase 1990-2000
Delaware	101,726	13	26
North Dakota	94,478	15	4
Vermont	77,510	13	17
District of Columbia	69,898	12	-10
Wyoming	57,693	12	22
Alaska	35,699	6	60

Source: Compiled by the Administration on Aging from Table DP-1. "Profile of General Demographic Characteristics for the United States: 1999–2001."

■ In nine states at least 1 in 7 people are elderly

The elderly constituted 14 percent or more of the total population in nine states in 2000: Florida (18 percent); Pennsylvania (16 percent); West Virginia (15 percent); Iowa (15 percent); North Dakota (15 percent); Rhode Island (15 percent); Maine (14 percent); South Dakota (14 percent); and Arkansas (14 percent) (Table 2.1).

■ Every state's elderly population grew between 1990 and 2000

Every state experienced growth in its elderly population between 1990 and 2000, ranging from a 1 percent increase in Rhode Island to a 72 percent increase in Nevada (see Table 2.1).

■ In 14 states the elderly population increased 20 percent or more between 1990 and 2000

In 14 states the elderly population increased by 20 percent or more between 1990 and 2000 (see Table 2.1). Nevada and Alaska had the highest increases (72 and 60 percent, respectively). Other states with large increases are: Arizona (40 percent); New Mexico (30 percent); Hawaii (29 percent); Utah (27 percent); Colorado (26 percent); Delaware (26 percent); South Carolina (22 percent); Wyoming (22 percent); Texas (21 percent); North Carolina (21 percent); Idaho (20 percent); and Georgia (20 percent).

■ The West and South had the highest growth in the elderly population between 1990 and 2000

The West experienced the highest percentage increase of the elderly population between 1990 and 2000, at 20 percent. The South's elderly population grew by 16 percent.

In contrast, the elderly population grew at a much lower rate in the Midwest (7 percent) and Northeast (5 percent).

FIGURE 2.1
Percent of Population Aged 65+ by County or Equivalent Area

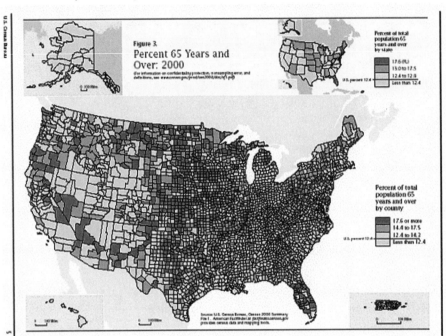

▦ Most elderly live in metropolitan areas

More than three-fourths of the elderly, 78 percent, live in metropolitan areas. About 50 percent live in the suburbs, 27 percent live in central cities, and 23 percent live in nonmetropolitan areas.

▦ While the number of elderly grew, people aged 65+ represented a smaller *portion* of the nation's population in 2000 than in 1990

Unlike previous decades, during the 1990s, the portion of the population that was elderly declined nationally, in two regions of the country, and in over half of the states. For example, nationally, 12.6 percent of the population was elderly in 1990, compared to 12.4 percent in 2000. In the Midwest, the portion aged 65+ declined slightly from 13.0 percent of its total population in 1990 to 12.8 percent in 2000, and the portion in the South also declined slightly, from 12.6 percent to 12.4 percent.

This portion remained at 13.8 percent in the Northeast, but in the West, the portion of people aged 65+ increased slightly from 10.9 percent in 1990 to 11.0 percent in 2000.

▦ The portion of elderly in counties follows regional trends

Figure 2.1 shows the portion of elderly in each of the 3,141 U.S. counties and equivalent areas. It shows a high concentration of elderly in counties extending through the Great Plains and south into central Texas. Many of these counties had percentages of elderly equaling or exceeding Florida's 17.6 percent.

The presence of this band in the Midwest suggests that the trends of young people leaving the area and residents' aging-in-place have continued in this region.

A similar band of counties with high concentrations of elderly is found in the Northeast region, stretching along Appalachia. By contrast, much of the West consists of counties with lower percentages of elderly than the U.S. portion of 12.4 percent, in part a result of higher net immigration and fertility.

The percentage of elderly in counties range from 2 to more than 35 percent

The portion of elderly in counties range from a low of 2 percent in Chattahoochee County, Georgia, which has a large military presence, to a high of 35 percent in Charlotte County, Florida. In 2000 at least 1 in 5 people was elderly in 381 counties. Thirty percent or more of the population were elderly in 10 counties, half of which were in Florida.

Of all 3,141 counties in the United States in 2000, 2,263 counties (72 percent) had a percentage of elderly that exceeded the national value of 12.4 percent (see Table 2.2). The Midwest had the highest percentage of counties that exceeded this value, followed by the Northeast, the South, and the West.

In 2000, a majority of the counties in 43 states had a portion of elderly that exceeded the national value of 12.4 percent. In seven states, more than 90 percent of the counties exceeded 12.4 percent. For example, in all of Rhode Island's five counties the share of elderly was higher than 12.4 percent, while in Maine this was true for 15 of 16 counties. (The five other states in which 90 percent of counties exceeded 12.4 percent were Nebraska, Iowa, West Virginia, Pennsylvania, and North Dakota.)

In seven states the majority of counties had elderly populations of less than 12.4 percent. These states were Alaska (in which there were no counties that exceeded the national percentage), Delaware, Utah, New Mexico, Colorado, Georgia, and Louisiana.

TABLE 2.2
Counties Exceeding the U.S. Portion of Elderly, United States and Regions: 2000

	Total Number of Counties	Number Exceeding U.S. Proportion	Percent Exceeding U.S. Proportion
United States	3,141	2,263	72
Northeast	217	170	78
Midwest	1,055	869	82
South	1,424	980	69
West	445	244	55

Source: U.S. Bureau of the Census, *2000 Census*. Washington, DC: U.S. Government Printing Office.

■ **Six of the top 10 places with high concentrations of elderly are in Florida**

Table 2.3 lists the 10 places with populations over 100,000 that had the highest percentage of elderly in 2000. Six of these places are located in Florida, while two are in Michigan, one is in Hawaii, and one is in Arizona. Clearwater, Florida, had the highest percentage of elderly (21 percent), followed by Cape Coral, Florida (20 percent), and Honolulu, Hawaii (18 percent).

■ **Eight of the top 10 places with low concentrations of elderly are in the West**

In 2000, 8 of the 10 places with the lowest percentage of elderly are western locations; two are in the South (see Table 2.4). Gilbert, Arizona, had the lowest proportion aged 65+ (3.8 percent), followed by Fontana, California (4.7 percent), and Plano, Texas (4.9 percent).

■ **Of the ten largest cities only Philadelphia exceeds the national average of elderly**

Table 2.5 lists the proportion aged 65+ of the ten largest cities in 2000. Of these cities, only Philadelphia, Pennsylvania, at 14.1 percent, had a proportion that exceeded the national level of 12.4 percent.

■ **The growth in the elderly population of states is expected to be uneven over the next 25 years**

According to projections by researchers at Harvard's Joint Center for Housing Studies, by 2025 no less than 10 percent of each state's population will be over age 65.[1] Some areas are, however, expected to gain more than others. Projections for 2025

TABLE 2.3
Top 10 Places with the Highest Portion of Elderly: 2000 (Places with Populations over 100,000)

Place	Total Population	Number of Elderly	Percent Elderly
Clearwater, Florida	108,787	23,357	21.5
Cape Coral, Florida	102.286	20.020	19.6
Honolulu, Hawaii	371,657	66,257	17.8
St. Petersburg, Florida	248,232	43,173	17.4
Hollywood, Florida	139,357	24,159	17.3
Warren, Michigan	138,247	23,871	17.3
Miami, Florida	362,470	61,768	17.0
Livonia, Michigan	100,545	16,988	16.9
Scottsdale, Arizona	202,705	33,884	16.7
Hialeah, Florida	226,419	37,679	16.6

Source: U.S. Bureau of the Census, *2000 Census*. Washington, DC: U.S. Government Printing Office.

TABLE 2.4
Places with the Lowest Portion of Elderly: 2000 (Places with Populations over 100,000)

Place	Total Population	Number of Elderly	Percent Elderly
Santa Ana, California	337,977	18,565	5.5
Anchorage, Alaska	260,283	14,242	5.5
Plano, Texas	222,030	10,911	4.9
Moreno Valley, California	142,381	7,809	5.5
Fontana, California	128,929	6,113	4.7
Palmdale, California	116,670	6,520	5.6
Gilbert, Arizona	109,697	4,118	3.8
Carrolton, Texas	109,576	5,711	5.2
West Valley City, Utah	108,896	5,858	5.4
Provo, Utah	105,166	6,020	5.7

indicate that increases in Alaska, Arizona, Colorado, Georgia, Idaho, Montana, New Mexico, Nevada, North Carolina, Oregon, South Carolina, Texas, Utah, Washington, and Wyoming will substantially outpace the national rate.

California, Florida, and Texas together are expected to account for 29 percent of the total increase in the senior population between now and 2025.

Although California and Florida are expected to show the largest growth in their elderly populations, their shares of the nation's seniors are expected to remain close to what they are today. Gains in Connecticut, District of Columbia, Illinois, Massachusetts, Michigan, New Jersey, New York, Ohio, Pennsylvania, and Rhode Island will significantly lag national growth trends. Even in many of these northern states, though, the proportion of seniors will rise sharply with the aging of the baby boomers and the continued outmigration of younger households.

TABLE 2.5
Percent of Elderly in the Ten Largest Cities: 2000

City	Total Population	Number of Elderly	Percent Elderly
New York, New York	8,008,278	937,857	11.7
Los Angeles, California	3,694,820	357,129	9.7
Chicago, Illinois	2,896,016	298,803	10.3
Houston, Texas	1,953,631	164,065	8.4
Philadelphia, Pennsylvania	1,517,550	213,722	14.1
Phoenix, Arizona	1,321,045	106,795	8.1
San Diego, California	1,223,400	128,008	10.5
Dallas, Texas	1,188,580	102,301	8.6
San Antonio, Texas	1,144,646	119,362	10.4
Detroit, Michigan	951,270	99,056	10.4

PATTERNS OF MOVING AND MIGRATION

■ Age strongly affects the likelihood that a person will move

Rates of moving usually peak between the ages of 18 and 30 and generally decrease until very late in life. The U.S. Bureau of the Census conducted an age-related migration analysis and published the results in a report titled "Internal Migration of the Elderly Population: 1995 to 2000." The report discusses migration of the elderly using 2000 census data. The following sections are adapted from this analysis.

Definitions: *Movers* can be classified by type of move and are categorized as whether they moved within the same county, to a different county within the same state, to a different county from a different state region, or were movers from abroad.

Migration is commonly defined as moves that cross jurisdictional boundaries (counties in particular). Migration can be differentiated as movement within the United States (*domestic*, or *internal*, migration) and movement into and out of the United States (*international* migration).

Residential mobility refers to moves within a jurisdiction.

Intercounty moves refers to moves between counties.

Intracounty moves refers to moves within the same county.

Inmigration is the number of migrants who moved into an area during a given period, while *outmigration* is the number of migrants who moved out of an area during a given period.

Net migration is the difference between inmigration and outmigration during a given time. A positive net, or *net inmigration*, indicates that more migrants entered an area than left during that time. A negative, or *net outmigration*, means that more migrants left an area than entered it.

GENERAL MOBILITY OF THE ELDERLY POPULATION

■ The elderly are much less likely to move than younger people

According to the 2000 Census most elderly people did not move between 1995 and 2000. Among the 34.7 million people aged 65+ who lived in the United States in 1995 and in 2000, only 7.9 million (23 percent) lived in a different residence at the end of the five-year period.

In contrast, people 55 to 64 years old in 2000 were more than twice as likely as the elderly to have moved during the same five-year period (48 percent compared with 23 percent, respectively).

■ Among the elderly, the oldest-old are the most likely to move

Among the elderly population, the oldest-old were most mobile. Between 1995 and 2000, one-third (33 percent) of the oldest-old moved, which was much higher than the percentages of movers aged 65 to 74 or 75 to 84 years old (21 percent and 22 percent, respectively).

▇ Most elderly movers relocate within the same county

Among moves made by the elderly, the majority were within the same county (60 percent), while about one-fifth (22 percent) were to a different county in the same state. About 1 in 5 (19 percent) relocated to a different state (see Table 2.6).

Among elderly movers, the young-old were slightly less likely than their oldest counterparts to have moved within a county (58 percent versus 61 percent), and more likely to have moved to a different state (21 percent versus 15 percent).

▇ Mobility patterns of the elderly differ by sex

The disproportionate share of women in the elderly population is even more pronounced among elderly movers—about 1.6 elderly women move for every elderly man who moves. Census 2000 data show that 4.9 million elderly women and 3.0 million elderly men moved between 1995 and 2000, 24 percent compared with 21 percent.

Although young-old women are about equally mobile as young-old men, oldest-old women are much more likely to have moved (34 percent) than their male counterparts (28 percent; see Table 2.6).

Elderly women are more likely than elderly men to move within the same county and less likely to move to another state. This is particularly true of young-old women.

▇ INTERNAL MIGRATION OF ELDERLY MOVERS[2]

▇ Between 1995 and 2000 the South experienced the greatest net gain of elderly people

Migration patterns of the elderly are quite similar to those of the general population. Elderly movers are going to the South and the West and away from the Northeast and the Midwest.

The South experienced the greatest net migration gain (and net migration rate) of the elderly population of all four regions between 1995 and 2000 (see Table 2.7). During this five-year period 437,000 elderly people moved to the South from other regions. This number was much higher than the number moving to the Northeast (90,000), the Midwest (133,000), or the West (177,000).

The elderly moving out of the South during this same period numbered 204,000, resulting in a net migration gain of 233,000, the highest gain among the four regions. This net gain translates into a net migration rate of 19.2 (19.2 elderly people migrating for every 1,000 elderly individuals living there in 1995) in the South. The South experienced net inmigration for all three age subgroups of elderly people, but most of the overall gain could be attributed to the young-old.

TABLE 2.6
General Mobility for the Elderly Population by Age and Sex: 1995 to 2000

	65+ Years	65-74 Years	75-84 Years	85+ Years
	%	%	%	%
Total	**100**	**100**	**100**	**100**
Nonmovers	77	79	78	68
Movers	23	21	22	32
Among movers:				
Same county	60	58	62	61
Different county, same state	22	21	21	24
Different state	19	21	17	15
Among out-of-state movers:				
Different state, same region	44	43	45	47
Different state, different region	56	58	55	53
Men	**100**	**100**	**100**	**100**
Nonmovers	79	79	80	72
Movers	21	21	20	28
Among movers:				
Same county	58	56	61	62
Different county, same state	22	22	21	23
Different state	20	23	18	16
Among out-of-state movers:				
Different state, same region	43	42	44	45
Different state, different region	57	58	56	55
Women	**100**	**100**	**100**	**100**
Nonmovers	76	79	77	66
Movers	24	21	23	34
Among movers:				
Same county	61	60	62	61
Different county, same state	21	20	21	24
Different state	18	20	17	15
Among out-of-state movers:				
Different state, same region	45	43	45	47
Different state, different region	56	57	55	53

▪ The South Atlantic division is enjoying the largest migration gains of elderly

Within the South, the South Atlantic division enjoyed the largest migration gains of the elderly population. Of the eight states and the District of Columbia in the South Atlantic division, five (Virginia, North Carolina, South Carolina, Georgia, and Florida) were ranked among the top 10 in terms of net migration gain.

TABLE 2.7

Inmigration, Outmigration, Net Internal Migration, and Rate of Net Internal Migration (per 1,000) of the Elderly, for the Population 65+ Years by Region, Division, State, and Age: 1995 to 2000

	65+ Years				65-74 Years		75-84 Years		85+ Years	
	In	Out	Net	Rate	Net	Rate	Net	Rate	Net	Rate
Northeast	**89,564**	**265,378**	**-175,814**	**-23.5**	**-122,249**	**-31.5**	**-40,986**	**-15.2**	**-12,579**	**-13.6**
New England	*46,341*	*68,627*	*-22,286*	*-11.7*	*-21,195*	*-21.9*	*-2,665*	*-3.9*	*1,574*	*6.4*
Maine	9,347	7,697	1,650	9.1	195	2.0	749	11.9	706	31.9
Vermont	4,736	4,717	19	0.2	-230	-5.6	30	1.1	219	22.6
New Hampshire	11,588	10,856	720	4.9	61	0.6	169	3.3	491	27.1
Massachusetts	22,360	36,784	-14,434	-16.6	-11,014	-25.2	-2,619	-8.3	-801	-7.0
Rhode Island	5,339	6,087	-748	-4.9	-1,029	-13.8	-10	-0.2	291	14.4
Connecticut	16,691	26,184	-9,403	-20.0	-9,178	-38.4	-983	-5.6	688	10.7
Middle Atlantic	*70,101*	*223,629*	*-153,528*	*-27.5*	*-101,054*	*-34.7*	*-38,321*	*-19.2*	*-14,153*	*-20.8*
New York	35,191	149,662	-114,171	-45.0	-71,721	-53.6	-29,666	-33.6	-12,784	-40.5
New Jersey	42,405	65,556	-23,151	-20.6	-18,239	-31.0	-4,496	-11.1	-738	-5.5
Pennsylvania	43,599	59,483	-15,884	-8.2	-11,094	-11.3	-4,159	-5.8	-631	-2.7
Midwest	**132,723**	**241,324**	**-108,601**	**-13.0**	**-85,036**	**-31.5**	**-19,290**	**-6.5**	**-4,275**	**-4.1**
East North Central	*97,317*	*191,251*	*-93,934*	*-16.3*	*-72,125*	*-23.8*	*-17,351*	*-8.5*	*-4,458*	*-6.5*
Ohio	33,063	51,652	-18,589	-12.2	-15,326	-18.9	-2,717	-5.0	-544	-3.2
Indiana	24,260	30,576	-6,315	-8.3	-6,556	-16.3	214	0.8	27	0.3
Illinois	30,294	73,413	-43,119	-28.1	-29,500	-36.9	-10,047	-18.5	-3,572	-18.8
Michigan	26,227	48,176	-21,949	-17.7	-16,637	-25.3	-4,385	-10.1	-867	-6.1
Wisconsin	19,046	23,008	-3,962	-5.6	-4,044	-11.2	-416	-1.7	498	5.4
West North Central	*60,042*	*74,709*	*-14,667*	*-5.7*	*-12,911*	*-9.9*	*-1,939*	*-2.1*	*183*	*0.5*
Minnesota	14,923	21,080	-6,137	-10.3	-6,107	-20.2	-826	-3.9	795	9.4
Iowa	10,843	16,770	-4,927	-11.2	-3,460	-15.0	-1,508	-9.4	41	0.6
Missouri	27,897	27,384	513	0.7	586	1.5	539	2.7	-512	-8.9
North Dakota	2,402	3,848	-1,546	-16.1	-624	-13.4	-586	-17.0	-338	-22.5
South Dakota	4,084	4,330	-246	-2.3	-230	-4.3	-16	-0.4	0	0.0
Nebraska	6,780	8,669	-1,889	-8.1	-1,477	-12.6	-272	-3.3	-140	-4.2
Kansas	14,357	14,792	-435	-1.2	-1,599	-9.0	730	5.7	434	8.7

continued

TABLE 2.7 (Continued)

	65+ Years				65-74 Years		75-84 Years		85+ Years	
	In	Out	Net	Rate	Net	Rate	Net	Rate	Net	Rate
South	**436,567**	**203,788**	**232,779**	**19.2**	**180,075**	**27.6**	**44,479**	**10.6**	**8,225**	**5.9**
South Atlantic	*370,822*	*171,664*	*199,158*	*30.0*	*154,017*	*43.7*	*37,738*	*16.0*	*7,403*	*9.8*
Delaware	8,268	5,589	2,679	27.2	2,141	39.4	316	9.3	222	21.9
Maryland	25,979	30,367	-4,388	-7.3	-7,878	-24.0	1,576	7.6	1,914	30.5
District of Columbia	2,860	8,047	-5,187	-69.5	-2,235	-58.5	-1,699	-63.7	-1,253	-128.9
Virginia	38,977	32,040	6,937	8.9	1,795	4.2	2,673	10.0	2,469	29.8
West Virginia	9,574	10,505	-931	-3.4	244	1.6	-489	-5.1	-686	-21.2
North Carolina	50,655	29,733	20,322	22.1	13,467	25.7	4,873	15.1	2,582	26.0
South Carolina	31,788	16,029	15,760	33.6	11,882	45.6	2,758	17.3	1,120	23.2
Georgia	42,444	28,518	13,926	18.1	6,590	15.2	5,132	20.3	2,204	26.3
Florida	256,808	137,368	149,440	56.9	128,011	97.8	22,598	22.8	-1,168	-3.6
East South Central	*69,538*	*54,972*	*14,566*	*6.9*	*13,507*	*11.7*	*1,980*	*2.8*	*-921*	*-3.8*
Kentucky	15,782	17,179	-1,997	-2.8	253	0.9	-754	-4.4	-896	-15.6
Tennessee	38,062	22,563	10,499	15.2	6,205	16.4	3,091	13.2	1,203	15.4
Alabama	19,765	16,734	3,031	5.3	3,682	11.6	-73	-0.4	-558	-8.4
Mississippi	13,437	11,004	2,433	7.1	3,387	18.3	-284	-2.5	-670	-15.4
West South Central	*94,827*	*75,772*	*19,055*	*5.7*	*12,551*	*6.8*	*4,761*	*4.2*	*1,743*	*4.5*
Arkansas	20,002	17,506	2,496	6.7	4,382	22.5	-1,136	-8.8	-750	-16.3
Louisiana	11,677	14,149	-2,472	7.8	-1,465	-5.1	-693	-4.0	-314	-5.4
Oklahoma	18,162	17,088	1,074	2.4	1,529	6.3	-249	-1.5	-206	-3.7
Texas	71,373	53,416	17,957	8.8	8,105	7.2	6,839	10.1	3,013	13.3

West	**176,696**	**145,060**	**51,636**	**7.6**	**27,210**	**7.6**	**15,797**	**6.6**	**8,629**	**11.1**
Mountain	*177,353*	*91,676*	*85,677*	*44.4*	*59,575*	*56.8*	*20,254*	*30.1*	*5,848*	*28.0*
Montana	6,911	6,020	891	7.4	311	5.0	383	9.0	197	13.1
Idaho	11,218	8,423	2,795	19.6	1,715	23.1	819	15.1	261	14.8
Wyoming	3,902	3,931	-29	-6.5	-172	-5.5	-38	-1.8	179	27.4
Colorado	28,104	26,110	1,994	4.8	-1,095	-4.8	1,282	9.2	1,807	40.0
New Mexico	16,362	13,882	2,500	12.0	2,157	18.6	93	1.3	250	11.1
Arizona	95,481	42,240	53,241	87.4	40,371	125.5	11,401	51.5	1,469	22.2
Utah	10,897	8,801	2,096	11.2	928	9.2	804	12.3	364	17.3
Nevada	41,857	19,668	22,189	114.2	15,380	132.7	5,508	86.6	1,821	88.0
Pacific	*109,554*	*143,595*	*-34,041*	*-7.0*	*-32,365*	*-12.7*	*-4,457*	*-2.6*	*2,781*	*4.9*
Washington	33,893	32,723	1,170	1.8	-2,278	-5.8	1,244	5.2	2,204	27.7
Oregon	28,551	27,211	1,340	3.1	588	2.7	2	0.0	752	13.6
California	94,557	128,728	-34,171	-9.6	-28,690	-15.2	-5,383	-4.3	-98	-0.2
Alaska	2,406	3,634	-1,428	-39.4	-1,375	-59.3	-211	-20.0	158	62.5
Hawaii	5,719	6,671	-952	-6.0	-608	-7.1	-109	-1.9	-235	-13.3

■ Outmigration of elderly people from the Pacific division was the main reason that the West had a low net migration increase from 1995 to 2000

Of the two divisions in the West, one (the Mountain division) experienced net inmigration of elderly people and the other (the Pacific division) had net outmigration from 1995 to 2000. The Mountain division's elderly net migration rate was the highest among the nine divisions and was primarily attributable to elderly people migrating to Nevada and Arizona. In contrast, the Pacific division had a net loss of over 30,000 elderly people and a net migration rate of about –7.0, indicating that the Pacific division lost 7 elderly people due to migration for every 1,000 elderly people living there in 1995. California alone had a net migration loss of 34,000 elderly people, the majority of whom were the young-old.

■ The Middle Atlantic division lost the largest number of elderly people between 1995 and 2000

The Middle-Atlantic division, consisting of New York, New Jersey, and Pennsylvania, lost the largest number of elderly people due to migration between 1995 and 2000, most of them in the young-old age group. Between 1995 and 2000, 224,000 elderly people moved out of the Middle Atlantic division, while only 70,000 moved in, resulting in a net outmigration of just over 150,000 and a net outmigration rate of 27.5.

■ Florida gained the largest number of elderly movers, but Nevada had the highest net migration rate between 1995 and 2000

The U.S. Bureau of the Census classifies states as "gaining states" if they experience an increase in their elderly population through migration, "losing states" if they see their elderly population decline through migration, and "stable states" if they had had very little change in their elderly population due to migration.

The top gaining states were in the South and the West. Between 1995 and 2000 Florida was the top gaining state, receiving 149,000 more elderly people than it lost through migration. Arizona was the second gaining state (53,000 net migration gain), and Nevada was third (22,000).

In terms of net migration rates of the elderly population, Nevada ranked first among the states, with a net migration rate of 114.2, gaining about 114 elderly people for every 1,000 in 1995 (Table 2.7). Arizona was again second in ranking, with a net migration rate of 87.4, while Florida was third at 56.9.

■ New York lost the largest number of elderly movers between 1995 and 2000

Five of the top-10 losing states were in the Northeast, while several others were in the Midwest. New York lost the largest number of elderly people through migration (114,000). As well as losing the largest number of elderly people through net migration, New York had one of the highest net outmigration rates of the elderly population, 45.0.

The District of Columbia had a greater net outmigration rate (69.5) than New York, due perhaps to its small size and functional status as a central city.

■ States gaining elderly migrants usually were in close proximity to or had milder climates than the states with net losses of elderly migrants

State-to-state migration flows illustrate the geographic origin of the gain or loss of a particular state. The top gaining state, Florida, received many migrants from the Northeast and the Midwest. Close to one-third of all elderly movers to Florida came from New York (61,000) and New Jersey (23,000).

Other top states sending elderly to Florida were the northeastern states of Pennsylvania and Massachusetts, and the midwestern states of Ohio, Michigan, and Illinois. Florida absorbed a large number of elderly movers from the Northeast and Midwest regions, who may have moved in search of a milder climate in which to retire.

Both Arizona and Nevada had a high net migration gain of elderly people, indicating that geographic proximity may also influence migration as one-quarter of elderly movers to Arizona came from California and Washington. Other top states sending elderly to Arizona were western states like Colorado, as well as midwestern states like Illinois. Similarly, Nevada gained mostly from inmigration from other western states like California (17,000), which represented 40 percent of its elderly inmigrants, and Arizona. Nevada also received a large number of elderly immigrants from Florida and Illinois.

Florida absorbed a large number of elderly movers from the Northeast and Midwest regions, who may have moved in search of a milder climate in which to retire.

Both Arizona and Nevada had a high net migration gain of elderly people, indicating that geographic proximity may also influence migration. One-quarter of elderly movers to Arizona came from California and Washington. Other top sending states to Arizona were western states like Colorado, as well as midwestern states like Illinois. Similarly, Nevada gained mostly from inmigration from other western states like California (17,000), which represented 40 percent of its elderly inmigrants, and Arizona. Nevada also received a large number of elderly immigrants from Florida and Illinois.

■ Patterns of top losing states varied

About three-fourths (72.8 percent) of New York's outmigrants moved to southern states along the eastern seaboard—Florida, North Carolina, Virginia, and South Carolina—or neighboring northeastern states—New Jersey, Pennsylvania, and Connecticut.

Illinois was the second-largest losing state, although its elderly outmigrants were more evenly distributed across the country than New York's outmigrants. Florida (15,000) received the largest number of elderly outmigrants from Illinois, while Arizona (7,000), Wisconsin, Indiana, and California also received many.

Geographic proximity (and perhaps cost of living) seems to play a greater role than climate for elderly California outmigrants, as more than half settled in other western states. Arizona (18,000), Nevada (17,000), Oregon (12,000), and Washington (10,000), along with Texas (8,000) and Florida (7,000), were favorite destinations for elderly people leaving California.

■ State-level migration rates between 1995 and 2000 varied by the age of the elderly population, suggesting a pattern of "return migration" at the oldest ages for some states

State-level migration rates between 1995 and 2000 varied by age within the elderly population. Many states that gained large numbers of the young-old saw migration rates drop by age, while other states that lost the young-old saw migration rates increase by age.

These changes in migration rates by age suggest that, at the oldest ages, many elderly people who initially moved away at retirement may have returned to their states of origin, perhaps to be closer to family or simply to return home.

Popular retirement states such as Florida and Arizona had net migration rates that decreased among their elderly populations. In fact, Florida experienced net outmigration of those aged 85+. On the other hand, many states that had high net outmigration of the young-old saw decreasing losses or even gains of advanced-age groups.

Examples of states with decreasing net outmigration by the age of the population are California, Massachusetts, Michigan, New Jersey, Ohio, and Pennsylvania. States that had a net loss of the young-old and a net gain of the oldest-old include Alaska, Colorado, Connecticut, Maryland, Minnesota, and Washington.

■ County-level migration rates of the elderly population between 1995 and 2000 followed patterns similar to state and regional findings

In general, county net migration rates for the population 65 years and elderly coincide with patterns found for regions and states, with migration gains in the South and the West, and migration losses in the Northeast and the Midwest. However, even in those states that lost elderly population, some counties gained elderly people, such as Riverside County (California), Ocean County (New Jersey), Barnstable County (Massachusetts), and Eaton County (Michigan). Within states that gained elderly people, of particular notice were the dichotomies between northeastern Arizona (lost) and the southwestern part of the state (gained), southern Florida (lost) and central Florida (gained), and northwestern Arkansas (gained) and southeastern Arkansas (lost).

The counties with the largest net gain of elderly people were Maricopa County (Arizona), and Palm Beach County (Florida). Many of the counties in Florida exhibited high net migration rates, led by Sumter County. Other counties with high net inmigration rates for the elderly population included Williamson County (Texas), James City County (Virginia), and Nye County (Nevada).

In terms of net migration loss, counties that lost the largest number of elderly people were Los Angeles County (California), and Cook County (Illinois), followed by Kings County (New York). Counties with high net outmigration rates of the elderly population included Chattahoochee County (Georgia), Prairie County (Montana), and Pope County (Illinois).

NOTES

1. Robert Schafer. (2000). "Housing America's Seniors." Joint Center for Housing Studies of Harvard University Graduate School of Design/John F. Kennedy School of Government. Cambridge, Massachusetts.
2. The net migration rate in this analysis is based on an approximated 1995 elderly population, which is the sum of people 65 years and over in 2000 who reported living in an area in both 1995 and 2000 and those who reported living in that area in 1995 but had moved elsewhere. The net migration rate divides net migration, which is inmigration minus outmigration, by the approximated 1995 population and multiplies the result by 1,000.

CHAPTER 3

Transportation and Housing

Transportation is the lifeline to independence and to integration into the community.

—Elizabeth D. Huttman, Social Services for the Elderly

Peace and rest at length have come
All the day's long toil is past,
And each heart is whispering,
"Home, Home at last."

—Thomas Hood

Access to transportation and housing determine where and how the elderly live. They are both key to healthy, happy lives. Unfortunately, very little data is collected about the myriad of options available in either topic area. Consequently we are necessarily limited in the amount and type of information we can present in this chapter. However, the following pages do include key statistics on a range of topics including: driving, vehicle ownership, traffic injuries and deaths, pedestrian deaths, the transportation preferences of the elderly, the type of housing the elderly live in, characteristics of housing environments such as neighborhood quality, minorities and housing, home improvement and modification, planning for the future, the major types of government-subsidized housing, and the assisted-living industry.

Highlights include:

- Four in 5 of the elderly have valid drivers' licenses.

- By 2030, one in 4 drivers will be elderly.

- People aged 80+ have the highest death rates per licensed driver of any group over age 25.

- Health and disability status rather than age determine mobility.

- The elderly head 1 in 5 households.

- The elderly spend less than any other age group on home improvements.

- Two in 5 low-income seniors receive housing assistance from the government.

- There are more than 36,000 assisted-living facilities in the United States.

▓▓ TRANSPORTATION

Driving

▪ The elderly are somewhat less likely than younger people to have a valid driver's license

Seventy-nine percent of the elderly have a valid driver's license, compared to 86 percent of younger people (aged 18 to 64),[1] and elderly men are 20 percent more likely to have a driver's license than elderly women (87 percent versus 73 percent).

Among those with a driver's license, 70 percent of the elderly have logged fewer than 10,000 miles in the past year, compared with 43 percent of younger people who have done so.[2] In fact, the elderly are twice as likely as younger people to have logged fewer than 5,000 miles over the past year (45 percent versus 24 percent).

▪ By 2030, 1 in 4 drivers will be elderly

By 2030 people aged 65+ are expected to represent 25 percent of the driving-age population and 25 percent of fatal crash involvements.[3]

▪ Daily driving decreases with age

With the exception of those aged 15 to 19, the elderly spend less time driving and drive fewer miles daily than any other age group (see Table 3.1).[4] In 2001 the elderly averaged 39 minutes and 17 miles of daily driving, compared to 58 minutes and 30 miles for people aged 55 to 64. The elderly also take fewer daily trips than any other age group, averaging three trips per day compared to four per day for people aged 55 to 64.

▪ Most elderly own at least one vehicle

Nearly all elderly (81 percent) own at least one automobile, but they are less likely to do so than younger people. In fact, the elderly are twice as likely as younger people

TABLE 3.1
Minutes and Miles Spent Driving Daily by Driver Age: 2001

	Minutes	Miles	Mean Number of Trips
15-19 years	24.6	12.2	4.0
20-24 years	51.7	28.9	4.1
25-54 years	64.1	35.0	4.6
55-64 years	57.7	29.7	4.1
65+ years	39.3	17.0	3.4

to be without a vehicle (19 percent versus 9 percent).[5] Among those who own a vehicle, half of the elderly (49 percent) own just one car, making them 50 percent more likely than younger people to do so (34 percent). Three percent of the elderly own a motorcycle or moped, half the level of younger people (7 percent).

■ American-made cars are the choice among the elderly

Eighty-eight percent of the elderly who own vehicles have at least one American car; this is comparable to 83 percent of younger people who do so.[6] One in 4 vehicle-owning elderly (23 percent) owns a foreign vehicle, compared with 1 in 3 younger people (36 percent).

Full or mid-size vehicles are the choice among both the elderly and younger people who own vehicles; 75 percent of the former and 63 percent of younger people own this type of vehicle.[7] Trucks are the next most popular type of vehicle, with 1 in 4 vehicle-owning elderly (23 percent) and 27 percent of younger people owning a pickup truck. Fewer than 1 in 10 elderly (7 percent) own a sports utility vehicle.

■ Driving provides enjoyment

Most elderly who drive enjoy doing so, and they enjoy it virtually as much as do younger people (see Table 3.2). Elderly drivers' attitudes about the functionality and image of cars is similar to that of younger people.

Traffic Injuries and Deaths

■ One in 7 fatal motor vehicle crashes involves the elderly

In 2002, 6,622 elderly people died in motor vehicle crashes. Such crashes included passenger vehicles, pedestrian accidents, motorcycle accidents, and related crashes.[8] The elderly constituted 16 percent of the driving age population and were involved in 15 percent of fatal motor vehicle crashes.

■ The number of seniors killed on motorcycles is small but increasing

While few elderly are killed while riding motorcycles, this number is increasing. About four times as many people aged 65+ (79) were killed on motorcycles in 2002 than in 1991 (21).[9]

TABLE 3.2
Automobile Attitudes of Those Owning a Vehicle, Percent Agreeing: 2002

	18-64 Years	65+ Years
	%	%
Enjoy driving	88	83
A car is just transportation	53	57
Cars say a lot about the driver	53	50

Source: NOP World, 2002.

■ The elderly account for 1 in 10 pedalcyclist fatalities

According to 2000 statistics, ten percent of pedalcyclist fatalities involved an elderly cyclist. People aged 55 to 64 accounted for 10 percent, people age 25 to 54, 43 percent, and the remainder involved people under age 24, including children.[10]

■ People aged 85+ and over have the highest motor vehicle–related death rates per licensed driver of any group over age 25

In 2002, people aged 85+ had more motor vehicle deaths per 100,000 licensed drivers (24) than other groups, with the exception of people younger than 25 (see Table 3.3).[11]

■ Men aged 85+ have the second highest rate of fatalities for licensed drivers

With the exception of men aged 16 to 19, males 85+ have the highest fatality rate per 100,000 licensed drivers (see Table 3.3). In 2002 their rate was 35 per 100,000.[12]

■ Most traffic deaths of drivers aged 75+ occur during the day

In 2002 most traffic fatalities involving drivers aged 75+ occurred during the daytime (81 percent), on weekdays (71 percent), and involved another vehicle (76 percent).[13]

■ Drivers aged 75+ are more likely to be the ones that are struck

In two-vehicle fatal crashes involving a driver aged 70+ and a younger driver, the vehicle driven by the older person was more than three times as likely to be the one

TABLE 3.3
Passenger Vehicle Driver Deaths per 100,000 Licensed Drivers: 2002

	Men	Women	Total
16-19 years	38	19	29
20-24 years	29	9	19
25-29 years	17	5	12
30-34 years	14	5	9
35-39 years	12	5	9
40-44 years	12	5	9
45-49 years	11	5	8
50-54 years	11	5	8
55-59 years	10	4	7
60-64 years	11	6	9
65-69 years	12	6	9
70-74 years	15	7	11
75-79 years	20	9	14
80-84 years	23	12	17
85+ years	35	14	24

that was struck (57 percent and 18 percent, respectively).[14] In 44 percent of these crashes, both vehicles were proceeding straight at the time of the collision; in 27 percent, the older driver was turning left—six times as often as younger drivers.

▉ When elderly drivers are involved in fatal crashes, alcohol is seldom the cause

Only 7 percent of fatally-injured drivers aged 65+ had a blood-alcohol concentration (BAC) of 0.08 or greater, compared with over 30 percent among drivers younger than age 65.[15] (See Table 3.4).

Safety
▉ People 70+ have the highest rate of restraint use

In 2000 almost three-fourths (73 percent) of all age 70+ occupants of passenger cars involved in fatal crashes were using restraints at the time of the crash, compared to 57 percent for other adult occupants (18 to 69 years old).[16]

Pedestrian Deaths
▉ The number of elderly pedestrian deaths is decreasing

Elderly pedestrian deaths peaked at 1,779 in 1975.[17] By 2002, this number had declined to 1,051.

▉ Individuals age 80+ have the highest pedestrian death rates of any age group

In 2002, people aged 80+ had the highest pedestrian death rates of any age group, at 4 per 100,000 people (see Table 3.5).[18] Among the older population, 85+ males have the highest rate of pedestrian deaths, at 7 per 100,000. This rate is three times higher than that of females the same age.

▉ Elderly pedestrian deaths seldom involve alcohol

During 2000, in 7 percent of all pedestrian deaths of people aged 70+ , the older person was intoxicated. This is the lowest rate for all age groups.[19] Comparatively, among people aged 55 to 59 the figure is 25 percent, and the highest rate is for people aged 21 to 34 (48 percent).

TABLE 3.4
Percentage of Drivers Killed with Blood Alcohol Concentration (BAC) ≥0.08 by Age: 2002

	Percent
16-24 years	34
25-64 years	38
65+ years	7

TABLE 3.5
Pedestrian Deaths per 100,000 People by Older Age Group: 2002

	Men	Women	Total
65-69 years	3	1	2
70-74 years	4	2	3
75-79 years	4	3	3
80-84 years	5	3	4
85+ years	7	2	4

The majority of pedestrian fatalities of people aged 70+ are not at intersections

For people aged 70+, 66 percent of pedestrian fatalities in 2000 occurred at non-intersection locations. For people of other ages, 80 percent of pedestrian fatalities occurred at non-intersection locations.

Transportation Needs and Preferences of the Elderly

In 2002 AARP published the results of its *Understanding Senior Transportation Survey*, a nationwide telephone survey of adults aged 50+.[20] (The survey was conducted from October 6, 1998, to January 8, 1999.) The survey focused on understanding transportation concerns of adults aged 75+. Key findings from the survey follow.

Age alone is not the best indicator of transportation mode use, transportation problems, or personal mobility

Health and disability status (HDS) is a strong predictor of mobility in the population aged 75+. Compared with those with poor HDS, those aged 75+ with excellent HDS are:

More likely to have gone out on the previous day or in a typical week;

More likely to drive;

More likely to walk regularly;

Less likely to be passengers in cars (to "ride share").

Health and disability status determine mobility for people age 85+

Individuals aged 85+ with *excellent* HDS are more mobile than their younger counterparts with *poor* HDS. Nearly all respondents aged 50+ with *excellent* HDS (97 percent) drive, but only three-quarters of those with *poor* HDS (74 percent) drive (see Chart 3.1).

As age increases, the percentages of individuals with *poor* HDS who continue to drive declines. Among respondents aged 85+, 4 out of 5 (82 percent) of those with *excellent* HDS are drivers compared with slightly less than half (44 percent) of those with *poor* HDS.

CHART 3.1
Percentage of Drivers by Health, Disability, Status, and Age, October 6, 1998, to January 8, 1999

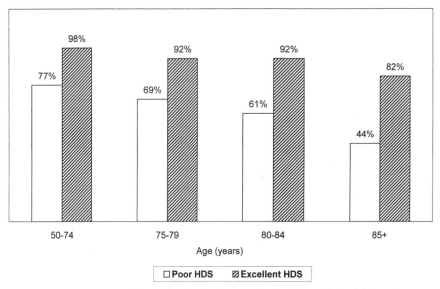

Source: AARP. (2003). "Understanding Senior Transportation Survey." Available online at http://aarp.org.

■ Driving is the usual mode of transportation for adults aged 75+

Nearly three-quarters (73 percent) of all AARP survey respondents who were aged 75+ said that they drive. The survey also found that the percentage of those who are licensed and who drive regularly declines slowly up to age 85, after which there is a substantial reduction in driving.

Individuals with *poor* HDS are far less likely to be drivers than individuals with *excellent* HDS. Among those aged 85+, for example, 82 percent of those with *excellent* HDS drive, compared with 44 percent of those with *poor* HDS.

■ Men aged 75+ are far more likely to drive than their female counterparts

There is a difference between men and women aged 75+ regarding the likelihood of being a driver. Nearly nine-tenths of men aged 75+ (91 percent) reported that they were drivers, compared to two-thirds of women (66 percent). Survey respondents with lower incomes were also less likely than all respondents to drive. Eighty-eight percent of people aged 75+ with incomes over $25,000 drive, compared to 68 percent for those with incomes under $25,000.

■ Most people aged 75+ avoid driving under certain conditions

Seventy-eight percent of current drivers reported that they avoid driving in at least one of the following situations: at night, during rush hour, or in the rain. Nearly two-thirds (63 percent) of drivers aged 75+ who still drive said they avoid traveling at night. Women (72 percent) were much more likely not to drive at night than men (53 percent). About one-third (34 percent) of drivers avoid driving in the rain, and over half (51 percent) of the drivers said they avoid driving during rush hour.

▧ As age increases and household size declines, the number of drivers per household similarly declines

Approximately 1 in 10 people age 75 to 79 (11 percent) and 1 in 7 respondents age 80 to 84 (14 percent) have no drivers in their home. The greatest change occurs among respondents aged 85+. For those age in this age group the average number of drivers per household declines to fewer than one (0.7).

Three in 10 respondents to AARP's survey aged 85+ (29 percent) say they have no driver in their household, compared with less than 1 in 10 respondents age 50 to 74 (7 percent).

Among respondents aged 75+, the percentage of respondents with *poor* HDS who say there is no driver in their household (29 percent) is more than three times as high as the percentage of respondents with *excellent* HDS who say there is no driver (9 percent).

▧ Inconsiderate drivers are the chief complaint of drivers aged 50+

Problems with driving commonly identified by individuals aged 50+ are: inconsiderate drivers, traffic congestion, night driving, poor roads, driving cost, crime, and fast traffic. Individuals with *poor* HDS are more likely than those with *excellent* HDS to consider these large problems.

Driving at night is the only problem that increases with age. Fewer than 1 in 5 respondents aged 75 to 79 (17 percent) report that driving at night is a *large problem* compared with about 1 in 4 respondents aged 80 to 84 (23 percent) or aged 85+ (24 percent). Fewer than 1 in 10 respondents aged 50 to 74 (9 percent) say that night driving is a *large problem*.

▧ Ride sharing increases with age

AARP's survey found that ride sharing is the second most common mode of transportation among adults aged 50+. More than 1 in 10 people in this age group (13 percent) rely on ride sharing as their usual mode of transportation.

Ride sharing as a usual mode of transportation increases with age. Although it is the usual mode for only 1 in 10 respondents aged 50 to 74 (10 percent), it is the usual mode for 2 in 10 respondents age 75 to 79 (19 percent), for 1 in 4 respondents age 80 to 84 (26 percent), and for 4 in 10 respondents aged 85+ (40 percent). Not surprisingly, more older nondrivers than older drivers report that ride sharing is their primary transportation mode.

▧ Trips from home decrease with age

Adults age 50 to 74 report leaving home an average of 3.5 times the previous day, while those aged 75+ report going out an average of only 2.5 times the previous day.

Individuals with *excellent* HDS are far more likely than individuals with *poor* HDS to be mobile. Older persons with *excellent* HDS go out more frequently in a typical week than do younger persons with *poor* HDS. Drivers aged 50+ also go out much more frequently in a typical week than their nondriving counterparts.

▓ One-third of people aged 75+ report walking monthly

One in 3 respondents aged 75+ (33 percent) reports walking on a monthly basis. HDS has a major influence on how frequently older respondents report walking. The percentage of respondents aged 75+ with *poor* HDS who report walking on a monthly basis (21 percent) is less than half the percentage of respondents aged 75+ with excellent HDS who report doing so (47 percent).

▓ Public transportation, taxis, and senior vans are uncommon transportation modes for older populations

A small percentage of respondents aged 50+ indicate that they use public transportation (5 percent), taxis (1 percent), or senior vans (1 percent) as their primary mode of transportation. A slightly larger percentage indicate that they use public transportation (9 percent), senior vans (4 percent), or taxis (2 percent) less frequently (monthly).

A small percentage (5 percent) of respondents aged 75+ say public transportation is their usual mode of transportation. There are no significant differences among the three older age segments (age 75 to 79, 80 to 84, and 85+). Among respondents aged 75+, public transportation is the usual mode for 1 in 7 nondrivers (14 percent) and for 1 in 100 drivers (1 percent). Furthermore, about 2 in 10 nondrivers (19 percent) in this population ride public transportation on a monthly basis, compared with less than 1 in 20 drivers (5 percent).

A similar trend occurs with the use of senior vans and taxis in the older population. Overall, taxi usage by respondents aged 75+ is not common, with only a small percentage of respondents (3 percent) identifying taxis as their usual transportation mode. Although virtually no drivers aged 75+ report taking taxis, about 1 in 10 nondrivers (10 percent) say it is their usual mode. One in 10 nondrivers (10 percent) takes taxis on a monthly basis, compared with fewer than one in 100 drivers (1 percent).

A small percentage (3 percent) of respondents aged 75+ indicate that senior vans are their usual mode of transportation. A larger percentage (8 percent) report using senior vans on a monthly basis. Substantially more nondrivers than drivers report that senior vans are their usual mode of transportation (9 percent and 1 percent, respectively). The percentage of nondrivers age 75+ who use senior vans on a monthly basis (17 percent) is higher than the percentage of drivers who say they use senior vans on a monthly basis (5 percent).

HOUSING

The Elderly and Housing

▪ The elderly head 1 in 5 households

Some 21.8 million elderly persons were head of households in 2002, equaling 1 in 5 households.[21]

▪ More than half of elderly households own a home with no mortgage

Home ownership, and especially mortgage-free homeownership, increases with age (see Charts 3.2 and 3.3). Eight in 10 elderly households own a home, with 70 percent of elderly homeowners aged 65 to 74, and 87 percent of those aged 75+, living in their home mortgage-free. Overall, this means that 57 percent of the younger elderly households and 68 percent of the older elderly households own their own home, free and clear of any mortgage (see Chapter 9, "Consumer Spending," for specific housing-related expenditures).

The elderly are just as conscious about home safety as younger people are. Half of elderly households (46 percent) have a smoke or fire detector, 32 percent have a fire extinguisher, and 11 percent have a burglar alarm.[22] These rates are quite similar to younger households.

CHART 3.2
Homeownership, by Age of the Household Reference Person: 2001

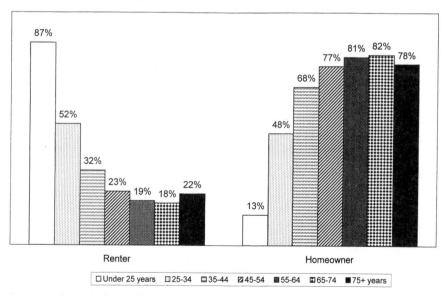

Source: Author calculations based on data from U.S. Department of Labor, Bureau of Labor Statistics, "2001 Consumer Expenditure Survey," www.bls.gov/cex/home.htm.

CHART 3.3
Mortgage Status among Homeowners, by Age of the Household Reference
Person: 2001

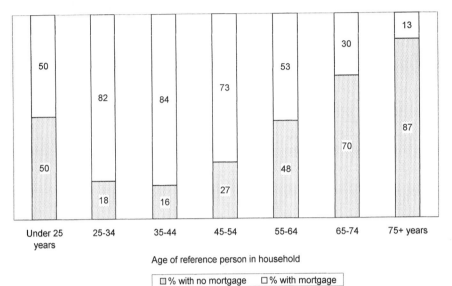

Age of reference person in household

□ % with no mortgage   □ % with mortgage

Source: Author calculations based on data from U.S. Department of Labor, Bureau of Labor
Statistics, "2001 Consumer Expenditure Survey," www.bls.gov/cex/home.htm.

▨ Higher income elderly less likely to live mortgage-free

Mortgage-free home ownership among the elderly declines with income. Fewer
than 1 in 4 elderly households with incomes below $40,000 have a mortgage com-
pared to 40 percent with incomes $70,000+ have one (see Chart 3.4). In part, this
could be driven by home values, which tend to increase with income. Also, higher
income elderly households are younger (and thus more likely to have a mortgage)
and have a higher likelihood of a member who works (thus increasing the ability to
support a mortgage; see the Pension and Social Security discussion in Chapter 9,
"Consumer Spending").

▨ Homes owned by the elderly average 87 percent of the value of those owned by the general population

In 2001, the median value of homes owned by the elderly was $107,398, compared
to a median home value of $123,887 for all homeowners.[23] Regionally, elderly house-
holds in the Northeast and West have the highest home values, about twice that of
their midwestern and southern counterparts (see Table 3.6). Those in the West are
the most likely to have a mortgage.

CHART 3.4
Mortgage Status and Home Value by Income

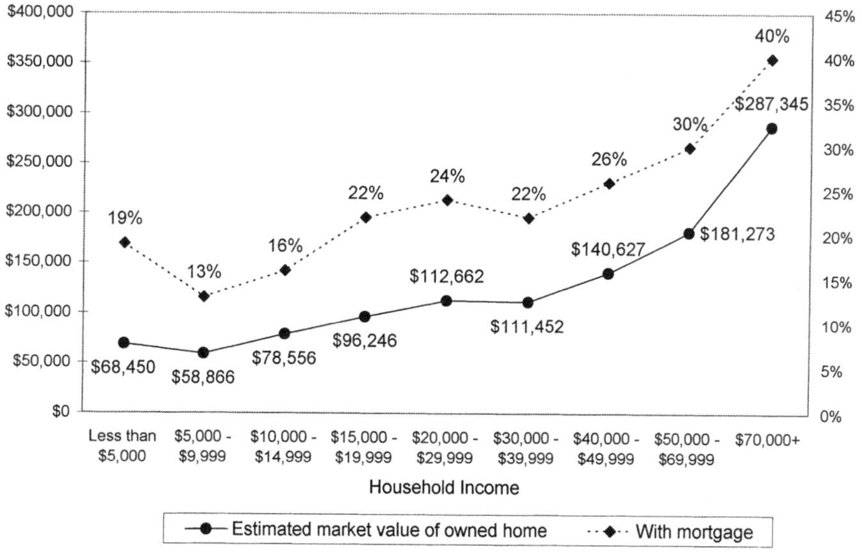

Source: Author calculations based on data from U.S. Department of Labor, Bureau of Labor Statistics, "2001 Consumer Expenditure Survey," www.bls.gov/cex/home.htm.

TABLE 3.6
Mortgage Status and Home Market Value in Households with an Elderly Reference Person, by Region: 2000 to 2001

	Northeast	Midwest	South	West
Without a mortgage	84%	81%	77%	72%
With a mortgage	16%	19%	23%	28%
Estimated market value of owned home	$161,001	$84,710	$86,276	$164,073

Source: U.S. Department of Labor, Bureau of Labor Statistics, "2001 Consumer Expenditure Survey," www.bls.gov/cex/home.htm.

▪ Elderly homeowners have twice the income of elderly renters*

In 2001 the median family income of elderly homeowners was almost twice that of elderly renters, $23,409 versus $12,233. Also, 41 percent of elderly householders spent more than one-fourth of their income on housing costs, compared to 39 percent for homeowners of all ages.

---

*Unless otherwise noted, the data in this section are from the 2001 or 2002 American Housing Survey. Available online at http://www.census.gov. Data for elderly include all households with householders aged 65+ years. This definition is narrower than that used by the Department of Housing and Urban Development, which counts as elderly all households where the householder or spouse is 62 or older or has a disability.

▦ Elderly-occupied housing is older than that of the general population

The median year of construction for homes occupied by the elderly in 2001 was 1963, compared to 1970 for all householders.

▦ One in 20 elderly-occupied housing units has physical problems

The American Housing Survey provides measures of structural, property, and neighborhood quality for households with an elderly householder. The following findings are for 2001:

- Five percent of elderly-occupied housing has moderate or severe physical problems.

- Five percent have had signs of mice in the last three months.

- Four percent were uncomfortably cold for 24 hours or more during the previous winter.

- Thirty-six percent of elderly homeowners say they live in a neighborhood that they rate as a 10 on a scale of 1 to 10, with 10 being the best.

- Forty-nine percent say they live in a neighborhood they rate as a 7, 8, or 9.

- Eleven percent report crime in their neighborhoods.

- Ninety-one percent feel that they have adequate police protection.

- Seventy-nine percent report satisfactory neighborhood shopping.

- Forty-one percent have community activities present.

- Ninety-two percent have trash, litter, or junk on their streets or properties within 300 feet of their house.

- Sixty-six percent say that no repairs are needed on their streets.

▦ Seven in 10 elderly housing units are single detached homes

In 2001, 69 percent of the 21,812,000 housing units headed by the elderly were single detached homes (14,981,000 elderly households). Seven percent of the elderly lived in manufactured housing or trailers, and another 7 percent lived in cooperatives or condominiums.

In the past year, elderly households were more likely than younger households to have used a housekeeping service (15 percent versus 11 percent) or property/garden maintenance service (17 percent versus 11 percent).[24]

Home Improvement

▦ The elderly spend less than any other age group on home improvements

According to a recent AARP housing survey, 83 percent of elderly Americans want to stay in their current homes for the rest of their lives.[25] However, as a group they spend less than younger homeowners on home improvements (see Chart 3.5).[26] From 1994 to 2001 elderly homeowners spent $1,050 on home improvements, compared to $1,620 for those aged 55 to 64.

Planning for Future Housing

■ The majority of the elderly do not think that they will have to move away from their present homes

According to a recent national telephone survey conducted by AARP, 61 percent of the elderly think that it is likely that they will be able to stay in their current home for the rest of their life.[27] Another 21 percent think that it is somewhat likely.

Other findings about the elderly's attitudes toward their future housing include:

- Half (51 percent) say that they have given a great deal or some thought to the home they will live in during their later years.

- Forty percent believe that it is likely that they will need to make changes to their home to be able to live there comfortably as they age.

- Fifty-six percent say that they have given a great deal or some thought to the community they will live in during their later years.

- Fifty-six percent say that they have given a great deal or some thought to the services they will need during their later years.

CHART 3.5
Average Annual Expenditures for Home Improvements by Age: 1994 to 2001

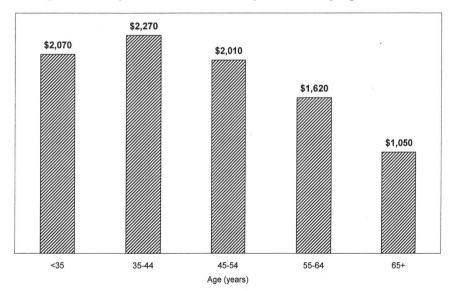

Source: Joint Center for Housing Studies of Harvard University. (2003). "Improving America's Housing 2003."

Secure and Age-Specific Communities
▓ Relatively few elderly live in secured communities

In 2001, 6 percent of the elderly lived in secured communities, in which community access is secured with walls and fences. Seven percent lived in multiunits in which access was secured.

Federal Rental Housing Programs

As a result of different housing policies instituted over the last seventy years, government-subsidized housing for people with low incomes is a patchwork of programs. It includes such widely diverse approaches as high-rise public housing projects, congregate housing for the elderly, and reverse mortgages, which allow older consumers to convert the equity in their homes to cash while retaining home ownership. This section covers the full range of these programs and includes statistics on the number of elderly they serve. Funding for federal housing assistance programs goes through the U.S. Department of Housing and Urban Development (HUD) to local housing agencies (HAs) that manage the programs. HUD furnishes technical and professional assistance in planning, developing, and managing these developments.

▓ Only 2 in 5 elderly renters with low incomes receive help from the government

According to the American Housing Survey, in 2001 about 1.3 million, or 40 percent, of elderly renter households with very low incomes received some form of rental assistance from a government housing program (see Chart 3.6).[28] The Department of Housing and Urban Development (HUD) considers most of the households who do not receive such assistance to be "rent burdened" because they spend more than 30 percent of their incomes on rent.

▓ Access to subsidized rental housing is limited

Waiting lists for many types of subsidized housing are long. It is estimated that the population of elderly who have unmet housing needs is nearly six times larger than the elderly who are currently served by rent-assisted housing.[29] For example, in 1999, approximately nine elderly applicants were on waiting lists for each Section 202 unit (see page 47) that became vacant within a year.[30] At the same time, low-income elderly Americans may lose a significant number of rental housing units. According to research by the Commission on Affordable Housing and Health Facility Needs for Seniors in the 21st Century, 324,000 Section 8 assisted units, which provide tenant-based rental assistance in senior properties, are currently at risk of "opting out" of the HUD program.[31]

▓ Assistance is limited for residents of subsidized housing

In a recent survey of 573 older residents in subsidized housing in Florida, one-third of the respondents (34 percent) replied that they had no one to turn to for help in the event that they were sick or disabled.

CHART 3.6
Housing Cost Burdens of Very Low-Income Elderly

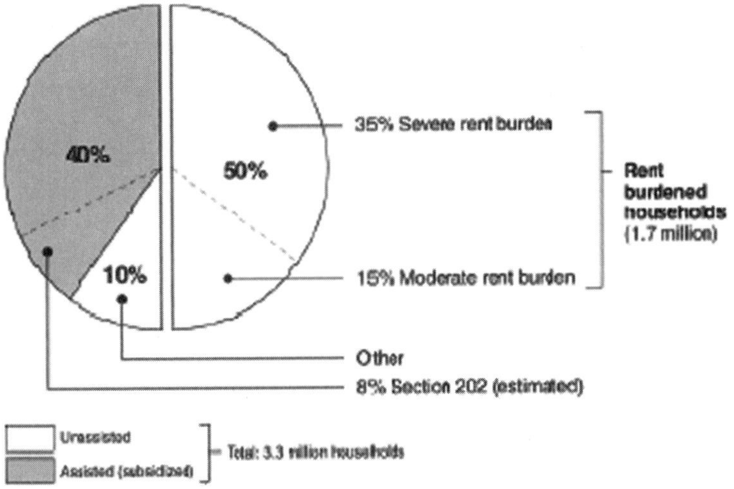

40%

50%

10%

35% Severe rent burden

15% Moderate rent burden

Rent
burdened
households
(1.7 million)

Other

8% Section 202 (estimated)

Unassisted

Assisted (subsidized)

Total: 3.3 million households

Source: General Accounting Office. (June 17, 2003). "Elderly Housing: Project Funding and Other Factors Delay Assistance to Needy Households." Testimony before the Special Committee on Aging, U.S. Senate.

Section 202 Housing. Section 202 Housing provides low-income elderly with housing options that allow them to live independently but in an environment that provides support activities such as cleaning, cooking, and transportation. The Housing Act of 1959 (P.L. 86-372) established the Section 202 program, which in its current form provides capital advances to private nonprofit organizations to pay for the costs of developing elderly rental housing. To be eligible to receive Section 202 housing assistance, households must have very low incomes and one member who is at least 62 years old. Section 202 tenants generally pay 30 percent of their income for rent. Section 202 can offer tenants a range of services that support independent living—for example, meal services, housekeeping, personal assistance, and transportation. According to a recent AARP study, the average age of the residents is 75, a large proportion of whom are frail.[32]

■ More than 1 in 5 residents in Section 202 housing are frail

In 1999 managers of 202 housing programs estimated that 22 percent of their residents were frail, up from 13 percent in 1988 (see Table 3.7). Managers also reported increases in specific disabilities, such as getting in and out of chairs and getting to and from places.

Through 2001, the Section 202 program provided housing for approximately 381,000 senior or disabled households in more than 9,000 facilities. The General

TABLE 3.7
Percent of 202 Housing Residents Having Difficulty Performing Various
Activities, as Reported by Manager

	1988	1999
	%	%
Getting out of chairs	11.0	30.5
Getting to and from places	11.4	34.0
Performing personal care	4.9	18.5
Taking prescribed medications	NA	18.9
Preparing meals	5.4	18.7
Finding way to apartment	0.8	1.9
Remembering to do things	4.0	11.2
Doing laundry	6.5	21.3
Doing housekeeping	9.4	26.6
Average of all activities	N/A	20.2

Note: NA = Not Available.
Source: Leonard Heumann, Karen Winter-Nelson, and James Anderson. (2001). *The
1999 National Survey of Section 202 Housing for the Elderly.* AARP Public Policy Report
#2001-02. Washington, DC: AARP.

Accounting Office estimates that Section 202 served around one-fifth of the 1.3 million very low-income elderly households in 2001.

▇ Section 202 housing is in high demand

In recent testimony before the House Financial Services Committee, Jane O'Dell Baumgarten, a member of the Board of Directors of AARP, testified that Section 202 units are in high demand. They have low vacancy rates (1 percent for one-bedroom units) and long waiting lists (nine applicants waiting for each vacancy that occurs in a given year).[33]

Although Section 202 is a highly popular and successful program, funding for it has dropped from an annual production level of 20,000 units in 1977 to today's production level of approximately 6,000 per annum.

Public housing. The hundreds of thousands of public housing units in the United States vary greatly in architecture and design—from single family houses to high-rise apartment buildings for the elderly. The Housing Research Foundation estimates that between 600,000 and 700,000 persons aged 62+ live in public housing. About half of this group live in public housing designed for the elderly only.[34] Much of this housing needs modernization.

Housing Choice Vouchers. Administered by local housing authorities, Housing Choice Vouchers (a tenant-based rental assistance program which was formerly the

Section 8 certificate and voucher program) is available to help with rent affordability for very low-income and extremely low-income persons in existing private rental housing. The Department of Housing and Urban Development estimated in 2002 that approximately 1.5 million vouchers were in use and that 17 percent of these went to elderly households.

The Housing Choice Voucher Program supplements tenants' rental payments in privately owned, moderately priced apartments chosen by the tenants. Currently, about 260,000 of the approximately 1.5 million voucher households are elderly.[35]

The elderly with physical limitations may have difficulty locating units that they can rent with their vouchers that are easily accessible. In a recently released HUD-commissioned study, 7 percent of respondents were elderly households. Of those respondents, persons aged 62+ had only a 54 percent success rate in finding appropriate housing using the voucher program.[36] By contrast, households headed by persons under age 25 had a 73 percent success rate, and households headed by persons aged 25 to 62 had a 68 percent success rate.

Section 221(d)(3) and 221(d)(4).   Section 221(d)(3) and 221(d)(4) insure mortgage loans to facilitate the construction or rehabilitation of multifamily rental or cooperative housing for moderate-income families, elderly, and the handicapped. Single Room Occupancy (SRO) projects may also be insured under this program. This program served 21,437 elderly in 1999.[37]

Section 236.   Section 236 Housing provides housing to low-income families and individuals. Rent is based on 30 percent of adjusted gross income or the minimum rent of the building, whichever is greater, up to a limit. Section 236 housing served 146,053 people aged 62+ in 1999.[38]

The New Rental Rehab Program.   The Voucher Rehab Loan program is a 3 percent interest-rate loan for landlords to fix up their rental units. In return for receiving a 3 percent loan, landlords must rent to families with Housing Choice Vouchers. Through 1999, this program served 343,673 people aged 62+.[39]

Low-Income Housing Tax Credit Program.   Currently more affordable housing is produced through the Low-Income Housing Tax Credit program (LIHTC) than any other federal housing program. Created by Congress in 1986, the program provides a tax credit to those who invest in affordable housing. Although LIHTC program rents must be "affordable," the rents are not capped at 30 percent of income as is other government-subsidized housing. Although not a program targeted exclusively to senior housing, each year about 13,200 units of senior housing are being created through the LIHTC.[40] In 1999 the program served 108,357 people aged 62+.[41]

Section 515 Rural Rental Housing Program.   Section 515 is a multifamily direct-loan program administered by the Rural Housing Service (RHS) of the U.S. Department of Agriculture. In recent years, Congress severely limited funding. Currently, the program receives allocations of only approximately 1,000 units per year. Approximately

40 percent of Section 515 developments are built and operated as senior housing properties that may contain community rooms that accommodate service delivery. Fifty-eight percent of all Section 515 units (in both elderly and family properties) are currently occupied by elderly or disabled households. Section 515 served 190,829 people age 62+ in 1999.[42]

Section 504 Home Repair Loan and Grant Program.   The Section 504 Home Repair Loan and Grant Program is a rural program offered to elderly persons and very low-income families who own homes that need repairs. Seniors may use grant funds to repair, improve, or modernize their dwellings, to remove health and safety hazards, or make a home accessible to family members with disabilities. Homeowners who are at least age 62 can receive home improvement grants of up to $7,500 if they cannot afford a loan at the 1 percent interest rate. There is no information currently available on how many elderly use this program annually.

HOME Investment Partnership Program.   HOME, a federally funded program for housing, was enacted in 1990 as part of the National Affordable Housing Act (NAHA). The program is intended to foster partnerships among federal, state, and local governments and the private sector. In FY2000, state agencies were awarded almost $72 million in funds for a range of housing activities targeted to seniors.[43] HOME served 20,106 seniors in 1999.[44]

Home Equity Conversion Mortgages (HECM).   Also known as "reverse mortgages," Home Equity Conversion Mortgage (HECM) loans enable homeowners aged 62+ to convert the equity in their homes into monthly income streams or lines of credit.

Based on AARP's 2000 survey on home modifications, slightly over half (51 percent) of all respondents aged 45+ say that they have heard of a reverse mortgage.[45] Of those who have heard of it and are homeowners, only 1 percent has a reverse mortgage, and 6 percent know someone who has one. About 1 in 5 (19 percent) says that this is an idea they might consider in the future.

Of the three types of reverse mortgages, the Home Equity Conversion Mortgage (HECM), which is insured by the federal Department of Housing & Urban Development, is the most popular. According to HUD, for the first nine months of fiscal year 2003, HECM volume was 12,255 loans. This compares to 9,595 HECMs a year earlier.

The actual current HECM volume activity is probably much larger than the numbers indicate. HUD has a second category for "unendorsed" HECMs. This largely includes pending reverse mortgages waiting to be insured by HUD. As of June 30, 2003, HUD reported 17,499 unendorsed HECMs, compared to 7,945 a year earlier.

Assisted Living
▪ Assisted living provides support services for the elderly

Assisted living is an increasingly popular housing and services program for seniors who need more assistance than that available in retirement communities but who do not require the medical and nursing care provided in nursing homes.

The National Academy for State Health Policy reports that in 2003 there were 36,399 assisted-living facilities in the United States, up 48 percent from 1998. These centers now house close to one million Americans.

Costs for assisted living vary greatly

Costs for assisted living residences depend on a number of factors, including the size of units, services provided, and location. The National Center for Assisted Living (NCAL) 2000 survey found that 16 percent of surveyed assisted-living residences charged less than $1,000 in average monthly rent and fees, 48 percent charged between $1,000 and $2,000, and another 23 percent charged between $2,000 and $3,000.[46] Nine percent charged more than $3,000 each month. The overall average monthly charge was $1,873; the median was $1,800.

Almost half of assisted-living residents move from home

According the NCAL 2000 survey, nearly half (46 percent) of residents move into assisted-living facilities directly from their homes, 20 percent come from another assisted-living residence, 14 percent come from a hospital, 10 percent come from a nursing home, and 12 percent come from other types of residences, such as independent living facilities.[47]

One-third of residents leave assisted-living facilities for nursing homes

As needs change, residents may leave assisted-living residences. NCAL's survey showed that the most common destination of residents who left assisted-living residences was a nursing home (33 percent); 28 percent had died, 12 percent moved back home, 14 percent went to another assisted-living facility, 11 percent went to a hospital, and 2 percent went to other types of residences.[48]

The average assisted-living facility houses 24 residents

The average size of an assisted-living residence is 23 units, with 30 beds and 24 residents.[49]

Most assisted-living residents pay out of their own pockets

According to the NCAL survey, about two-thirds (67 percent) of assisted-living residents paid with their own funds, 8 percent relied on family funding, 14 percent paid with Supplemental Security Income, and the remainder paid through programs such as long-term care insurance and managed care plans.[50] According to NCAL, assisted living is covered in a growing number of long-term care insurance policies. In 2000 the Health Insurance Association of America reported that all 11 of the leading insurance companies that sell long-term care insurance offer assisted-living coverage.

Medicare does not cover assisted living. Some services provided in assisted-living facilities may be paid under Supplementary Security Income and Social Services Block Grant programs. In 2000, 38 states reimbursed or planned to reimburse for assisted-living services as a Medicaid service. In addition, states have the option to pay for assisted living under Medicaid by including services in the state's Medicaid plan or petitioning the U.S. Department of Health and Human Services for a waiver.

▥ Over one-third of assisted-living facilities are in three states

In 2000 over 36 percent of assisted-living beds were located in three states: California (136,719), Florida (77,292), and Pennsylvania (73,075). Between 1998 and 2000, the number of licensed facilities has soared in Delaware (by 214 percent), Iowa (144 percent), New Jersey (139 percent), and Wisconsin (119 percent).[51] Ten states reported growth in licensed facilities of between 40 percent and 100 percent in the past two years: Alaska, Arizona, Indiana, Kansas, Massachusetts, Minnesota, Nebraska, New York, South Dakota, and Texas.

▥ Statistics are not available on other housing programs for seniors

Other housing programs for the elderly are available in local communities throughout the United States. However, national statistics are not collected on these programs. They include the following:

Continuing Care Retirement Communities (*CCRCs*) are residential campuses that provide a continuum of care—from private units to skilled nursing care, all in one location. CCRCs are designed to offer active seniors an independent lifestyle from the privacy of their own home, but also include the availability of services in an assisted-living environment and on-site intermediate or skilled nursing care if necessary.

Shared Housing is a housing arrangement where two or more unrelated people choose to share a house, an apartment, or another living arrangement. Each person usually has his or her own bedroom but shares the common areas of the home.

Elder Cottage Housing Opportunity (*ECHO*) *units*, or "granny flats," are small, free-standing, removable housing units that are located on the same lot as a single-family house.

Retirement Communities are also referred to as Congregate Living or Senior Apartments. These communities are designed for seniors who are able to live on their own, but desire the security and conveniences of community living. Some offer common recreational areas and organized social and recreational programs.

Alzheimer's Facilities are designed for individuals with Alzheimer's disease and related disorders. They are staffed with professional care providers experienced in handling behavior associated with memory impairments. Many facilities have specially designed features for residents such as color-coded hallways, visual cues, and secure wandering paths.

Board and Care Facilities provide shelter, food, and protection to frail and disabled individuals. Typically, residents have their own bedroom and bathroom, or share them with one other person, but all other rooms are shared space. The board and care business is riddled with fraud and abuses.

Please note: For information on nursing home care see Vierck and Hodges' book *Aging: Demographics, Health, and Health Services* (2003).

NOTES

1. Mediamark Research Inc., 2003.
2. Ibid.
3. S. Lyman, et al. (2001). "Older Driver Involvements in Police-Reported Crashes and Fatal Crashes: Trends and Projections." Arlington, VA: Insurance Institute for Highway Safety.
4. U.S. Department of Transportation. "2001 National Household Travel Survey." Available online at http://www.bts.gov.
5. NOP World, 2002.
6. Ibid.
7. Ibid.
8. Insurance Institute for Highway Safety. (2002). "Fatality Facts: Older People 2002." Available online at http://www.highwaysafety.org.
9. Ibid.
10. U.S. Department of Transportation. National Highway Traffic Safety Administration. "Fatality Analysis Reporting System (FARS)." Available online at http://www.dot.gov.
11. Insurance Institute for Highway Safety.
12. Ibid.
13. U.S. Department of Transportation, National Highway Traffic Safety Administration. (2000). "Traffic Safety Facts 2000, Older Population." Available online at http://www.nrd.nhtsa.dot.gov.
14. Ibid.
15. Insurance Institute for Highway Safety.
16. U.S. Department of Transportation, "Traffic Safety Facts 2000."
17. Insurance Institute for Highway Safety.
18. Ibid.
19. U.S. Department of Transportation, "Traffic Safety Facts 2000."
20. American Association of Retired Persons (AARP). (2002). "Understanding Senior Transportation: Report and Analysis of a Survey of Consumers Age 50+." Available online at http://research.aarp.org.
21. Bureau of the Census. (2002). "Housing Vacancies and Homeownership Annual Statistics: 2002." Available online at http:www.census.gov.
22. Mediamark Research Inc., 2003.
23. Bureau of the Census.
24. Mediamark Research Inc., 2003.
25. AARP. (2003). "These Four Walls . . . Americans 45+ Talk about Home and Community." Available online at http://aarp.org.
26. Joint Center for Housing Studies of Harvard University. (2003). "Improving America's Housing 2003." Available online at http://jchsharvard.edu.
27. AARP. "These Four Walls."
28. General Accounting Office. (2003). "Project Funding and Other Factors Delay Assistance to Needy Households." Available online at http://www.gao.gov GAO.
29. Commission on Affordable Housing and Health Facility Needs for Seniors in the 21st Century. (2002). "A Quiet Crisis Is Looming for America's Seniors." Available online at http://www.seniorscommission.gov.

30. Stephen M. Golant. (January 2002). "The Housing Problems of the Future Elderly Population." Commission on Affordable Housing and Health Facility Needs for Seniors in the 21st Century.
31. Leonard Huemann, Winter-Nelson, and James R. Anderson. (2001). "The 1999 National Survey of Section 202 Elderly Housing," Washington, DC: Public Policy Institute of the American Association of Retired Persons.
32. Ibid.
33. Jane O'Dell Baumgarten. (2001). "Elderly Housing And Affordability Issues for the 21st Century." Testimony before the Housing and Community Opportunity Subcommittee of the House Financial Services Committee.
34. Abt Associates. (2001). *A Study on Section 8 Voucher Success Rates.* Vol. 1: *Quantitative Study of Success Rates in Metropolitan Areas.* Washington, DC: U.S. Printing Office.
35. General Accounting Office.
36. Abt Associates.
37. Andrew Kochera. (2001). "A Summary of Federal Rental Housing Programs." Available online at http://aarp.org.
38. Ibid.
39. Ibid.
40. National Council of State Housing Agencies (2000). *State HFA Factbook: 2000 Annual Survey Results.* Washington, DC: Author.
41. Kochera.
42. Ibid.
43. National Council of State Housing Agencies.
44. Kochera.
45. Ada-Helen Bayer. (2000). "Fixing to Stay: A National Survey on Housing and Home Modification Issues." Available online at http://aarp.com.
46. National Center for Assisted Living. (2001). "Assisted Living Resident Profile." Available online at http://www.ncal.org/about/resident.htm.
47. Ibid.
48. National Center for Assisted Living. (2001). "Assisted Living: Independence, Choice and Dignity." Available online at http://www.ncal.org.
49. Ibid.
50. Ibid.
51. Ibid.

CHAPTER 4

Community Life, Social Activity, and Leisure

We belong to the community.

—Henry David Thoreau

Life is lived in common.

—Michael Harrington, The Other America

It is from leisure that one constructs the true fabric of self.

—Adapted from Agnes Repplier (1855–1950)

This chapter covers the elderly's involvement in their communities, their social lives, participation in leisure activities, and religious affiliations. Highlights from this chapter include:

- Club or organizational membership is highest among the elderly.

- The rate of volunteering decreases with age. However, of all age groups, elderly volunteers devote the most time.

- The elderly have the highest rate of voter participation of all age groups.

- Virtually all retired people give money to charity when asked.

- One in 4 elderly are gamblers.

- As is the case for people of all ages, television is the most dominant form of entertainment for the elderly.

- One in 4 elderly own a pet.

- Elderly men like watching football; elderly women like watching figure skating.

- Walking for exercise is by far the elderly's most common source of physical activity.

- Cards and crossword puzzles are among the most popular games the elderly play.

- Outdoor gardening is a favorite solitary leisure activity in which the elderly engage.

- About one-half the elderly took an extensive trip last year.

- The elderly have the highest rate of memberships in religious institutions of all age groups.

POLITICAL ACTIVITY

▓ Two in 5 elderly have been involved in political or community activity over the last year

Thirty-seven percent of the elderly have been involved in some type of political or community activity in the past year.[1] The elderly are somewhat less active than younger people, of whom 42 percent have had some past-year involvement. Petition signing is the most common activity, with 22 percent of the elderly having done so in the past year (see Table 4.1). Fifteen percent of the elderly have contacted a politician in the past year, and 1 in 10 attended a public meeting. Fewer than 1 in 10 have been motivated enough to publicly express their opinion, attend a political rally, be an officer or committee member of an organization, or be a member of a politically active group.

▓ The elderly have the highest rate of voter participation of all age groups

The voting rate is much higher among the elderly than younger age groups (see Chart 4.1 and Table 4.2). The peak age group for voting participation is 65 to 74 years; 72 percent of citizens in this age group voted in the 2000 election. The lowest voting rate (36 percent) is for 18 to 24-year-old citizens, who were half as likely to vote as people aged 65 to 74 years.

TABLE 4.1
Political and Community Involvement (Past Year), by Age: 2003

	18-64 Years	65+ Years
	%	%
Signed a petition	27	22
Contacted a politician	13	15
Attended public meeting (governmental or school)	16	10
Expressed an opinion through a letter to the editor or on a radio/TV show	6	8
Attended political rally, speech, or protest	8	6
Served on local organization's committee	8	6
Served as club or organization officer	6	5
Been an active member of politically involved group	6	5

Source: NOP World, 2003.

CHART 4.1
Reported Voting and Registration among Age Groups: 2000

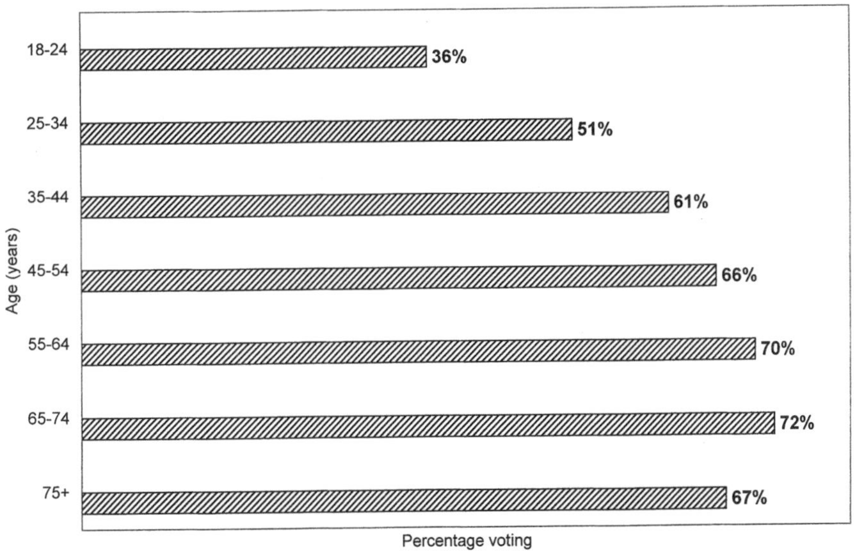

Source: U.S. Census Bureau. (November 2000). "Current Population Survey."

A key difference between these two groups is voter registration—while 79 percent of older citizens were registered, 51 percent of younger citizens were registered.

■ In most presidential elections the elderly had the highest rate of any age group of voter registration

Voting and registration rates are historically higher in years in which there is a presidential election. Table 4.2 shows the elderly's participation in voter registration for the last nine presidential elections compared to three younger age groups. Although in 1968, 1972, 1976, and 1980 the age group 45 to 64 outpaced them, in most presidential elections the elderly had the highest rate of voter registration. In general, three-fourths of the elderly have been registered to vote in each of the nine elections.

TABLE 4.2
Registration in Presidential Election Years by Age: November 1964 to 2000

	Presidential Election Year of:								
	1968	1972	1976	1980	1984	1988	1992	1996	2000
18-24 years	56*	59	51	49	51	48	53	49	45
25-44 years	72	71	66	66	67	63	65	62	60
45-64 years	81	80	76	76	77	76	75	74	71
65+ years	76	76	71	75	77	78	78	77	76

*Prior to 1972, data are for people 21 to 24 years of age with the exception of those aged 18 to 24 in Georgia and Kentucky, 19 to 24 in Alaska, and 20 to 24 in Hawaii.
Source: U.S. Census Bureau, Current Population Survey, November 2000 and earlier years.

CLUB OR ORGANIZATIONAL MEMBERSHIP

■ Club or organizational membership is highest among the elderly

Generally, the elderly are more likely to be members of a club or organization than younger people are (see Chart 4.2). Predictably, one major exception is union membership, as the elderly are much less likely to be working.

Elderly men are most commonly members of a veterans club or a fraternal order and are substantially more likely to be such members than are their female or younger counterparts. Elderly women most commonly belong to a religious club, with 13 percent doing so. Women, both elderly and younger, are more likely than men to belong to a charitable organization.

CHART 4.2
Club and Organization Membership, by Age and Sex: 2003

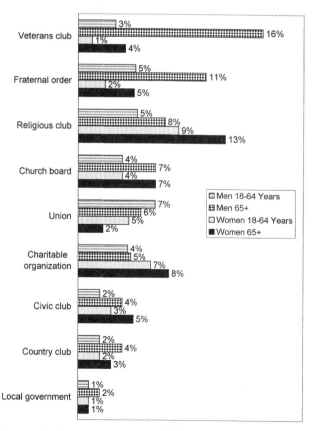

Source: Mediamark Research Inc., 2003

VOLUNTEERING

■ The rate of volunteering decreases with age

According to the Bureau of Labor Statistics, during the September 2001 to 2002 period 7,492,000 elderly volunteered. Among all age groups, 35- to 54-year olds were the most likely to volunteer, with 1 in 3 having donated their time. Along with those in their early twenties, volunteer rates were lowest among persons aged 65+ (23 percent).

■ Among the older age groups volunteering decreases with age

Among the elderly, the volunteer rate decreases with age. For example, between September 2001 and September 2002, twenty-six percent of 65- to 69-year-olds volunteered, compared with 16 percent of those age 80 and older (see Table 4.3).

■ Elderly men volunteer slightly less often than elderly women

During the September 2001 to September 2002 period, 3 million elderly men volunteered (21 percent) and 4.5 million elderly women volunteered (24 percent).

■ Elderly white women have the highest volunteer rates among the elderly

Of racial and ethnic groups over age 65, white females have the highest rate of volunteering (25 percent) and Hispanic males have the lowest (6 percent; see Table 4.4).

■ Of all age groups, elderly volunteers devote the most time to volunteering

While the elderly volunteer less often, when they do volunteer they devote more time. The elderly devote a median of 96 hours annually to volunteering, more than any other age group and more than twice that of people aged 16 to 34 (see Chart 4.3 and Table 4.5). One in 10 elderly volunteer 500 or more hours a year.

TABLE 4.3
Percent of Elderly Volunteering
by Age Group: September 2002

	Percent
65-69 years	26
70-74 years	25
75-79 years	23
80+ years	16

Source: Bureau of Labor Statistics. (2002). "Volunteering in the United States." Available online at http://bls.gov.

TABLE 4.4
Percent Volunteering by Age, Race, Ethnic Group, and Sex

	45-54 Years	55-64 Years	65+ Years
	%	%	%
Total	31	28	23
Men	28	25	21
Women	35	30	24
White	34	29	24
Men	29	26	22
Women	38	31	25
Black	20	21	14
Men	19	19	15
Women	21	22	13
Hispanic	16	13	7
Men	15	12	6
Women	17	14	7

Source: Bureau of Labor Statistics. (2002). "Volunteering in the United States."
Available online at http://bls.gov.

CHART 4.3
Volunteers by Median Annual Hours of Volunteer Activities: September 2002

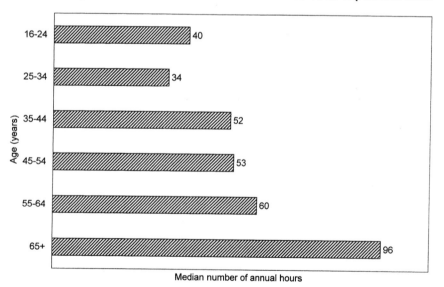

Source: Bureau of Labor Statistics. (2002). "Volunteering in the United States." Available
online at http://bls.gov.

TABLE 4.5
Hours Volunteers Work by Age

	45-54 Years	55-64 Years	65+ Years
Median hours worked annually	53	60	96
Distribution of hours			
1-14 hours	21%	18%	14%
15-49 hours	23%	22%	19%
50-99 hours	16%	14%	13%
100-499 hours	30%	32%	35%
500+ hours	6%	7%	10%
Not reporting hours	5%	6%	8%

Source: Bureau of Labor Statistics. (2002). "Volunteering in the United States." Available online at http://bls.gov.

■ The elderly who volunteer are more likely to volunteer for religious organizations than younger people

Forty-five percent of elderly volunteers performed volunteer activities, mainly through or for a religious organization, compared with 29 percent of volunteers aged 25 to 34 (see Table 4.6). After religious organizations, other leading types of organizations that the elderly contribute time to are social or community service organizations (18 percent), hospital and health (11 percent), civic (8 percent), and educational (7 percent).

TABLE 4.6
Percent Distribution of Volunteers by Type of Organization: September 2002

	16-24 years	16-19 years	20-24 years	25-34 years	35-44 years	45-54 years	55-64 years	65+ years
	%	%	%	%	%	%	%	%
Religious	30.5	30.7	30.3	28.6	29.3	34.5	41.1	45.2
Social or community service	12.9	13.2	12.6	11.5	9.5	11.0	13.4	17.6
Hospital or other health care	9.0	7.7	10.7	8.6	6.6	8.7	10.4	10.5
Civic, political, professional, or international	4.8	4.6	5.0	5.5	4.6	6.4	9.3	7.9
Educational or youth service	31.0	34.1	27.3	34.3	39.3	25.5	13.0	6.5
Sport, hobby, cultural, or arts	3.1	3.1	3.0	3.2	3.9	5.1	4.0	4.2
Public safety	1.7	1.0	2.5	1.9	1.2	1.4	1.1	1.2
Environmental or animal care	1.8	1.6	2.0	1.8	1.4	1.6	2.3	1.0
Other	3.5	2.8	4.4	3.4	3.1	3.8	3.8	4.0
Not determined	1.6	1.2	2.2	1.1	1.0	2.0	1.7	2.0

Source: Bureau of Labor Statistics. (2002). "Volunteering in the United States." Available online at http://bls.gov.

■ **One in 3 elderly who volunteer organizes, supervises, or helps with events or activities**

The top five groups of volunteer activities that people aged 65+ perform, in order of participation, are: organizing, supervising, or helping with events or activities (35 percent); collecting, making, serving, or delivering goods (29 percent); participating as a board member or neighborhood association member (20 percent); canvassing, campaigning, or raising funds (16 percent); and consulting or administrative work (15 percent).[2]

A DIFFERENT APPROACH TO MEASURING VOLUNTEERING

In 2003 AARP published results of their survey, *Time and Money: An In-Depth Look at 45+ Volunteers and Donors*. The study oversampled African-Americans, Asian-Americans, and Hispanics and used a new definition of volunteering and giving based on adding behaviors not captured by traditional research questions in this area. These behaviors include activities such as neighborhood clean-up projects, mowing the lawn for an elderly neighbor, a letter-writing campaign to troops in Iraq, or any other positive social behaviors that result in the betterment of one's community.

AARP's innovative approach to measuring volunteering and giving resulted in a higher percentage of individuals as volunteers or donors than that found by other research organizations that commonly gather statistics on volunteering, such as the Bureau of Labor Statistics or the Independent Sector. For example, about 51 percent of the middle-aged and older population reported volunteering, when asked the traditional question about serving in their communities (whether they volunteer for non-profit charities, schools, hospitals, religious organizations, neighborhood associations, civic or other groups). However, an additional 36 percent reported behaviors that were not captured by the traditional volunteering question, but are services to communities and individuals. Findings from AARP's survey include the following.

■ **80 percent or more of people over age 58 say they volunteer for organizations and others in need**

AARP's respondents were asked whether they had volunteered for a non-profit organization, charity, school, hospital, religious organization, neighborhood association, civic or any other group. In addition, they were asked questions such as "Aside from an organized group, in the last 12 months have you volunteered your time, on your own, to help your community or someone who was in need? That is, given your time, without pay, to help your community or to help someone who is not a member of the family?" When the responses to such questions were compiled, 86 percent of aged 58 to 69 and 80 percent of those age 70+ said they had volunteered in the last 12 months.

▣ Nearly 9 in 10 people aged 58 to 69 say they give money to organizations, family members, or others

AARP's *Time and Money* survey asked respondents whether they gave money or financial contributions to organizations or to family members and non-related individuals in the last year. Eighty-seven percent of people aged 58 to 69 said they had participated in such giving.

▣ The elderly respond generously when asked to give money to charity

The Independent Sector, in its 2001 *Giving and Volunteering in United States* survey, found that virtually all (95 percent) of their retired respondents, most of whom were aged 65+, gave to charity when asked. In addition, the average contribution was nearly double that of the 70 percent of those who gave without being asked. Charitable giving is covered in more detail in Chapter 9, "Consumer Spending."

▣ Two in 5 elderly who volunteer are asked by others to participate

Forty-one percent of volunteers aged 65+ are asked to volunteer by an employer, relative, or someone else. This percentage is slightly less than that of people aged 55 to 64 (43 percent). Forty-three percent of elderly volunteers approach the organization themselves. This is the highest rate for any group. (The remaining 14 percent of volunteers did not answer this question or answered "other.")

▣ The elderly who attend religious services donate money generously

Retired respondents to the 2001 Independent Sector survey, most of whom are over age 65, are more likely to give to charity, and they give more, when they attend religious services weekly. The amount given is nearly double that of those who do not attend weekly services ($2,010 versus $1,139). Ninety-three percent of retired people who are weekly attendees donate, compared to 81 percent of those who do not attend weekly services.

▣ The elderly who volunteer also donate money generously

Retired respondents to the 2001 Independent Sector survey, most of whom are over age 65, donate significantly more money than their counterparts who do not volunteer. Retired volunteers showed an average contribution of $2,300, compared to the average of $1,346 for those who do not volunteer.

SOCIAL LIFE AND LEISURE ACTIVITIES

Gambling

▣ One in 4 elderly is a gambler

Both the elderly and younger people (aged 18–64) are about evenly divided on their opinions of the casino or gambling industry; 53 percent of the elderly and 49 percent

TABLE 4.7
Past-Year Gambling Behavior, by Age: 2002

	18-64 Years	65+ Years
	%	%
Played state-run lottery game	45	27
Played games of chance sponsored by church groups or charitable organizations	9	17
Gambled at casino	20	15

Source: NOP World, 2002.

of younger people have unfavorable opinions.[3] However, the elderly are more likely than younger people to feel that casinos take money from people who can least afford it (59 percent versus 52 percent) and that opening more casinos threatens values and morality (50 percent versus 34 percent).

Nevertheless, one quarter (27 percent) of the elderly played a state-run lottery game in the past year, and even fewer played church-sponsored games of chance or gambled at a casino (see Table 4.7). Except for games of chance, the elderly are less likely than younger people to engage in gambling behavior. However, when the elderly play the lottery, they play as intensively as younger people, nine times on average in the last 30 days versus eight times, respectively.[4]

Technology

▤ The elderly are technology fuddy-duddies

Compared with younger people (aged 18–64), the elderly are less positive about technology.[5] Specifically, the elderly are more likely to state that technology decreases sociability, complicates lives, and gives people less control over their lives. The elderly also are less likely than younger people to say technology saves time or improves the quality of life.

Three in 10 elderly feel that technology is beyond their capabilities, and they are 50 percent more likely to feel this way (see Table 4.8). At the other extreme, the eld-

TABLE 4.8
Opinions about Computers and Technology, by Age: 2003

	18-64 Years	65+ Years
	%	%
New technology:		
is beyond me	19	29
must be mastered to remain up-to-date	35	23
is scary	6	22
is exciting	32	9

Source: NOP World, 2003.

erly are also least likely to find new technology exciting; 1 in 10 does so, one-third the level of younger people. About 1 in 5 elderly finds new technologies frightening and is more than three times as likely to feel this way as a younger person.

Given these opinions, it is not surprising to find that the elderly are substantially less likely than younger people to own new technologies such as computers, cell phones, video cameras, or caller ID (see Table 4.9).

Social Discourse

As a group the elderly favor communicating with people by telephone or in person; half use the mail for such communications (see Table 4.10).[6] These rates are similar to that of younger people. Not surprisingly, it is with the more technologically driven vehicles, such as cell phones and computer-related sources, that the elderly substantially lag behind younger people.

Keeping Informed

■ Television and newspapers are the elderly's preferred informational and news sources

More than three-quarters of the elderly use television and newspapers to keep informed.[7] They use these sources at levels similar to younger people (see Table 4.11). The elderly are somewhat less likely to rely on the radio for information and news than are younger people. Again, the elderly use the technology-driven sources far less.

TABLE 4.9
Percent Having Various Type of Appliance, Electronic Product, or Service in Their Household: 2002

	18-64 Years	65+ Years
	%	%
Color TV set	98	97
Microwave oven	96	96
Cordless phone	79	71
Video cassette recorder/player	81	67
Audio/stereo system	80	59
Large screen TV	49	41
Computer	66	35
Caller ID	55	26
Cellular telephone	58	24
Compact disc player	58	21
Portable radio/tape/CD player	57	19
Video camera	32	14

Source: NOP World, 2002.

TABLE 4.10
Sources Used When Wanting to Communicate with Other People Verbally
or in Writing, by Age: 2003

	18-64 Years	65+ Years
	%	%
Telephone	95	96
In-person	85	82
Mail or delivery service	50	52
Cell phone	55	30
E-mail	49	24
Computer	37	17
Online service/Internet	26	10

Source: NOP World, 2003.

Three-quarters of the elderly (78 percent) read a newspaper, levels that are similar to younger people aged 18–64.[8] Among those who do read a newspaper, the elderly tend to be more broad-based readers. They are more likely than younger people to read the major sections, with the exception of the classified ads and movie listings and reviews, which are more preferred by younger people. The latter is not surprising given the elderly's lower incidence of movie attendance.

Elderly men and women differ in the parts of the newspaper they read (see Table 4.12). Elderly women are more likely to read the TV/radio listings, the movie listings/reviews, and the food, home, or fashion sections. Elderly men are more likely to read the sports, classifieds, and science and technology sections.

TABLE 4.11
Sources Used When Wanting to Be Informed on a Variety of Different
Subjects: 2003

	18-64 Years	65+ Years
	%	%
Television	82	84
Newspapers	75	76
Radio	59	52
Magazines	34	23
In-person	29	22
Books	27	21
Computer	39	14
Online service/Internet	31	12
E-mail	17	7

Source: NOP World, 2003.

TABLE 4.12
Sections of Daily Newspaper Read, among Those Reading a Newspaper: 2003

	18-64 Years	65+ Years	Men 65+	Women 65+
	%	%	%	%
General news	77	85	83	87
Editorial page	37	65	64	67
TV or radio listings	29	54	48	58
Sports	46	47	66	32
Food/cooking	32	46	24	63
Comics	38	45	46	44
Business/finance	39	45	56	37
Home, furnishings, gardening	27	33	21	43
Travel	25	28	28	28
Movie listings and reviews	36	27	20	32
Classified	51	26	29	23
Fashion	18	25	10	37
Science and technology	24	22	28	18

Source: Mediamark Research Inc. 2003.

Entertainment—TV

Virtually all elderly own a color TV set (97 percent).[9] Of the elderly who own a TV, 61 percent own one or two TV sets, somewhat more likely than the 49 percent of younger people who do so.[10]

Television is the most dominant entertainment vehicle among people of all ages, followed by radio, although to a substantially lesser degree (see Table 4.13). About 1 in 4 elderly finds books a source of entertainment. Newer technologies such as com-

TABLE 4.13
Sources Used When Wanting to Be Amused or Entertained, by Age: 2003

	18-64 Years	65+ Years
	%	%
Television	87	90
Radio	59	51
Books	37	28
Magazines	36	28
Newspapers	23	20
Compact disc (CD)	39	15
Computer	30	14
Internet	20	6

Source: NOP World, 2003.

TABLE 4.14
Percent Viewing Particular Type of Television Show, by Age: 2003

	18-64 Years	65+ Years
	%	%
Early evening news programs (weekend or weekday)	32	58
Early evening weekday news programs	26	48
Early evening weekend news programs	18	35
Early morning programs	19	26
Weekend news/information programs	14	25
Early morning news	14	21
Daytime soaps	14	17
Late night shows	15	17

Source: Mediamark Research Inc., 2003.

pact discs, computers, and the Internet are rarely sources of entertainment for the elderly and much less so than for younger people.

The elderly are more likely viewers than are younger people of many types of television programming (see Table 4.14), even late-night shows. The elderly are especially fond of news programs. Interestingly, elderly women are just as likely as younger women to watch daytime soaps (21 percent versus 20 percent).

Entertainment—Dining Out and Other Social Activities
■ The elderly go out for entertainment less often than younger people

According to December 2002 NOP World data, half of the elderly went out for entertainment in the past week, compared with 71 percent of younger people.[11] When they did go out, 60 percent of the elderly went out just once in that one-week period, compared with 35 percent of younger people. The most popular entertainment for the elderly was a restaurant dinner, followed by visiting a friend at their home (76 percent versus 38 percent).

Dining out, attending a movie, and entertaining are major sources of leisurely activities that provide social contact for the elderly (see Chart 4.4).[12] As a leisure activity, half of the elderly dined out in the past year and one-third entertained friends or family. Those who dine out for leisure purposes do so frequently, with more than half of the elderly (56 percent) dining out at least once a week, somewhat more often than do younger people who dine out leisurely (49 percent at least once a week).[13]

Entertaining and especially attending a movie are much less intensive leisure activities. One-quarter of the elderly (24 percent) who entertain do so at least once a week, and only 5 percent of movie-attending elderly do so on a weekly basis. Playing cards places a distant third and is more than twice as popular as board games or dancing, with the elderly.[14]

CHART 4.4
Percent Participating in Particular Social Leisure
Events in the Past 12 Months, by Age and Sex:
2003

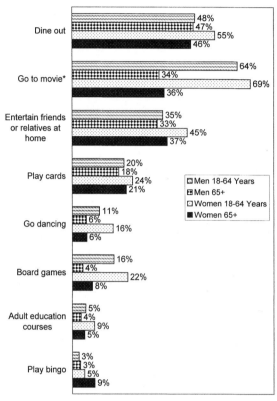

*Past 6 months.
Source: Mediamark Research Inc., 2003.

▨ When the elderly dine out for any reason (including leisure events), they most frequently dine in fast-food outlets

Nearly 6 in 10 elderly dined in a fast-food restaurant in the past month (see Table 4.15).[15] However, they are about 30 percent less likely to have frequented such an outlet as younger people. Those elderly who ate fast food did so about four times in the past month, compared with nearly twice that level among younger people. Location, prices, and the food are the dominant reasons people choose this type of outlet.

Family-style restaurants where alcohol is not served are the next most frequented dining environment with the elderly. About half of the elderly ate at such an

TABLE 4.15
Restaurant Behavior and Attitudes: 2002

	18-64 Years	65+ Years
Fast food chain		
Ate at past 30 days	80%	57%
Mean # of times (excluding none)	7.3	4.0
Reasons for eating at this type restaurant:		
Convenient location	62%	63%
Prices	66%	59%
The food	52%	53%
Service	26%	28%
Family-style chain (no alcohol served)		
Ate at past 30 days	55%	45%
Mean # of times (excluding none)	3.1	3.3
Reasons for eating at this type restaurant:		
The food	68%	70%
Service	38%	49%
Wide menu variety	45%	47%
Prices	44%	45%
Convenient location	42%	45%
Casual dining chain (alcohol served)		
Ate at past 30 days	45%	31%
Mean # of times (excluding none)	2.4	2.2
Reasons for eating at this type restaurant:		
The food	70%	65%
Wide menu variety	46%	53%
Prices	36%	44%
Service	47%	44%
Convenient location	35%	41%

Source: NOP World, 2002.

establishment over a 30-day period, somewhat less likely than younger people. But when they did, they frequented such outlets just as often (about 3 times a month). The food is the dominant reason.

The elderly are about 30 percent less likely than younger people to eat at a casual dining establishment (one which serves alcohol). But the elderly who frequent such outlets do so just as often as younger people. The food and menu variety are the dominant reasons for eating at such an outlet.

Animal Companionship
■ One in 4 elderly owns a pet

Elderly households are 40 percent less likely to have a pet than younger households (27 percent versus 44 percent, respectively), and more likely to have a pet that

TABLE 4.16
Pet Ownership, by Age: 2003

	18-64 Years	65+ Years
Pet ownership	44%	27%
Pet owners with a dog	72%	69%
Pet owners with a cat	52%	48%
Average number of dogs owned	1.6	1.5
Average number of cats owned	1.9	1.8
Age of dog (s):		
< 2 yrs	25%	16%
2-6 years	42%	39%
7+ years	33%	46%
Age of cat(s)		
< 2 yrs	26%	18%
2-6 years	41%	37%
7+ years	33%	45%

Source: Mediamark Research Inc., 2003.

is at least seven years old (see Table 4.16). However, when the elderly own a pet they are just as likely as younger people to have a cat or a dog and to have the same number of them, on average.

The elderly are enthusiastic greeting card purchasers

Two-thirds of the elderly (65 percent) bought greeting cards in the past 6 months. And in the past 30 days, this group bought 13 cards.[16] Younger people are just as likely to buy greeting cards, but they buy fewer of them—67 percent of younger people bought greeting cards and averaged 9 cards in the last 30 days.

Spectator Sports

▉ Elderly men go for football, elderly women for skating

Elderly men's interest in spectator sports is dominated by professional football. Three-quarters are interested in watching this sport. Professional basketball, baseball, and college football are the next most popular spectator sports, with 6 in 10 elderly interested in watching them (see Table 4.17). Except for professional bowling, elderly men are less interested in spectator sports than are younger men.

Elderly women, on the other hand, are most interested in watching ice skating or Olympic competition; half of them are interested in doing so (see Tables 4.17 and 4.18). About 1 in 4 elderly women is interested in watching the more male-dominated spectator sports of football, baseball, and basketball. Except for ice skating, elderly women are less interested in spectator sports than are younger women.

TABLE 4.17
Men's Interest in Various Spectator Sports, Percent Interested: 2002

	18-64 Years	65+ Years
	%	%
Professional football	81	74
Professional basketball	65	59
Baseball	69	58
College football	60	57
College basketball	57	46
Olympic competition	55	42
Golf	42	37
Professional bowling	17	32
Boxing	51	30
Auto racing	53	28

Source: NOP World, 2002.

Exercise and Sports

▮ Walking for exercise is by far the elderly's most dominant source of physical activity

One in 3 elderly walked for exercise in the past year.[17] Elderly men are more likely to walk than younger men, while elderly women are somewhat less likely to walk than younger women. For other sports, the elderly are consistently less likely participants than younger people. Among those who walk for exercise, three-quarters of these elderly walk at least twice a week, compared with 6 in 10 younger walkers. (See Chart 4.5).

Predictably, hunting, fishing, and golf are more dominant among elderly men than elderly women. Elderly men are twice as likely to fish than hunt (18 percent versus

TABLE 4.18
Women's Interest in Various Spectator Sports, Percent Interested: 2002

	18-64 Years	65+ Years
	%	%
Ice skating	45	53
Olympic competition	56	52
Gymnastics	46	34
College football	32	28
Professional football	46	27
Baseball	34	26
Professional basketball	33	25
College basketball	27	24

Source: NOP World, 2002.

CHART 4.5
Percent Participating in Particular Sport in the
Past 12 Months, by Age and Sex: 2003

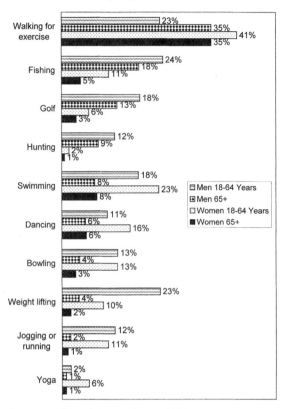

Source: Mediamark Research Inc. 2003.

9 percent) and three times more likely to golf (13 percent) than bowl (4 percent) or lift weights (4 percent).

Swimming is the second most popular sport activity among elderly women, although less than 1 in 10 participated in such exercise in the past year.

One in five elderly (21 percent) owns some type of exercise equipment, such as a stationary bicycle, a treadmill, a stair stepper, a rowing machine, or weight-lifting equipment. This is somewhat less than the 29 percent of younger people do so.

Entertainment—Cultural
■ **The elderly are less likely than younger people to engage in cultural events.**

Music performances are the most popular cultural event that the elderly attend, although fewer than 1 in 5 did so in the past year (see Chart 4.6). About 1 in 10 elderly visited a museum in the past year. The elderly are less likely than younger people to engage in cultural events.

CHART 4.6
Percent Attending Particular Cultural Event in the Past 12 Months,
by Age and Sex: 2003

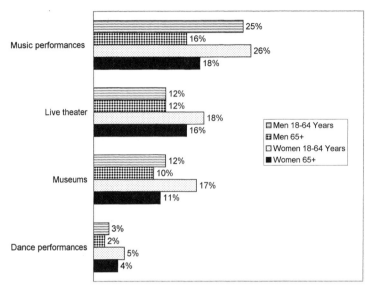

Source: Mediamark Research Inc. 2003.

Entertainment—Games

▦ Cards and crossword puzzles are among the most popular games the elderly play.

About 1 in 5 elderly have played cards in the past year (see Chart 4.7).[18] Elderly women are the most likely to do crossword puzzles, with 1 in 4 doing so over the past year. Elderly female "crosswords" are as intense about their passion as their male counterparts; 75 percent of elderly women who do crosswords do so at least twice a week compared with 80 percent of their male counterparts.

Card playing is a less intensive endeavor, with 30 percent of elderly women card players and 24 percent of elderly men card players managing at least two games a week. However, more than half of elderly women card players (52 percent) manage at least a weekly game, and 43 percent of their male counterparts do so.

Women of all ages are bigger game players than men.

Entertainment–Solitary Endeavors

▦ Outdoor gardening is one of the more prominent solitary leisure activities that the elderly engage in

In the past year, nearly half of elderly men and women gardened an average of 47 days (see Chart 4.8). Reading is another popular endeavor, with one-third of elderly

CHART 4.7
Percent Playing Particular Game in the Past 12 Months, by Age
and Sex: 2003

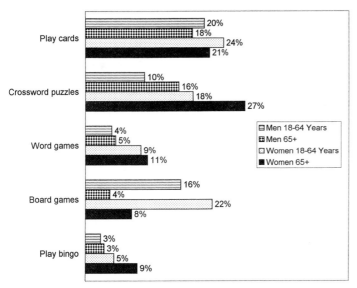

Source: Mediamark Research Inc. 2003.

men and half of elderly women reading for pleasure over the past year. Elderly book-worms are somewhat more voracious than their younger counterparts, with 73 per-cent of the former and 61 percent of the latter reading books at least twice a week. However, the elderly are less likely than younger people to have bought a book over the past year (42 percent versus 55 percent), although they tend to buy the same number of books, on average (9 versus 10).

Elderly women bookworms slightly edge out their male counterparts in frequency of reading—75 percent versus 69 percent read books at least twice a week.

Elderly women also like to do crossword puzzles and cook for fun. Elderly men also like to do crossword puzzles and are as equally as likely to do woodworking as cook-ing. Photography, bird watching, and painting or drawing are of interest to fewer than 1 in 10 elderly.

Forty percent of the elderly have a garden, and 46 percent gardened outdoors an average of 47 days in the past year.

Leisure—Travel

▪ About one-half the elderly took an extensive trip last year

Similar to younger people, 90 percent of the elderly have taken an extensive vaca-tion of at least 5 nights away from home at some point in time.[19] Among those elderly

CHART 4.8
**Percent Participating in Particular Hobby in the Past
12 Months, by Age and Sex: 2003**

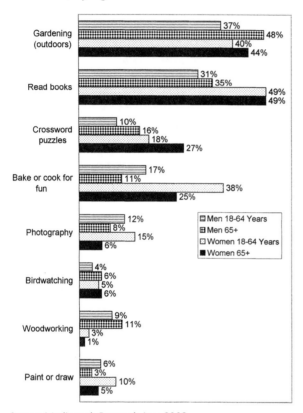

Source: Mediamark Research Inc. 2003.

who have taken such a vacation, about half (47 percent) did so in the past year. In comparison, 59 percent of younger people who took such trips did so in the past year. Compared with younger people, the elderly have taken an extensive trip much less recently. For 32 percent it has been more than three years since taking such a trip, nearly twice the level of younger people.

In the past 12 months, 1 in 4 elderly (24 percent) stayed in a hotel or motel for personal or vacation purposes for an average of 6.7 days (see Table 4.19).[20] Younger people are more likely to do so (35 percent), but at about the same frequency (6.1 days).

▇ Half of all the trips the elderly take are to a lake or beach

Over a 12-month period, two-thirds of the elderly (67 percent) participated in at least one of 21 vacation options.[21] However, they are substantially less likely to have done so than 84 percent of younger people. Trips to the lake, shore, or beach are the

TABLE 4.19
Past 12-Month Participation in Selected Vacation Activities: 2002

	18-64 Years	65+ Years
	%	%
Any of 21 vacation activities	84	67
Selected vacation activities (among those who participated in at least one such trip):		
Trip to lake, shore, or beach	67	52
Weekend getaway and stayed at hotel or motel	32	24
Driving tour	23	21
Casino or gambling trip	23	18
Resort vacation	15	15
Cruise	4	10
Camping or hiking trip	25	9
Guided tour	5	9
Trip outside U.S.	12	9
Package tour	4	6

Source: NOP World, 2002.

most common vacation activity among the elderly—more than half of all elderly (52 percent) who participated in some type of vacation activity did so. One-quarter (24 percent) of the vacationing elderly had a weekend getaway at a hotel or motel.

One in 5 elderly would like to take a trip outside the United States in the future

While only 1 in 10 vacationing elderly took a cruise or guided tour in the past year, they are substantially more likely than their younger vacationing counterparts to have done so.[22] (See Table 4.20). Interest in a future cruise is substantial, with 25 percent of the elderly interested in taking a cruise in the future, a rate lower than the 38 percent of younger people. Interest in a future trip outside the United States is also significant; although only 9 percent of the elderly took a trip outside the country in the past year, 22 percent are interested in doing so in the future.

The vacationing elderly are also more likely than younger people to have taken a guided or package tour.[23]

One in 5 elderly took a foreign vacation in the last year

Twenty-two percent of the elderly have a valid passport, comparable to the 25 percent level among younger people.[24] In the past three years, 21 percent of the elderly have taken a foreign vacation (or to Alaska or Hawaii), and those people averaged 1.9 trips during that period. On average, the last such trip they took lasted 13 days (see Table 4.21). This compares with 25 percent of younger people who averaged two trips lasting a somewhat shorter time, 10 days. Both the elderly and younger

TABLE 4.20
Domestic and Foreign Travel Statistics, by Age: 2003

	Domestic Travel		Foreign Travel	
	18-64 Years	65+ Years	18-64 Years	65+ Years
Took trip (past 12 months domestically; past 3 years foreign)	57%	46%	25%	21%
Number of nights away with last trip	4.8	5.9	10.2	12.7
Percent of trips taken in:				
January-March	19%	21%	22%	18%
April-June	28%	30%	28%	30%
July-September	34%	29%	32%	33%
October-December	19%	20%	18%	19%
Round trip distance traveled with last trip:				
less than 500 miles	33%	29%	NA	NA
500-999 miles	30%	26%	NA	NA
1000+ miles	36%	45%	NA	NA
Traveling with:				
1 person	35%	40%	NA	NA
2 people	41%	58%	NA	NA

Source: Mediamark Research Inc., 2003.

TABLE 4.21
Opinions about Travel (Agree Completely), by Age: 2002

	18-64 Years	65+ Years
	%	%
Seek safety and security	67	69
Seek comfort and convenience	49	58
Very budget-conscious	52	52
Expect good service	40	37
Willing to pay for quality	42	31
Eager to see new places	55	30
Travel is a way for self enrichment	34	25
Enjoy taking trips on short notice	33	20
Willing to make financial sacrifices to travel	24	19
Very knowledgeable about travel	19	16
Prefer planning on the spot rather than making advance plans	32	14
Willing to "rough it"	28	12

Source: NOP World, 2002.

people prefer the spring and summer months for foreign travel, with 6 in 10 traveling between April and September.

■ Almost half the elderly took a domestic trip in the last year

Not surprisingly, the elderly are more likely to have taken a domestic trip, with 46 percent having done so in the past 12 months, somewhat less likely, though, than the 57 percent of younger people.[25] The elderly who have traveled domestically have done so an average of 2.4 times during the past year, somewhat less often than younger people, who averaged 2.8 times.

Forty percent of the elderly who traveled domestically did so by themselves, a figure only slightly higher than the 35 percent level among younger people.[26]

Fourteen percent of the elderly belong to a frequent-flyer program.[27]

For both the elderly and younger people, safety and security are the most important aspects when traveling (see Table 4.21).[28] The elderly are more likely than younger people to seek comfort and convenience when traveling, and budget considerations are an equal consideration among the generations. The elderly are less interested in seeing new places, roughing it, or taking spur-of-the-moment trips.

Religious Participation

■ Religion is important to most of the elderly

A recent Gallup poll shows that 73 percent of seniors identify religion as being very important to them.[29] Table 4.22 shows that about half of adults age 18 to 29 say that religion is very important to them compared to almost three-quarters of the elderly.

■ Seven in 10 elderly are Protestant Christians

Seventy percent of American seniors are Protestant Christians (see Table 4.23).[30] Another 20 percent are Catholic. There is a dramatic contrast between the percentage of older and younger age groups who are Protestant and Catholic (39 and 29 percent respectively for people age 18 to 29). Very small percentages of the elderly are Jewish, Mormon, or other religions.

TABLE 4.22
How Important Is Religion in Your Life?

	18-29 years	30-49 years	50-64 years	65+ years
	%	%	%	%
Very Important	51	60	62	73
Fairly important	31	28	25	22
Not very important	17	12	13	4
Don't know	1	–	1	1

Source: Gallup, 2002. Data purchased by Elizabeth Vierck.

■ The elderly have the highest rate of attendance at religious institutions

Many elderly, particularly of advanced age, cannot participate in organized religious activities due to physical limitations. Yet people age 65+ have the highest rate of attendance at a religious institution of any age group (see Table 4.24).

■ The elderly have the highest membership rate in churches, synagogues, or other religious institutions

As Table 4.25 shows, seniors have the highest membership rate in churches, synagogues, or other religious institutions of any age group. Seventy-seven percent of seniors are members of such religious organizations, compared to 48 percent of adults aged 18 to 29.[31]

TABLE 4.23
Religious Preference of Americans by Age Group

	18-29 years	30-49 years	50-64 years	65+ years
	%	%	%	%
Protestant	39	50	60	70
Roman Catholic	29	29	24	20
Orthodox churches	2	–	1	–
Mormon	4	2	2	2
Other Christian	20	7	2	–
Jewish	2	1	1	2
Muslim	1	–	–	–

Note: Percentage may not add to 100 due to rounding.
Source: Gallup, 2002. Data purchased by Elizabeth Vierck.

TABLE 4.24
Attendance at a Religious Institution

	18-29 years	30-49 years	50-64 years	65+ years
	%	%	%	%
Yes	30	41	50	53
No	70	59	50	47

Source: Gallup, 2002. Data Purchased by Elizabeth Vierck.

TABLE 4.25
Membership in Religious Institution

	18-29 years	30-49 years	50-64 years	65+ years
	%	%	%	%
Yes	48	66	72	77
No	52	34	29	23

Source: Gallup, 2002. Data purchased by Elizabeth Vierck.

NOTES

1. NOP World, 2003.
2. Bureau of Labor Statistics. (2002). "Volunteering in the United States." Available online at http://bls.gov.
3. NOP World, 2002.
4. Ibid.
5. Ibid., 2003.
6. Ibid.
7. Ibid.
8. Mediamark Research Inc., 2003.
9. NOP World, 2002.
10. Mediamark Research Inc., 2003.
11. NOP World, 2002.
12. Ibid.
13. Ibid.
14. Ibid.
15. Ibid.
16. Mediamark Research Inc., 2003.
17. Ibid.
18. Ibid.
19. NOP World, 2002.
20. Mediamark Research Inc., 2003.
21. NOP World, 2002.
22. Ibid.
23. Ibid.
24. Mediamark Research Inc., 2003.
25. Ibid.
26. Ibid.
27. Ibid.
28. NOP World, 2002.
29. Gallup, 2002. Data purchased by Elizabeth Vierck.
30. Ibid.
31. Ibid.

CHAPTER 5

Crime and the Elderly

Commit a crime and the earth is made of glass.

—Ralph Waldo Emerson (1803–1882)

If crime went down 100 percent, it would still be 50 times higher than it should be.

—Councilman John Bowman,
on the high crime in Washington

This chapter covers criminal victimization of the elderly, crimes committed by the elderly, and elder abuse. There is actually a fair amount of good news here. For example, people aged 65+ are crime victims less often than younger people, and the rate of violence against this group is decreasing. Other highlights include:

- Victimization rates for personal crimes are similar for elderly whites and blacks.

- Elderly victims often know the perpetrator of the crime.

- One in 25 murder victims is elderly.

- Two in 5 crimes against the elderly occur near home.

- Significant numbers of elderly are injured or killed by loved ones every year.

- The elderly have the lowest rate of arrests of all age groups.

- Self-neglect and physical abuse are the top two types of elder abuse.

- Information on elder abuse in nursing homes is piecemeal but strongly points to a widespread problem.

■ More than 1.5 million elderly were victims of crime in 2001*

Some 1,572,000 elderly people were victims of personal and property crimes in 2001, at a loss of more than $1.042 billion.

Definitions: *Household head* is the person providing information to surveyors about household characteristics and data on burglaries, motor vehicle thefts, or property thefts occurring within the household.

Nonlethal violent crimes include rape, robbery, and aggravated and simple assault.

Personal crimes include crimes of violence, robbery, assault, and purse snatching and pocket picking.

Property crimes include household burglary, motor vehicle and other theft.

Simple assault is an attack without a weapon, resulting either in no injury or in a minor injury, such as cuts or bruises. Simple assault includes attempted attacks and verbal threats to attack or kill the victim.

Violence includes murder, rape and sexual assault, robbery, and simple and aggravated assault.

PERSONAL CRIMES

■ People aged 65+ are crime victims less often than younger people

In 2001 the personal crime rate for victims aged 65+ was 3.8 per 1,000 persons, compared to a high of 58.8 per 1,000 persons for victims age 16 to 19 (see Chart 5.1 and Table 5.1). In fact, the elderly's rate was the lowest of all age groups for most major types of crime. The exception was robbery, where the rate for people age 50 to 64 was similar to that for the elderly.

Note: Data from the 2001 National Crime Victimization Survey (NCVS) are presented here to provide information that is as current as possible. However, for some data (such as those providing details on age, race, and sex) the findings are based on about 10 or fewer sample cases. For data with larger sample sizes see the Bureau of Justice Statistics report *Crimes against Persons Age 65 or Older, 1992–97*. (Select details from this report appear later on this chapter.)

A Note about Frauds against the Elderly

It is important to note that the NCVS does not collect data on frauds against the elderly, even though there is much "informal" information that such crimes are a significant problem. In fact, numerous congressional hearings have highlighted the problem, but no hard data is currently available.

---

*Unless otherwise noted all data in this section is from the Bureau of Justice Statistics, "Criminal Victimization in the United States, 2001." Available online at http://www.ojp.usdoj.gov.

CHART 5.1

Victimization Rates for Personal Crimes, Persons Aged 12 and Over: 2001

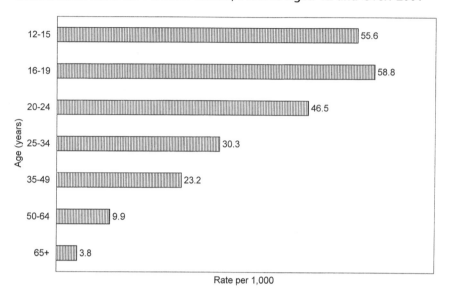

Rate per 1,000

Source: U.S. Department of Justice, Bureau of Justice Statistics, *Criminal Victimization in the United States, 2001*. Available online at http://www.ojp.usdoj.gov/bjs/cvictgen.htm.

TABLE 5.1

Personal Crime Victimization Rates for Persons Aged 12 and Over, by Types of Crime and Age of Victims: 2001

	Age (Years)						
	12-15	16-19	20-24	25-34	35-49	50-64	65 +
All personal crimes	55.6	58.8	46.5	30.3	23.2	9.9	3.8
Crimes of violence	55.1	55.8	44.7	29.3	22.9	9.5	3.2
Completed violence	17.4	18.9	17.8	10.0	6.1	2.1	1.2
Attempted/threatened	37.7	36.9	26.9	19.3	16.8	7.4	2.0
Rape/Sexual assault	1.7*	3.4	2.4	1.1	1.0	0.2*	0.1*
Robbery	5.2	6.4	4.2	3.6	2.1	1.2	1.3
Completed/property taken	2.8	4.5	2.7	2.6	1.4	0.8	1.0
Attempted taking property	2.4	1.9	1.5*	1.1	0.6	0.4*	0.3*
Assault	48.3	46.1	38.1	24.6	19.7	8.2	1.8
Aggravated	8.7	12.3	10.7	6.5	5.2	2.0	0.4*
Simple	39.6	33.8	27.4	18.1	14.5	6.2	1.4
With minor injury	9.9	7.6	8.8	4.9	2.7	0.8	0.1*
Without injury	29.6	26.2	18.6	13.2	11.9	5.4	1.3
Purse snatching/Pocket picking	0.5*	3.0	1.8	1.0	0.4*	0.3*	0.7*

Source: U.S. Department of Justice, Bureau of Justice Statistics, *Criminal Victimization in the United States, 2001*. Available online at http://www.ojp.usdoj.gov/bjs/cvictgen.htm.
*Estimate is based on about 10 or fewer cases.

TABLE 5.2
Average Annual Rate (per 1,000) of Violent Crimes, by Age: 1999–2000 and 2001–2002

	1999-2000	2001-2002
12-15 years	67	50
16-19 years	71	57
20-24 years	59	46
25-34 years	36	28
35-49 years	24	21
50-64 years	14	10
65+ years	4	3

Source: U.S. Department of Justice, Bureau of Justice Statistics, *Criminal Victimization in the United States, 2001.* Available online at http://www.ojp.usdoj.gov/bjs/cvictgen.htm.

■ The rate of violent crime against the elderly decreased slightly between 1999 and 2001

Following a pattern affecting all age groups, the rate of violent crime against the elderly has been decreasing since the early 1900s. In fact, between 1999 and 2002 the rate for the elderly decreased only slightly compared to that for all age groups (see Table 5.2).

■ Elderly women are slightly more likely to be crime victims than elderly men

According to 2001 data, in most areas of personal crime, elderly females are slightly more likely to be victims of crime than elderly males (see Table 5.3). Elderly males have slightly higher rates of being robbed than elderly females.

TABLE 5.3
Victimization Rates (per 1,000) of the Elderly by Sex: 2001

	Men	Women
Crimes of violence	2.7	3.5
Robbery	1.4	1.2
Assault	1.4	2.1
Purse snatching/pocket picking	0.2	1.0

Source: U.S. Department of Justice, Bureau of Justice Statistics, *Criminal Victimization in the United States, 2001.* Available online at http://www.ojp.usdoj.gov/bjs/cvictgen.htm.

■ Victimization rates for personal crimes are similar for elderly whites and blacks

Based on 2001 data, elderly whites are slightly more likely to be victims of violent crime than elderly blacks (see Table 5.4). The reverse is true for robbery.

■ Elderly victims often know the perpetrator of the crime

Personal crimes are often conducted by people whom the victims know. In 2001, for example, 44 percent of the time that the elderly were victims of violent crimes, they knew the perpetrator. This figure is 65 percent for assault but only 13 percent for robbery. Half the time that elderly women were victims of rape, they knew the rapist.

■ Elderly victims of crime often try to defend themselves

In 2001, when the elderly were victims of violent crime, 70 percent of the time they tried to defend themselves. For elderly women who were sexually assaulted, the figure is 100 percent, and for robbery and assault combined, the figure is 66 percent.

■ The elderly are the most likely age group to report crime

The rate of reporting crimes to the police increases with age. Two-thirds (66 percent) of elderly crime victims reported the crime to police in 2001, compared to one-third of people age 12 to 19 (see Chart 5.2).

■ Three in 5 robberies of the elderly result in injury

In 2001, an elderly person who was robbed sustained physical injury 59 percent of the time. However, the elderly are the least likely age group to sustain an injury from an assault (6 percent).

TABLE 5.4
Victimization Rates (per 1,000) of the Elderly, by Race: 2001

	White	Black
Crimes of violence	3.3	2.6
Robbery	1.3	2.2
Assault	1.9	1.4
Purse snatching/pocket picking	0.6	0.7

Source: U.S. Department of Justice, Bureau of Justice Statistics, Criminal Victimization in the United States, 2001. Available online at http://www.ojp.usdoj.gov/bjs/cvictgen.htm.

CHART 5.2
Percent Reporting Crimes to the Police, by Age: 2001

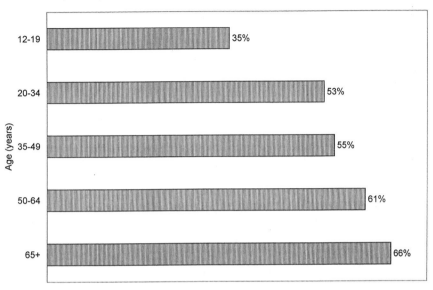

Source: U.S. Department of Justice, Bureau of Justice Statistics, *Criminal Victimization in the United States, 2001*. Available online at http://www.ojp.usdoj.gov/bjs/cvictgen.htm.

PROPERTY CRIMES

■ The elderly are victims of property crime far less often than younger age groups

In 2001 the rate (66 per 1,000) for property crimes, such as household burglary and motor vehicle theft, committed against elderly households was half that of households headed by someone aged 50 to 64 (133 per 1,000) and one-sixth of the rate for victims aged 12 to 19 (393 per 1,000) (see Table 5.5).

ELDERLY MURDER VICTIMS

■ One in 25 murder victims is elderly

In 2001, the United States recorded 607 murders of elderly people, which represented 4 percent of all murders.[1] Elderly murder victims were more likely to be men (57 percent) than women (43 percent), and more likely to be white (72 percent) than black (24 percent); the race of 3 percent was "other" or unknown.

In 2001, firearms accounted for 33 percent of all murders of elderly victims. Knives and other cutting instruments were used in 20 percent of the murders, blunt objects were used in 14 percent, and 12 percent were with "personal weapons" such as hands, fists, and feet. The remaining 23 percent were by other means, such as fire and strangulation.

TABLE 5.5
Property Crime Victimization Rates (per 1,000), by Age of Head of Household: 2001

	12-19 Years	20-34 Years	35-49 Years	50-64 Years	65+ Years
All property crimes	393.1	213.6	211.7	132.5	66.1
Household burglary	66.9	37.1	32.1	24.0	16.6
Completed	57.6	31.5	28.1	20.2	13.8
Forcible entry	12.8*	13.7	10.2	9.0	4.6
Unlawful entry without force	44.7	17.7	17.9	11.2	9.3
Attempted forcible entry	9.3*	5.6	4.0	3.8	2.8
Motor vehicle theft	27.5	12.1	11.4	7.5	3.3
Completed	20.5*	8.7	8.3	5.0	2.5
Attempted	7.0*	3.4	3.1	2.5	0.7*
Theft	298.7	164.4	168.2	101.0	46.2
Completed	288.9	159.3	162.8	97.0	45.0
Less than $50	76.1	49.1	58.6	34.4	17.4
$50 - $249	96.5	59.6	59.4	30.5	12.6
$250 or more	108.8	43.6	32.1	23.6	9.1
Amount not available	7.4*	6.9	12.7	8.6	5.9
Attempted	9.8*	5.1	5.4	4.0	1.2*

Source: U.S. Department of Justice, Bureau of Justice Statistics, *Criminal Victimization in the United States, 2001.*
Available online at http://www.ojp.usdoj.gov/bjs/cvictgen.htm.
*Estimate is based on about 10 or fewer cases.

NATIONAL CRIME VICTIM SURVEY RESULTS ON CRIMES AGAINST THE ELDERLY

The Bureau of Justice Statistics report *Crimes against Persons Age 65 or Older, 1992–97* (2000 revision), is the most recent in-depth analysis of crimes against the elderly. The report draws on the National Crime Victimization Survey (NCVS). The study features data aggregated across six years, which provides a large enough number of cases for more detailed analyses than are possible with data from only one or two years. Key findings from this report appear below.

■ Two in 5 crimes against the elderly occur near home

From 1992 to 1997, 43 percent of violent, nonlethal crimes against the elderly occurred in or near their homes, compared to 30 percent for people aged 50 to 64 and 32 percent for people aged 25 to 49.

■ As is true for younger people, personal theft from the elderly takes place in a variety of locations

Among elderly victims of purse snatching and pocket picking, 31 percent of thefts occur in commercial places and 22 percent occur on the open street (see Table 5.6).

TABLE 5.6
Purse Snatching and Pocket Picking: Place of Occurrence and Time of Day, by Age: 1992–1996

	12-64 Years	65+ Years
	%	%
Place of occurrence	100	100%
Own home or friend's	7	4
Commercial place	31	41
Parking lot or garage	6	6
Open area of street	22	23
Public transportation	11	17
Other	23	10
Time of occurrence	100	100
Day	64	87
Night	34	12
Unknown	2	1

Source: U.S. Department of Justice, Bureau of Justice Statistics. (2000). Crimes against Persons Age 65 and Older, 1992–97.

Sixty-four percent of such crimes against elderly persons occurs during the day. The locations of such crimes do not significantly differ from that for younger people.

▧ The elderly report that most car thefts occur at night but that other thefts occur about equally at night and during the day

The Bureau of Justice Statistics analysis separates purse snatching and pocket picking from other forms of theft—household burglary, motor vehicle theft, and theft from a house or car (see Table 5.7). During 1992 to 1997, for those who knew whether the crime was committed during day or night, about three-fourths of the elderly reported that motor vehicles thefts occurred at night, while household burglary and theft from a house or car were roughly evenly divided between night and day. These findings were similar for younger people.

The location of motor vehicle theft and theft from a house or car were also similar for the two age groups. The most frequent locations were near the victim's home or in a parking lot or garage. However, younger people were more likely than the elderly to have a theft near their homes or the home of a friend or neighbor.

▧ Property crime rates for elderly-headed households are highest for blacks and Hispanics

Property crimes committed against elderly-headed households are least likely among those who are white (see Table 5.8). The crime rates for those who are Hispanic or black are nearly twice the level of those who are white.

TABLE 5.7
Property Crime: Place of Occurrence and Time of Day, by Age: 1992–1997

	12-64 Years %	65+ Years %
Time of Day		
Household burglary	100	100
Unknown time of day	32	41
Known time of day	68	59
Day*	53	49
Night*	47	51
Motor Vehicle Theft	100	100
Unknown time of day	12	15
Known time of day	88	85
Day*	26	26
Night*	74	74
Theft from car or home	100	100
Unknown time of day	23	31
Known time of day	77	69
Day*	51	52
Night*	49	48
Place of Occurrence		
Motor Vehicle Theft	100	100
Near victim's home	44	55
Near friend or neighbor's home	8	7
Parking lot or garage	33	26
Open area, near public transportation	10	8
Other	5	5
Theft from car or home	100	100
Victim's, friend's, neighbor's home	48	59
Commercial place, parking lot	23	22
School	14	4
Open area, public transportation	6	5
Other	8	10

*Percent based on known time of day.
Source: U.S. Department of Justice, Bureau of Justice Statistics. (2000). *Crimes against Persons Age 65 and Older, 1992–97.*

TABLE 5.8
Average Annual Property Crime Rates per 1,000
Elderly-Headed Households: 1992–1997

	Per 1,000
Crimes against elderly-headed :	
White households	110
Non-Hispanic households	115
Hispanic households	168
Black households	184

Source: U.S. Department of Justice, Bureau of Justice Statistics. (2000). *Crimes against Persons Age 65 and Older, 1992–97.*

■ **Among households with an elderly head of household, property crime rates are higher for those having annual incomes over $50,000**

Between 1992 and 1997, the average annual rate of property crimes per 1,000 households with an elderly head of household ranged from 103 crimes against households with less than $15,000 per year to 179 crimes against households with more than $50,000 per year.

■ **About two-thirds of nonlethal violence by loved ones of elderly victims occur at home**

Sixty-nine percent of the nonlethal violence toward the elderly that was conducted by a relative, an intimate, or a close acquaintance occurred in the victim's home. In addition, 36 percent of the nonlethal violence toward the elderly conducted by strangers or casual acquaintances occurred at home.

■ **Males commit over three-fourths and whites commit almost half of the nonlethal violence against the elderly**

Males committed over three-fourths (76 percent) of the nonlethal violence against the elderly in the years 1992 to 1997; white offenders committed almost half (48 percent).

■ **Nonlethal violence against the elderly is most typically between a white victim and a white offender**

Almost half of the nonlethal violence against persons age 65 or older involved a white offender and a white victim (48 percent); almost a fifth (19 percent) involved a black offender and a white victim; and about an eighth involved a black offender and a black victim (12 percent).

■ **Money and credit cards top the list of items most often stolen from elderly households**

Cash, wallets, or credit cards, followed by motor vehicle parts and gasoline, top the list of objects most often stolen from households with a household head age 65 or older (see Chart 5.3).

■ **Significant numbers of elderly are injured or killed by loved ones every year**

Between 1992 and 1997, an average of 500 elderly were killed by loved ones each year, accounting for 26 percent of all yearly murders of the elderly. In addition, 36,000 elderly persons were injured by a relative, an intimate, or a close acquaintance annually over the six-year period.

CHART 5.3
Items Stolen from Elderly Households, 1992–1997

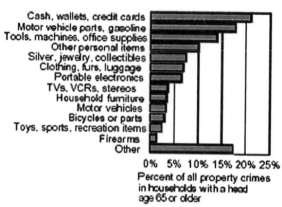

Source: U.S. Department of Justice, Bureau of Justice Statistics. (2000). *Crimes against Persons Age 65 and Older, 1992–97.*

■ One third of murders of elderly people are by people aged 25 to 49

Between 1992 and 1997, murders of elderly people were most commonly committed by people aged 25 to 49 (33 percent). People younger than 25 accounted for 17 percent, and elderly people committed 11 percent of the murders.

THE ELDERLY ON "THE OTHER SIDE" OF THE LAW

■ Within elderly age groups, people aged 75+ are the most likely to commit murder

In 2001, only 154 elderly persons committed murder, less than 1 percent of all such offenders. Thirty-nine percent of elderly murderers were aged 75+. Most elderly murderers were men (88 percent); 12 percent were women; 77 percent were white, 20 percent were black, and 3 percent were "other" or unknown races.

■ The elderly seldom get in trouble with the law

Along with children under age 10 and people age 60 to 64, the elderly are seldom arrested. The elderly have the lowest percentage of all arrests (0.6 percent).[2]

■ Three percent of the state and federal prison population are aged 55+

The federal and state prison systems consider inmates aged 55+ to be elderly. In 2002, the elderly state and federal prison population (excluding those in local jails) stood at 40,800 and represented 3 percent of the entire prison population aged 18+ (see Table 5.9). Nine in 10 elderly prisoners were male, and over half were black.

TABLE 5.9

Sentenced Prisoners Aged 55+ under State and Federal
Jurisdiction, by Race, Hispanic Origin, and Age: 2002

	Number	Percent
Total 55+	**40,800**	**100**
Men	**38,900**	**95**
White	21,500	53
Black	10,800	26
Hispanic	4,800	12
Other*	1,800	4
Women	**1,900**	**5**
White	1,200	3
Black	500	1
Hispanic	200	0.5
Other*	–	–

*Includes American Indians, Alaska Natives, Asians, Native Hawaiians,
and other Pacific Islanders.
Source: National Criminal Justice Reference Center. (2002). "Prisoners
2002." Available online at http://ncjrs.org.

■ More than half of elderly prisoners are incarcerated for nonviolent offenses

In 1997 the National Center on Institutions and Alternatives (NCIA) surveyed states and the Federal Bureau of Prisons to distinguish between violent and nonviolent elderly offenders. They found that the majority of elderly inmates, 52 percent, are incarcerated for nonviolent offenses; 48 percent were in prison for violent offenses.[3]

NCIA found great variation between federal and state prisons. Thirty-four states in their study were able to categorize inmates based on offense; 28 of them reported that the majority of elderly prisoners were incarcerated for a violent offense. Six states reported a majority of nonviolent elderly inmates. The Federal Bureau of Prisons reported that 97 percent of its elderly inmates were sentenced for nonviolent offenses.

■ Costs for elderly prisoners are two or three times higher than for younger inmates

Jonathan Turley, founder and director of the Project for Older Prisoners (POPS), and his students at George Washington University Law School studied California's prison system, the largest in the nation, with 61,412 inmates.[4] Turley estimates that by 2024 the state's projected population of prisoners above the age of 60 years will reach an estimated 47,647 inmates. Unfortunately, national statistics are not available on this issue.[5] He also estimates that older prisoners are two to three times more expensive to maintain than younger prisoners. Unofficial estimates are that elderly prisoners cost about $70,000 per year.

According to a federal study of state recidivism statistics, older parolees and probationers are reincarcerated very infrequently.[6] In 1991, the most recent data available for the elderly, 51 percent of new prison admissions were parolees or probationers between the ages of 18 and 29; only 1 percent were 55 or older.

ELDER ABUSE

■ Self-neglect is the leading type of elder abuse

According to a 2000 survey of Adult Protective Services Administrators by the National Center on Elder Abuse (NCEA)* there were 472,813 elder/adult abuse reports for the most recent year for which data were available prior to 2000.[7] Of these, 396,398 were investigated and 166,019 reports were substantiated, for a 42 percent overall substantiation rate.

State report totals over this period ranged from a low of 108 to a high of 70,424 reports. Complainants were most often family members (14 percent), followed by health care professionals (11 percent), and social service agency staff (10 percent).

Based on information from forty states, the most frequently occurring substantiated allegation of elder abuse involved self-neglect (42 percent), followed by physical abuse (20 percent) and caregiver neglect or abandonment (13 percent).

■ Elder abuse victims are usually women

The NCEA study found that victims in substantiated reports of elder abuse were predominantly women (56 percent). More than half of the victims were Caucasian (66 percent), followed by African-Americans (17 percent). For substantiated reports that excluded self-neglect, about half (47 percent) of abused older adults were aged 80+. For substantiated cases of self-neglect, about a third (34 percent) involved persons aged 80+.

■ Perpetrators of elderly abuse are usually male

The NCEA survey found that perpetrators of elder abuse were most typically males (52 percent) between the ages of 36 and 50 (25 percent). Sixty-two percent of perpetrators were family members (spouse, parents, children, grandchildren, siblings, and other family members), and in particular, spouses or intimate partners (30 percent). The second largest category of perpetrators were adult children (18 percent). Four percent of elder abuse was by facility or institutional staff.

---

*Adult Protective Services (APS) are those services provided to older people and people with disabilities who are in danger of being mistreated or neglected, are unable to protect themselves, and have no one to assist them.

ABUSE AND NEGLECT IN INSTITUTIONS

Information on elder abuse in nursing homes is piecemeal but strongly points to a widespread problem

Dr. Catherine Hawes, an expert on elder abuse, remarked in testimony before the U.S. Senate Committee on Finance in 2002, "There are no reliable data on the prevalence of abuse or neglect in nursing homes or residential long-term care facilities. However, the piecemeal evidence we do have suggests the problem is serious and widespread."[8]

The following findings are examples of evidence reported by Hawes in her testimony:

- The Atlanta Long Term Care (LTC) Ombudsman Program conducted a study of abuse in 23 nursing homes in Georgia. Forty-four percent of the residents reported that they had been abused, while 48 percent said that they had been treated roughly. In addition, 38 percent of the residents reported that they had seen other residents being abused, and 44 percent said they had seen other residents being treated roughly.

- In a 1993 survey, 17 percent of Certified Nursing Assistants (CNAs), who provide care in nursing homes, reported that they had pushed, grabbed, or shoved a resident. More than half (51 percent) reported they had yelled at a resident in anger during the last year, while one-quarter (23 percent) had insulted or sworn at a resident.

- In a training project designed to reduce abuse and neglect in nursing homes, 77 CNAs from 31 different nursing facilities were interviewed. More than half (58 percent) of the CNAs said they had seen a staff member yell at a resident in anger, 36 percent had seen staff insult or swear at a resident, and 11 percent had witnessed staff threatening to hit or throw something at a resident. They also reported witnessing incidents of rough treatment and physical abuse of residents by other staff. One-quarter (25 percent) of the CNAs witnessed staff isolating a resident beyond what was needed to manage his or her behavior; 21 percent witnessed restraint of a resident beyond what was needed; 11 percent saw a resident being denied food as punishment.

- In the training project mentioned above, CNAs also reported witnessing more explicit instances of abuse. For example, 21 percent saw a resident pushed, grabbed, shoved, or pinched in anger; 12 percent witnessed staff slapping a resident; 7 percent saw a resident being kicked or hit with a fist; 3 percent saw staff throw something at a resident; and 1 percent saw a resident being hit with an object.

- An estimated 20,000 complaints, 10 percent of the complaints received by nursing home ombudsmen during fiscal year 1998, involved allegations of abuse, gross neglect, or exploitation. However, Hawes points out that formal complaints underestimate actual instances of abuse or neglect, since residents and families are often unwilling to file a formal complaint due to fear of retaliation and a belief that complaining would be futile.

- The Minority Staff of the Special Investigations Division of the House Committee on Government Reform issued a report in 2001 asserting that abuse of residents "is a major problem in U.S. nursing homes." They analyzed complaint investigations during a two-year period. The report concluded that during that time, nearly one-third of all certified facilities had been cited for some type of abuse violation that had the potential to cause harm or had actually caused harm to a nursing home resident. In addition, 10 percent of the nursing homes in the U.S. were cited for abuse violations that caused actual harm to residents or placed them in immediate jeopardy of death or serious injury.

NOTES

1. Federal Bureau of Investigation. (2002). *Crime in the United States*. Available online at http://www.fbi.gov.
2. Ibid.
3. National Center on Institutions and Alternatives. (1997). "Elderly Study." Available online at http://NCIANET.org.
4. GW News Center. (February 24, 2003). GW Professor Jonathan Turley to Testify on California's Prison Overcrowding and Budgetary Crisis before the State Senate February 25." Available online at http://www.gwu.edu.
5. Mark Martin. (February 26, 2003). "State Warned on Elderly Inmate Crisis." *San Francisco Chronicle*.
6. U.S. Department of Justice, Bureau of Justice Statistics. (1991), *Survey of State Prison Inmates*. Available online at http://www.ojp.usdoj.gov.
7. The National Center on Elderly Abuse. (2000). *A Response to the Abuse of Vulnerable Adults: The 2000 Survey of State Adult Protective Services*. Available online at http://www.elderabusecenter.org.
8. Catherine Hawes. (June 18, 2002). "Elder Abuse in Residential Long-Term Care Facilities: What Is Known about Prevalence, Causes, and Prevention." Testimony Before the U.S. Senate Committee on Finance.

CHAPTER 6

Citizenship, Language, and Education

Immigration is the sincerest form of flattery.

—Jack Paar

Language exerts hidden power, like a moon on the tides.

—Rita Mae Brown, Starting from Scratch, *1988*

Education is what survives when what has been learned has been forgotten.

—B. F. Skinner

This chapter covers the citizenship status of the elderly, the language they speak at home, and their educational levels. Highlights include:

- One in 10 elderly is foreign born.

- The oldest elderly are most dominant in Europe, while Latin America is for the youngest elderly.

- Thirteen percent of the elderly speak a language other than English at home, most commonly an Indo-European language (but non-Spanish).

- One in 4 elderly men and 1 in 5 elderly women have a college degree.

- The elderly in the West, especially Colorado, and those in metropolitan areas are more educated.

CITIZENSHIP

One in 10 elderly is foreign born

The U.S. Census Bureau defines "**foreign born**" as anyone who was not a U.S. citizen at birth. **Natives** are those who were born in the United States or a U.S. island area (like Puerto Rico or the U.S. Virgin Islands) or were born abroad and had at least one parent who was a U.S. citizen.

In 2002, 10 percent of the elderly population was foreign born (see Table 6.1). The elderly are the least likely age group to be foreign born, and they are half as likely as those aged 30–34. Most foreign-born elderly are naturalized citizens.

The foreign-born elderly have been in this country for many years (see Table 6.1). Overall, 6 in 10 of them arrived in the United States before 1970. Interestingly, 15 percent arrived within the last 12 years.

One-third of the foreign-born elderly are of European descent, and an equal percentage are Latin American (35 percent and 34 percent, respectively); one-quarter are Asian (23 percent). However, the proportions are very different by age—the European influence diminishes with younger people, and the Latin American influence increases (see Chart 6.1). In fact, half of all foreign-born elderly aged 85+ came from Europe. This drops dramatically to 30 percent of the youngest elderly aged 65–74, for whom the Latin component then becomes dominant, at 37 percent of the foreign born. The foreign-born elderly are also the least likely age group to be Asian.

LANGUAGE

More than 1 in 10 elderly speak a language other than English

Thirteen percent of the elderly speak a language other than English at home (see Table 6.2). Indo-European languages (other than Spanish) are the most commonly

TABLE 6.1
Citizenship Status and Period of Entry, by Age: March 2002

	20-24 Years	25-29 Years	30-34 Years	35-44 Years	45-54 Years	55-64 Years	65-74 Years	75-84 Years	85+ Years	65+ Years
	%	%	%	%	%	%	%	%	%	%
Native born	85	81	80	84	88	88	89	91	91	90
Foreign born	15	19	20	16	12	12	11	9	9	10
Naturalized	2	4	5	6	6	7	7	7	7	7
Not a citizen	12	16	15	10	6	5	4	2	2	3
Among the foreign born:										
Period of entry										
Before 1970	NA	NA	1	6	14	34	53	64	74	59
1970-1979	2	9	10	15	30	27	17	11	9	14
1980-1989	20	20	28	38	30	19	12	12	8	12
1990-2002	78	71	61	41	26	21	18	12	8	15

Source: Author calculations based on data from U.S. Census Bureau, "Foreign-Born Population of the United States Current Population Survey—March 2002. Detailed Tables (PPL-162)." Tables 1.1 and 2.1. Available online at www.census.gov/population/www/socdemo/foreign/ppl-162.html.

CHART 6.1
World Region of Birth, by Age: March 2002

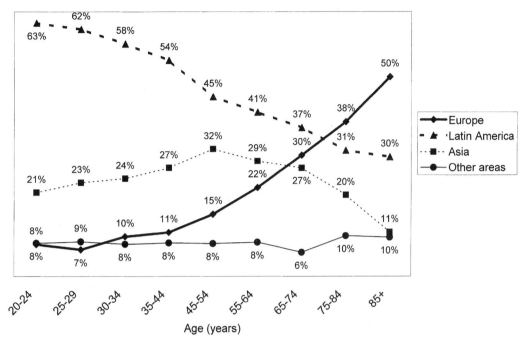

Source: Author calculations based on data from U.S. Census Bureau, "Foreign-Born Population of the United States Current Population Survey—March 2002. Detailed Tables (PPL-162)." Tables 3.1. Available online at www.census.gov/population/www/socdemo/foreign/ppl-162.html.

spoken language, with 44 percent of the non-English-speaking elderly conversing in these languages. Spanish is a close runner-up.

Elderly Indo-European speakers are very fluent in English, with 8 in 10 of them able to speak English "very well" or "well." These speakers are more fluent in English than are those who speak Spanish or Asian/Pacific Island languages (60 percent and 51 percent, respectively, speak English "very well" or "well").

The elderly in Hawaii, New Mexico, and California are most likely to speak a language other than English; more than 25 percent of them do so (see Table 6.3). In contrast, no more than 2 percent of the elderly in the southern states of Arkansas, Tennessee, Mississippi, Alabama, and Kentucky speak a non-English language.

There are eight states where elderly residents are substantially more likely than their younger counterparts to speak a language other than English: Hawaii, Alaska, Louisiana, New Hampshire, Maine, North Dakota, South Dakota, and Vermont.

TABLE 6.2
Language Spoken at Home and Ability to Speak English, by Age: 2000

	18-64 Years %	65+ Years %	Ratio of 65+ to 18-64
Speak only English	81	87	1.08
Speak other than English	19	13	0.67
Among those speaking other than English			
Speak Spanish	60	38	0.63
Speak other Indo-European languages	20	44	2.16
Speak Asian and Pacific Island languages	16	14	0.90
Speak other languages	4	4	0.97
Among those speaking Spanish			
Speak English "very well"	48	39	0.80
Speak English "well"	20	21	1.05
Total "well" or "very well"	68	60	0.87
Speak English "not well"	20	21	1.04
Speak English "not at all"	12	19	1.67
Among those speaking other Indo-European languages			
Speak English "very well"	66	60	0.90
Speak English "well"	21	21	1.00
Total "well" or "very well"	88	81	0.93
Speak English "not well"	11	14	1.28
Speak English "not at all"	2	5	3.21
Among those speaking Asian and Pacific Island languages			
Speak English "very well"	48	28	0.58
Speak English "well"	30	23	0.76
Total "well" or "very well"	78	51	0.65
Speak English "not well"	18	30	1.61
Speak English "not at all"	3	19	5.74
Among those speaking other languages			
Speak English "very well"	69	54	0.78
Speak English "well"	22	24	1.11
Total "well" or "very well"	91	78	0.86
Speak English "not well"	7	14	1.91
Speak English "not at all"	2	7	4.44

Source: Author calculations based on data from U.S. Census Bureau, Census 2000 Summary File 3 (SF 3)—Sample Data, "P17, Age by Language Spoken at Home by Ability to Speak English for the Populations 5 Years and Older." Available online at http://factfinder.census.gov.

EDUCATION

More than half of the elderly have a high school education or less; about one-quarter have a college degree

Educational attainment has risen through the generations, and this is reflected in the statistics. Today's elderly are much less educated than the generations that will

TABLE 6.3
Percent Who Speak a Language Other than English at Home for the
Total U.S. and States, by Age: 2000

	18-64 Years	65+ Years	Ratio of 65+
	%	%	to 18-64
Hawaii	26.5	38.8	1.47
New Mexico	38.8	34.3	0.88
California	40.5	27.4	0.68
New York	29.3	23.0	0.78
Rhode Island	19.5	20.5	1.05
Texas	32.7	19.9	0.61
Alaska	14.3	19.1	1.34
New Jersey	27.4	18.6	0.68
Connecticut	18.9	16.7	0.88
Florida	24.9	16.5	0.66
Massachusetts	19.2	16.5	0.86
Louisiana	9.3	15.1	1.63
Arizona	27.4	14.2	0.52
New Hampshire	8.1	14.0	1.73
Nevada	24.0	13.4	0.56
Maine	7.7	12.8	1.67
Illinois	20.4	12.7	0.62
Total United States	**18.8**	**12.6**	**0.67**
Colorado	15.6	12.6	0.81
North Dakota	5.5	12.5	2.29
Washington	14.8	9.0	0.61
Maryland	13.7	8.5	0.62
Michigan	8.7	8.2	0.94
Vermont	5.9	8.1	1.37
Utah	14.0	7.8	0.55
Pennsylvania	8.6	7.5	0.88
South Dakota	6.4	7.4	1.15
Minnesota	8.5	6.6	0.78
Wisconsin	7.2	6.4	0.89
Delaware	10.2	6.3	0.62
Wyoming	6.7	6.0	0.89
Oregon	12.9	5.9	0.46
Ohio	6.3	5.9	0.93
Virginia	12.2	5.5	0.45
Montana	5.4	5.2	0.96
Idaho	10.0	4.8	0.48
Nebraska	8.4	4.7	0.56
Kansas	9.5	4.4	0.47
Indiana	6.9	4.2	0.61
Georgia	10.9	3.8	0.35
Oklahoma	8.2	3.5	0.43

continued

TABLE 6.3   (Continued)

	18-64 Years	65+ Years	Ratio of 65+ to 18-64
	%	%	
Iowa	6.3	3.3	0.53
Missouri	5.5	3.2	0.59
North Carolina	9.0	2.8	0.31
South Carolina	5.8	2.6	0.45
West Virginia	2.9	2.2	0.75
Arkansas	5.5	2.0	0.36
Tennessee	5.5	2.0	0.36
Mississippi	4.1	1.9	0.47
Alabama	4.4	1.9	0.43
Kentucky	4.4	1.7	0.40

Source: Author calculations based on data from U.S. Census Bureau, Census 2000 Summary File 3 (SF 3)—Sample Data, "P17, Age by Language Spoken at Home by Ability to Speak English for the Populations 5 Years and Older." Available online at http://factfinder.census.gov.

succeed them. About 60 percent of elderly men and about 65 percent of elderly women have, at best, a high school education (see Chart 6.2 and Table 6.4). In other words, about 40 percent of elderly men and one-third of elderly women have at least some college experience. This compares with more than 50 percent of younger men

CHART 6.2
Educational Attainment of the Population, by Age and Sex: 2002

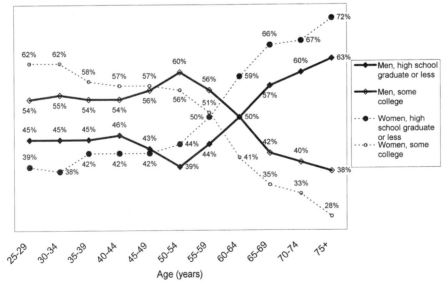

Source: Author calculations based on data from U.S. Census Bureau, "Educational Attainment in the United States: March 2002; Detailed Tables (PPL-169)." Table 1. Available online at www.census.gov/population/www/socdemo/education/ppl-169.htm.

TABLE 6.4
Educational Attainment of the Population, by Age and Sex: 2002

	Age in Years										
	25-29	30-34	35-39	40-44	45-49	50-54	55-59	60-64	65-69	70-74	75+
	%	%	%	%	%	%	%	%	%	%	%
Men											
High school											
graduate or less	45	45	45	46	43	39	44	50	57	60	63
No degree	15	15	13	12	11	11	15	18	25	30	34
Degree	30	30	32	34	32	28	29	32	32	30	29
Some college											
experience	54	55	54	54	56	60	56	50	42	40	38
No degree	20	17	17	16	18	18	16	15	14	14	14
Degree	34	38	37	38	38	42	40	35	28	26	24
Women											
High school											
graduate or less	39	38	42	42	42	44	50	59	66	67	72
No degree	12	11	11	10	10	11	15	19	25	27	34
Degree	27	27	31	32	32	33	35	40	41	40	38
Some college											
experience	62	62	58	57	57	56	51	41	35	33	28
No degree	21	19	18	18	18	17	18	16	14	13	12
Degree	41	43	40	39	39	39	33	25	21	20	16

Source: Author calculations based on data from U.S. Census Bureau, "Educational Attainment in the United States: March 2002; Detailed Tables (PPL-169)." Table 1. Available online at www.census.gov/population/www/socdemo/education/ppl-169.htm.

and women. In fact, about 1 in 4 elderly men and 1 in 5 elderly women have a college degree (two- or four-year), the least likely of any age group.

■ The elderly who work are more highly educated than those who do not work

Elderly men and women who are still in the labor force are about 40 percent more likely to have some college education than those who are not in the labor force (see Table 6.5).

■ More education results in more earnings

Elderly working men's earnings are substantially higher among those with more education (see Chart 6.3). Specifically, those who have at least a bachelor's degree have median earnings that are twice that of those who have a high school degree or less. Elderly working women's median earnings vary much less by educational attainment.

■ Native-born elderly and those in metropolitan areas are more educated

Native-born elderly are somewhat more educated than their foreign-born counterparts, with 40 percent of elderly native-born men having some college experience,

TABLE 6.5
Educational Attainment of the Elderly, by Labor Force Status and Sex: March 2002

	Not In Labor Force	In Labor Force	Ratio of in Labor Force to Not in Labor Force
	%	%	
Men			
High school degree or less	63	49	0.78
At least some college	37	51	1.38
Women			
High school degree or less	70	57	0.81
At least some college	30	43	1.43

Source: Author calculations based on data from U.S. Census Bureau, "Educational Attainment in the United States: March 2002; Detailed Tables (PPL-169)." Table 5a. Available online at www.census.gov/population/www/socdemo/education/ppl-169.htm.

CHART 6.3
Earnings in 2001 by Educational Attainment of the Elderly, by Sex: March 2002

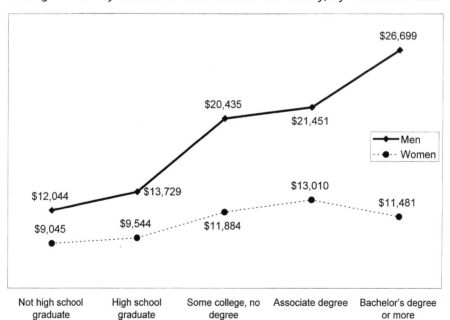

Source: Author calculations based on data from U.S. Census Bureau, "Educational Attainment in the United States: March 2002; Detailed Tables (PPL-169)." Table 9. Available online at www.census.gov/population/www/socdemo/education/ppl-169.htm.

compared with 35 percent of their foreign-born counterparts (see Table 6.6). For elderly women, the comparable figures are a little more divergent, 32 percent versus 24 percent. However, native and foreign-born elderly are equally as likely to have some sort of college degree, whether a two-year or four-year degree.

The elderly in nonmetropolitan areas are less educated than those who reside in metropolitan areas (see Table 6.7). The differences are primarily in the likelihood of a college degree, with the elderly in nonmetropolitan areas substantially less likely to have such a degree than those in metropolitan areas.

■ Westerners are more educated

The elderly in the West are the most educated (see Table 6.8). Four in 10 elderly women (39 percent) and half of elderly men (51 percent) who live in the Western

TABLE 6.6
Educational Attainment of the Elderly, by Nativity, Period of Entry, and Sex: March 2002

	Nativity		Foreign Born					
			Citizenship		Period of Entry			
	Native Born	Foreign Born	Naturalized	Not a Citizen	Before 1970	1970-1979	1980-1989	1990-2002
	%	%	%	%	%	%	%	%
Men								
High school graduate or less	60	65	61	76	64	64	70	67
No degree	29	41	34	56	38	42	48	43
Degree	31	24	26	20	25	23	22	24
Some college experience	40	35	39	24	36	36	30	33
No degree	14	8	9	4	9	8	5	7
Degree	26	27	30	20	28	28	25	26
Women								
High school graduate or less	68	76	73	83	74	71	86	84
No degree	29	44	38	59	39	40	64	56
Degree	40	32	35	24	35	31	22	28
Some college experience	32	24	27	17	26	29	14	16
No degree	14	8	9	6	11	7	1	4
Degree	18	16	18	11	16	22	13	12

Source: Author calculations based on data from U.S. Census Bureau, "Educational Attainment in the United States: March 2002; Detailed Tables (PPL-169)." Table 10. Available online at www.census.gov/population/www/socdemo/education/ppl-169.htm.

TABLE 6.7

Educational Attainment of the Elderly, by Metropolitan and Nonmetropolitan Residence and Sex: March 2002

	Total	Central City	Balance of Metropolitan Area	Nonmetropolitan Area
	%	%	%	%
Men				
High school graduate or less	60	59	57	68
No degree	30	31	26	38
Degree	30	28	31	30
Some college experience	40	41	43	32
No degree	14	14	14	13
Degree	26	27	29	18
Women				
High school graduate or less	69	67	69	73
No degree	30	32	27	35
Degree	39	36	42	38
Some college experience	31	33	31	27
No degree	13	14	12	13
Degree	18	19	19	14

Source: Author calculations based on data from U.S. Census Bureau, "Educational Attainment in the United States: March 2002; Detailed Tables (PPL-169)." Table 11. Available online at www.census.gov/population/www/socdemo/education/ppl-169.htm.

United States have at least some college experience, substantially higher than the elderly in the remaining part of the country.

■ Colorado has the most educated elderly

Overall, the elderly in Colorado are the most educated, with 2 in 10 having at least a bachelor's degree (see Table 6.9). At the other extreme are elderly West Virginians, of whom fewer than 1 in 10 have such degrees.

Colorado and Maryland have the most educated elderly men. Nearly 3 in 10 elderly men in these states have at least a bachelor's degree. In contrast, elderly men in North Dakota and West Virginia are the least educated, with barely 1 in 10 having a four-year degree.

Vermont has the most educated elderly women, while West Virginia has the least educated (17.2 percent versus 7.7 percent with at least a bachelor's degree).

TABLE 6.8
Educational Attainment of the Elderly, by Region and Sex: March 2002

	Northeast	Midwest	South	West
	%	%	%	%
Men				
High school graduate or less	64	65	62	49
No degree	30	31	34	22
Degree	34	34	28	27
Some college experience	36	35	38	51
No degree	10	14	14	18
Degree	27	21	25	33
Women				
High school graduate or less	72	70	71	61
No degree	30	28	35	25
Degree	42	42	37	37
Some college experience	28	30	29	39
No degree	10	14	12	16
Degree	18	17	16	22

Source: Author calculations based on data from U.S. Census Bureau, "Educational Attainment in the United States: March 2002; Detailed Tables (PPL-169)," Table 12. Available at www.census.gov/population/www/socdemo/education/ppl-169.htm.

TABLE 6.9
Percent of the Elderly Population with at Least a Bachelor's Degree for the Total U.S. and States, by Sex: 2000

	Total	Men	Women	Ratio of Men	Rankings		
	%	%	%	to Women	Total	Men	Women
Colorado	21.1	28.2	16.0	1.76	1	1	2
Vermont	20.1	24.2	17.2	1.40	2	10	1
Maryland	20.0	27.5	14.9	1.85	3	2	8
California	19.8	26.4	15.0	1.76	4	4	6
Washington	19.5	25.6	15.0	1.71	5	5	7
New Hampshire	19.4	25.4	15.0	1.69	6	6	5
Utah	19.2	26.8	13.3	2.01	7	3	14
Arizona	19.1	25.1	14.4	1.75	8	7	10
New Mexico	18.7	23.3	15.2	1.53	9	14	4
Connecticut	18.6	24.7	14.4	1.71	10	8	9
Virginia	18.0	24.5	13.6	1.81	11	9	12
Massachusetts	17.7	24.1	13.5	1.78	12	11	13
Florida	17.6	23.6	13.0	1.82	13	12	16

continued

TABLE 6.9   (Continued)

	Total %	Men %	Women %	Ratio of Men to Women	Rankings Total	Men	Women
Delaware	17.4	23.5	12.9	1.81	14	13	18
Alaska	17.3	19.3	15.5	1.25	15	23	3
Oregon	17.3	22.2	13.7	1.63	16	16	11
New York	16.4	21.3	13.1	1.63	17	18	15
Hawaii	16.1	20.5	12.6	1.63	18	21	20
Texas	15.7	21.4	11.8	1.82	19	17	25
New Jersey	15.7	22.3	11.2	1.99	20	15	28
Maine	15.6	19.3	13.0	1.49	21	24	17
South Carolina	15.5	20.5	12.1	1.69	22	20	23
Total United States	**15.4**	**20.5**	**11.8**	**1.73**	**23**	**19**	**24**
Montana	15.3	18.5	12.8	1.44	24	32	19
Wyoming	15.2	18.5	12.6	1.47	25	30	21
Kansas	14.9	18.9	12.2	1.55	26	27	22
North Carolina	14.7	19.2	11.7	1.64	27	26	26
Nevada	14.4	19.5	10.0	1.95	28	22	36
Idaho	14.4	18.6	11.1	1.68	29	29	29
Minnesota	14.2	18.4	11.3	1.63	30	33	27
Georgia	14.1	19.2	10.8	1.77	31	25	30
Oklahoma	13.9	18.5	10.7	1.72	32	31	31
Rhode Island	13.7	18.6	10.5	1.77	33	28	33
Illinois	13.4	17.9	10.5	1.71	34	34	35
Louisiana	12.8	16.2	10.5	1.55	35	38	34
Wisconsin	12.7	15.6	10.7	1.46	36	42	32
Michigan	12.6	16.5	9.9	1.67	37	36	38
Ohio	12.5	16.7	9.6	1.74	38	35	41
Alabama	12.0	16.1	9.3	1.73	39	39	43
Pennsylvania	11.9	16.3	9.0	1.81	40	37	46
Tennessee	11.8	15.9	9.0	1.76	41	40	45
Missouri	11.8	15.7	9.1	1.72	42	41	44
Mississippi	11.8	15.1	9.6	1.57	43	43	42
Nebraska	11.7	14.3	10.0	1.44	44	46	37
Iowa	11.5	13.9	9.9	1.41	45	47	39
South Dakota	11.2	13.4	9.7	1.39	46	48	40
Arkansas	11.0	14.6	8.5	1.71	47	45	49
Indiana	11.0	14.6	8.5	1.72	48	44	48
Kentucky	10.2	12.9	8.4	1.54	49	49	50
North Dakota	9.8	11.2	8.8	1.28	50	50	47
West Virginia	9.1	11.1	7.7	1.44	51	51	51

Source: Author calculations based on data from U.S. Census Bureau, Census 2000 Summary File 3 (SF 3)— Sample Data, "Pct25, Sex by Age by Educational Attainment for the Population 18 Years and Over." Available online at http://factfinder.census.gov.

Utah, New Jersey, and Nevada are where the education differential among elderly men and women is greatest. In these states, elderly men are twice as likely as elderly women to have at least a bachelor's degree. At the other extreme are Alaska and North Dakota, where elderly men are only 25 percent more likely than elderly women to have at least a four-year degree.

Work and Money

CHAPTER 7

Income and Poverty

All progress is based upon a universal innate desire on the part of every organism to live beyond its income.

—Samuel Butler

Money is better than poverty, if only for financial reasons.

—Woody Allen

It is pretty hard to tell what does bring happiness; poverty and wealth have both failed.

—Kin Hubbard

This chapter is primarily based on data from the Social Security Administration report *Income of the Population 55 and Older*.[1] At the time this book went to publication, the most recent report accessed data from the U.S. Census Bureau's March 2000 Current Population Survey (CPS).

Unlike most other CPS-sourced publications, the Social Security Administration uses the concept of "aged units," not households, families, or unrelated individuals. An aged unit is either a married couple living together (at least one of whom is aged 55+) or a nonmarried person aged 55+. A nonmarried person is one who is unmarried (widowed, divorced, or never married), separated, or married but living apart from their spouse (for example, someone whose spouse resides in a nursing home). This aged unit definition includes the aged population whether or not they live with other relatives. For the purposes of this chapter, the authors have further concentrated on the elderly aged unit (those aged units where at least one person is aged 65+). This is a broader definition than that used with many other CPS-sourced publications that classify someone aged 65+ living with a younger relative, who is considered the householder, as a "family under 65." Thus, the elderly aged unit definition is broader. In fact, Census data indicate that in 2000 there were 21,828,000 households with a householder aged 65+, while the Social Security elderly aged unit definition encompasses 16 percent more households, or 25,230,000. The age of a married-couple aged unit is the age of the husband, unless he is under 65, in which case it is the age of the wife. In this chapter, the terms *elderly, elderly aged units*, and *aged units aged 65+* are used synonymously.

In this chapter, income specifically refers to money income that is the total income received by an aged unit before any deductions for taxes, union dues, or Medicare premiums. This income is from any source that is regularly received and includes wages and salaries, self-employment income (including losses), Social Security, Supplemental Security Income, public assistance, interest, dividends, rent, royalties, estates or trusts, veterans' payments, unemployment compensation, workers' compensation, private and government retirement and disability pensions, alimony, and child support. Capital gains and losses and lump-sum or one-time payments such as life insurance are excluded. Nonmoney transfers such as food stamps, health benefits, subsidized housing, payments in kind, and fringe benefits are not included.

This chapter also covers the poverty status of the elderly. Among other things, it points out that the measure that the government uses to define poverty is lower for the elderly than for younger people. For example, in 2002 the poverty threshold for a single person was $9,359 for an individual under age 65, but $8,628 for a person aged 65+.

Highlights from this chapter include:

- Nine in 10 elderly receive Social Security benefits, and 4 in 10 receive some sort of pension or annuity.

- Among nonmarried black women who receive Social Security, for 45 percent of them, it is their only income source.

- Six in 10 elderly receive income from assets.

- Among the elderly who work, earnings account for at least half of their income, and the working elderly have median incomes 2.5 times larger than those who do not work.

- One-quarter of the elderly have median incomes of $35,000 or more, while a similar percentage have income under $10,000.

- Some 3.4 million elderly live in poverty.

- Poverty rates for the elderly have decreased dramatically since 1965.

- One in 4 of the oldest-old has a very low income.

- One in 10 elderly blacks has an income below 75 percent of the poverty level.

- Elderly women are far more likely to be poor than elderly men.

INCOME SOURCES AND THE IMPORTANCE OF INCOME SOURCES

▨ Almost all elderly receive Social Security

Social Security is the single most common income source among the elderly, with 90 percent of elderly aged units receiving Social Security retirement benefits in 2000 (See Chart 7.1; see Chapter 11 for more detailed Social Security statistics). Assets generate the second most common income source for the elderly, with 6 in 10 receiving income from assets, followed by 4 in 10 who receive pensions, and 2 in 10 who receive earnings income.

▨ The likelihood of the elderly receiving income from pensions or assets has fluctuated during the last quarter-century

Since 1976, the percent of the elderly who receive Social Security has remained relatively unchanged (see Chart 7.2). One of the greatest changes during this period was for pension income and asset-generated income. Fewer than 1 in 3 elderly received pension income in 1976, but this steadily increased to 45 percent in 1992 and then declined somewhat to 41 percent in 2000. Those elderly who received asset-

CHART 7.1
Percent of Elderly Aged Units with Income from Specified Source: 2000

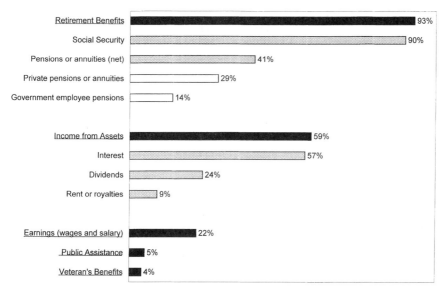

Source: Social Security Administration, *Income of the Population 55 or Older, 2000*, Table 1.1.

CHART 7.2
Percent of Elderly Aged Units with Income from Specified Source: 1976–2000

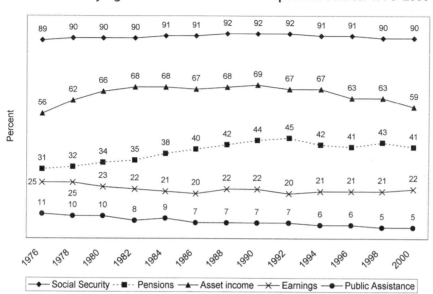

Source: Social Security Administration, *Income of the Aged Chartbook, 2000*. Detailed data provided to the authors.

generated income rose from 56 percent in 1976 to 69 percent in 1990, but the percentage has since declined to 59 percent in 2000.

One in 4 elderly aged units received earnings-generated income in 1976. This declined to a low of 20 percent in both 1986 and 1992, with some slight increase to 22 percent in 2000.

Reliance upon public assistance has steadily declined over the past quarter-century, with the elderly in 2000 half as likely as their 1976 counterparts to be receiving public assistance (5 percent versus 11 percent).

■ Virtually all elderly receive some type of retirement benefit

Overall, more than 9 in 10 elderly (93 percent) receive some type of retirement benefit (see Chart 7.1); 7 percent receive no retirement benefit. Social Security is the most common retirement benefit, with 90 percent of the elderly receiving it in 2000. Four in 10 elderly (41 percent) receive some type of non–Social Security retirement benefit, most commonly private pensions or annuities (received by 29 percent). Fourteen percent receive some type of government employee pension: military (2 percent), federal (5 percent), or state or local (8 percent).

Social Security is the single largest income source for the elderly

On average, Social Security accounts for nearly 40 percent of the aggregate income of the elderly (see Chart 7.3). Earnings account for nearly 25 percent of aggregate income, followed by asset-generated income and pensions.

Social Security has been, and continues to be, the dominant income source for the elderly (see Chart 7.4). Between 1976 and 2000, Social Security ranged between 36 and 42 percent of the aggregate income of the elderly.

Asset-generated income peaked in importance in 1984 when it accounted for 28 percent of the total income of the elderly. Since then it has declined to less than 20 percent of aggregate income.

Earnings, on the other hand, dramatically declined in importance between 1976 and 1984 and then began increasing, rising back to the 1976 level of 23 percent in 2000. This pattern parallels the elderly's labor force participation trends (see Chapter 10, Work and Retirement).

Pension income has fluctuated between 15 and 20 percent of the elderly's total income over the last quarter-century.

Social Security is an important income source for the elderly

Among the elderly who receive Social Security, for 20 percent of them Social Security is their only income source, and for two-thirds it represents at least half of their

CHART 7.3
Percent of Aggregate Income among Elderly Aged Units, by Source: 2000

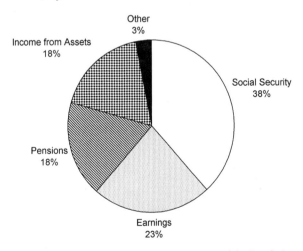

Source: Social Security Administration, *Income of the Population 55 or Older, 2000*, Table 7.1.

CHART 7.4

Percent of Aggregate Income among Elderly Aged Units, by Source: 1976–2000

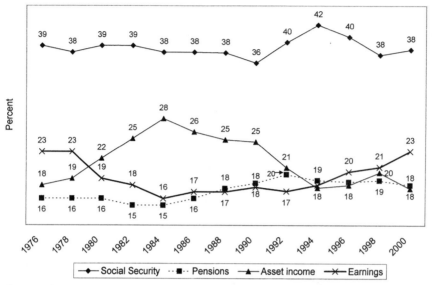

Source: Social Security Administration, *Income of the Aged Chartbook, 2000*. Detailed data provided to the authors.

income (see Table 7.1). The older elderly (aged 75+) are more dependent on Social Security than are the younger elderly (aged 65–74). For 73 percent of the older elderly, Social Security accounts for at least half of their income compared with 55 percent of the younger elderly (aged 65–74).

TABLE 7.1

Relative Importance of Social Security Income for Elderly Aged Units among Those Receiving Social Security, by Age: 2000

	65+ Years	65-74 Years	75+ Years	Ratio of 75+ to 65-74
	%	%	%	
Proportion of income accounted for by Social Security				
100%	20	17	23	1.35
90% or more	31	25	38	1.52
80% or more	38	31	46	1.48
50% or more	64	55	73	1.33
Less than 50%	36	45	27	0.60
Less than 20%	10	13	7	0.54

Source: Social Security Administration, *Income of the Population 55 or Older, 2000*, Table 6.B1.

CHART 7.5
Percent of Aggregate Income among Elderly Aged Units, by Source and Age: 2000

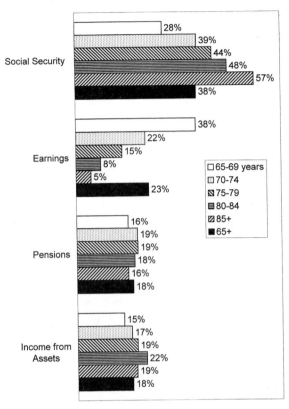

Source: Social Security Administration, *Income of the Population 55 or Older, 2000*, Table 7.1.

These statistics are reflected in the elderly's aggregate income. More specifically, with age, Social Security accounts for a larger share of the elderly's aggregate income, ranging from 28 percent among those aged 65–69, to 57 percent among those aged 85+ (see Chart 7.5).

■ Social Security is a more important income source for blacks, especially nonmarried women

Overall, elderly blacks are about twice as dependent upon Social Security as their white counterparts (see Table 7.2), regardless of their marital status. Elderly black nonmarried women are the most dependent upon Social Security; nearly half of them totally depend upon Social Security for all their income, compared with one-quarter of their white counterparts. Elderly black nonmarried men fare only somewhat better, with 39 percent of them totally dependent upon Social Security, compared with 23

TABLE 7.2
Percent of Elderly Aged Units Who Derive 100 Percent of Their Income from Social Security, by Race and Marital Status: 2000

	Total	White	Black	Ratio of Black to White
	%	%	%	
Married couples	11	10	21	2.10
Nonmarried men	25	23	39	1.70
Nonmarried women	26	24	45	1.88

Source: Social Security Administration, *Income of the Population 55 or Older, 2000*, Table 6.B3.

percent of their white male counterparts. Black married couples fare the best, with only 1 in 5 totally dependent upon Social Security, but it is still twice the level of their white counterparts.

■ Assets generate the second most common type of income the elderly receive

Asset-generated income is the second most common type of income that the elderly receive; 59 percent receive income from assets, most commonly interest income (57 percent; see Chart 7.1). Fewer than half as many elderly receive dividend income (24 percent), and only 9 percent receive income from rent or royalties.

■ Asset income is a less dominant income source for the elderly

The elderly who receive asset-generated income are far less dependent upon that income source than they are for other types of income. For only 14 percent of them does it represent at least half of their income, and for 60 percent it represents less than 20 percent of their income (see Table 7.3).

TABLE 7.3
Relative Importance of Asset Income for Elderly Aged Units among Those Receiving Asset Income, by Age: 2000

	65+ Years	65-74 Years	75+ Years
	%	%	%
Proportion of income accounted for by assets			
100%	1	1	2
90% or more	2	2	2
80% or more	3	3	4
50% or more	14	12	16
Less than 50%	86	88	84
Less than 20%	60	63	57

Source: Social Security Administration, *Income of the Population 55 or Older, 2000*, Table 6.B1.

Elderly nonmarried women are more dependent upon asset-generated income than are elderly nonmarried men or elderly married couples (accounting for at least half the income for 38 percent, 32 percent, and 22 percent of these groups, respectively).

■ Working provides a substantial source of income for the elderly

Earnings encompass the third most common source of income for the elderly; 22 percent of the elderly receive income from working (see Charts 7.1 and 7.6). Since labor force participation rates decline dramatically with age, the likelihood of earnings income varies greatly by age, declining from 44 percent of elderly aged units aged 65 to 69, to 4 percent of those aged 85+ (see Chart 7.6; also see Chapter 10, "Work and Retirement," for labor force participation rates).

Consequently, with age, earnings income becomes less important overall. Among all elderly aged 65 to 69, earnings represent 38 percent of their total aggregate income. This declines to 5 percent among all elderly aged 85 and older (see Chart 7.6).

Nonetheless, earnings are an important income source for the working elderly, especially the younger elderly (see Table 7.4). For 49 percent of the elderly who work, those earnings represent at least half of their income; this varies from 52 percent of younger elderly workers to 39 percent of older elderly workers (aged 75+). For 6 percent of the working elderly, those earnings represent their entire income.

CHART 7.6
Earnings Income among Elderly Aged Units, by Age: 2000

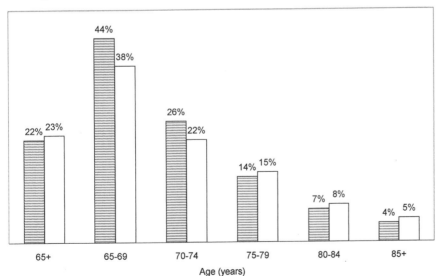

Source: Social Security Administration, *Income of the Population 55 or Older, 2000*, Tables 1.1 and 7.1

TABLE 7.4

Relative Importance of Earnings Income for Elderly Aged Units among Those Receiving Earnings, by Age: 2000

	65+ Years	65-74 Years	75+ Years
	%	%	%
Proportion of income accounted for by earnings			
100%	6	6	6
90% or more	12	12	10
80% or more	18	19	16
50% or more	49	52	39
Less than 50%	51	48	61
Less than 20%	19	17	25

Source: Social Security Administration, *Income of the Population 55 or Older, 2000*, Table 6.B1.

▪ For the few elderly who receive public assistance, it is a major income source

Only 5 percent of the elderly receive public assistance, generally Supplemental Security Income (SSI). However, those funds are an important source of income (see Table 7.5). For 28 percent of these elderly, public assistance is their sole income source; for more than one-third (37 percent), public assistance accounts for at least half of their income. Among the elderly receiving public assistance, there is minimal variation in the importance of public assistance by age or marital status.

TABLE 7.5

Relative Importance of Public Assistance Income for Elderly Aged Units among Those Receiving Public Assistance, by Age: 2000

	65+ Years	65-74 Years	75+ Years
	%	%	%
Proportion of income accounted for by public assistance			
100%	28	28	28
90% or more	29	29	29
80% or more	30	31	29
50% or more	37	38	36
Less than 50%	63	62	64
Less than 20%	31	32	30

Source: Social Security Administration, *Income of the Population 55 or Older, 2000*, Table 6.B1.

INCOME LEVELS

Median income declines rapidly with age

Median income for the elderly is nearly $19,000 and less than half that of those aged 55 to 61 (see Chart 7.7). Median income drops substantially with age, with the median income of the youngest elderly, aged 65 to 69, being twice that of their oldest counterparts aged 85+ ($25,873 versus $12,964).

One in 20 elderly aged units (5.2 percent) have an income of less than $5,000, while nearly 10 percent have incomes of $65,000 or more (see Chart 7.8). Just as many elderly (about 1 in 4) have incomes below $10,000 as above $35,000.

The median income of elderly aged units who work is substantially greater than those who do not. Specifically, those who have earnings have a median income 2.5 times larger than those who do not have earnings ($38,800 versus $15,400).

Elderly aged units who have asset income also have substantially higher median incomes than those who do not have asset income, $26,000 versus $11,500. Among the 52 percent of elderly aged units whose only retirement benefit is Social Security, their median income is half that of those who receive Social Security and a private pension ($13,300 versus $26,400).

CHART 7.7
Median Income of Aged Units, by Age: 2000

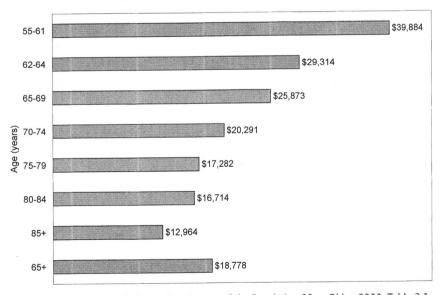

Source: Social Security Administration, *Income of the Population 55 or Older, 2000*, Table 3.1.

CHART 7.8
Distribution of Income Received by Elderly Aged Units: 2000

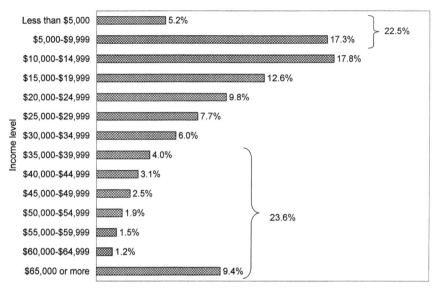

Source: Social Security Administration, *Income of the Population 55 or Older, 2000*, Table 3.1.

■ Nonmarried women have the lowest median income

With each successive five-year age group, median income among married couples drops precipitously with age up through age 79, at which point it continues to decline but at a much lower rate (see Chart 7.9 and Table 7.6). Overall, elderly married couples have a median income of $31,188, twice that of elderly nonmarried men ($15,682) and 2.6 times higher than that of elderly nonmarried women ($12,035). Nonmarried elderly women have the lowest median income—three-quarters that of their nonmarried male counterparts.

While the median income of nonmarried men and women is less consistent with age, the general trend is downward, with the oldest nonmarried people having the lowest median income (see Chart 7.9 and Table 7.6).

■ Nonmarried black women have even lower incomes

Black nonmarried elderly women have a median income of less than $9,000 (see Chart 7.10), two-thirds the median income of their white counterparts. Black nonmarried elderly men have a median income that is 62 percent that of their white counterparts ($10,192 versus $16,537). Black married elderly couples fare better, with a median income that is 82 percent that of their white counterparts ($26,192 versus $31,775).

CHART 7.9
Median Income of Aged Units, by Age and
Marital Status: 2000

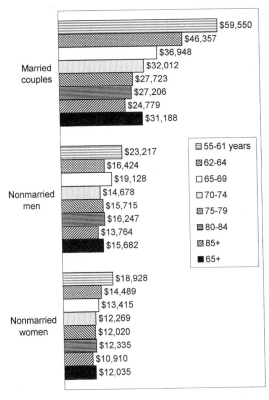

Married couples
- $59,550
- $46,357
- $36,948
- $32,012
- $27,723
- $27,206
- $24,779
- $31,188

Nonmarried men
- $23,217
- $16,424
- $19,128
- $14,678
- $15,715
- $16,247
- $13,764
- $15,682

Legend:
- 55-61 years
- 62-64
- 65-69
- 70-74
- 75-79
- 80-84
- 85+
- 65+

Nonmarried women
- $18,928
- $14,489
- $13,415
- $12,269
- $12,020
- $12,335
- $10,910
- $12,035

Source: Social Security Administration, *Income of the Population 55 or Older, 2000*, Table 3.1.

TABLE 7.6
Percent Difference in Median Income and Ratio of Median Income among Aged Units, by Age and Marital Status: 2000

	Percent Difference in Median Income versus Prior Age Group			Ratio of Median Income		
	Married Couples	Nonmarried Men	Nonmarried Women	Married Couples to Nonmarried Men	Married Couples to Nonmarried Women	Nonmarried Men to Nonmarried Women
55-61 years	NA	NA	NA	2.6	3.1	1.2
62-64	-22%	-29%	-23%	2.8	3.2	1.1
65-69	-20%	16%	-7%	1.9	2.8	1.4
70-74	-13%	-23%	-9%	2.2	2.6	1.2
75-79	-13%	7%	-2%	1.8	2.3	1.3
80-84	-2%	3%	3%	1.7	2.2	1.3
85+	-9%	-15%	-12%	1.8	2.3	1.3
65+	NA	NA	NA	2.0	2.6	1.3

Source: Calculations based on median incomes in Chart 7–9.

CHART 7.10

Median Income, by Age, Marital Status, and Race: 2000

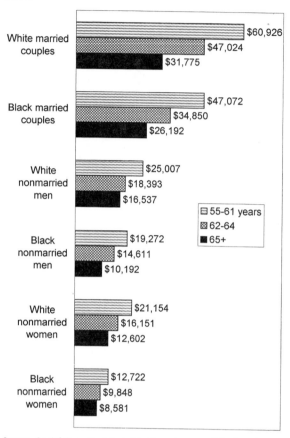

Source: Social Security Administration, *Income of the Population 55 or Older, 2000*, Table 3.3.

Elderly divorcees have higher incomes

Divorced seniors have the highest median income of any elderly who are unmarried (see Chart 7.11). Divorced elderly women have median incomes about 10 percent higher than their widowed or never-married counterparts. In contrast, divorced elderly men have median incomes about 6 percent higher than their widowed counterparts and 23 percent higher than never-married elderly men.

CHART 7.11
Median Income of Elderly Nonmarried Persons, by Sex and Marital Status: 2000

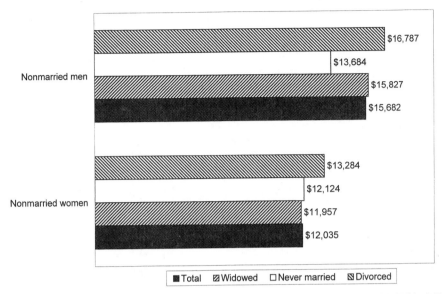

Source: Social Security Administration, *Income of the Population 55 or Older, 2000*, Table 3.7.

POVERTY

◼ 3.4 million elderly live in poverty

Based on 2002 statistics, 10 percent of the elderly (3.4 million people) are poor.[2] This is a number greater than the entire population of the state of Connecticut.

◼ The elderly must be worse off financially than younger people to be considered poor

The level that the U.S. Bureau of the Census uses to measure poverty is called the *poverty threshold*. In 2002 the poverty threshold for a single person under age 65 was an annual income of no more than $9,359, but it was $8,628 for a single person aged 65+. The threshold for two persons with the householder under age 65 was $12,047, compared to $10,885 for those in which the householder was 65+. The poverty threshold is lower for older people under the assumption that they spend less on food than younger people, but it does not account for the increased cost of health care, medicines, and related expenditures.

■ Poverty rates for the elderly have decreased dramatically since 1965

Chart 7.12 shows the dramatic reduction in poverty for the elderly since the founding of Social Security in 1965. In 1965 the elderly had the highest poverty rates in the United States. By 1974 the rates for children aged 18 and younger surpassed them. This trend continues today.

POVERTY RATES BY AGE: 1959 TO 2002

■ Elderly people are more likely than younger people to have marginal incomes

If the poverty level for the elderly was raised by 25 percent, 17 percent of this group would be poor. With the exception of those under age 24, the elderly are far more likely than other age groups to have incomes clustered above the poverty line (between 100 and 125 percent of the poverty level). For example, while 17 percent of the elderly had incomes below 125 percent of poverty in 2002, this figure was 14 percent for people 60 to 64 and 11 percent for those 55 to 59.

■ Elderly women are far more likely to be poor than elderly men

Twelve percent of elderly women were poor in 2002, compared to 8 percent of elderly men. This trend is consistent for all racial and ethnic groups (see Table 7.7).

CHART 7.12
Poverty Rates by Age: 1959 to 2002

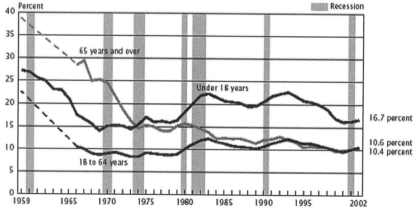

Note: The data points represent the midpoints of the respective years. Data for people 18 to 64 and 65 and older are not available from 1960 to 1965.
Source: Bureau of the Census. *Poverty in the United States: 2002.* Figure 2.

TABLE 7.7
Elderly Living in Poverty (100 Percent of Poverty Level), by Sex and Race: 2002

	Men	Women
	%	%
All Races	8	12
White	7	11
Black	18	27
Asian	8	10
Hispanic	19	23

Note: All race and Hispanic statistics refer to "alone or in combination."
Source: Bureau of the Census, *Poverty in the United States: 2002.*

■ Elderly blacks and Hispanics are more than twice as likely to be poor as elderly whites and Asians

Elderly blacks and Hispanics have higher rates of poverty than elderly whites and Asians. One-quarter, 24 percent, of elderly blacks lives in poverty compared to 9 percent of both white and Asian elderly (see Table 7.8). This trend carries out for males and females of all racial and ethnic groups, with black women having the highest rate of poverty, 27 percent, and white males the lowest, 7 percent (see Table 7.7). This trend also holds true for those with incomes below 125 percent of poverty (see Table 7.9).

■ Foreign-born elderly are more likely to live in poverty

Poverty is more common among the foreign-born elderly, and the differential is greatest among elderly men (see Table 7.10.). Elderly foreign-born men are more than

TABLE 7.8
Percent of Elderly Living in Poverty (100 Percent of Poverty Level), by Age and Race: 2002

	65+ Years	65-74 Years	75+ Years
	%	%	%
All Races	10	9	12
White	9	8	11
Black	24	23	24
Asian	9	7	11
Hispanic	43	39	49

Note: All race and Hispanic statistics refer to "alone or in combination."
Source: Bureau of the Census, *Poverty in the United States: 2002.*

TABLE 7.9
Percent of Elderly with Incomes below 125 Percent of the Poverty
Level, by Sex and Race: 2002

	Men	Women
	%	%
All Races	31	34
White	11	19
Black	26	38
Asian	11	16
Hispanic	31	34

Note: All race and Hispanic statistics refer to "alone or in combination."
Source: Bureau of the Census, Poverty in the United States: 2002.

twice as likely as their native-born counterparts to live in poverty (14 percent versus 6 percent).

■ One in 4 oldest-old has a very low income

People aged 85+ are particularly vulnerable to the effects of poverty due to their increased risk of needing long-term care and related services. Fourteen percent of the oldest-old are poor, and 23 percent have incomes below 125 percent of the poverty level (Table 7.11 and 7.12). Blacks of advanced age, particularly black women, have the highest rates of poverty of all age, race, and ethnic groups. Almost half of black women who are aged 85+ are poor.

TABLE 7.10
Percent of Elderly below 100 Percent of the Poverty Level, by
Citizenship Status and Sex: March 2002

	Total	Men	Women
	%	%	%
Native born	10	6	12
Foreign born	15	14	15

Source: Author calculations based on data from U.S. Census Bureau, "Foreign-Born Population of the United States Current Population Survey—March 2002. Detailed Tables (PPL-162)," Table 1.1.

TABLE 7.11
Percent of Oldest-Old Living (Aged 85+) in Poverty (100 Percent of Poverty Level),
by Sex, Race, and Ethnic Background: 2002

	Total	Men	Women
	%	%	%
All Races	14	8	16
White	12	8	15
Black	29	21	31
Asian	13	---	---
Hispanic	29	---	30

Note: All race and Hispanic statistics refer to "alone or in combination."
Source: Bureau of the Census, *Poverty in the United States: 2002*.

◼ One in 10 elderly blacks has an income below 75 percent of the poverty level

Poverty disproportionately touches older blacks, 10 percent of whom had incomes below 75 percent of the poverty level in 2002.

◼ Eleven jurisdictions had elderly poverty rates of 13 percent or more from 1998 to 2000

Some areas of the country have particularly high poverty rates for their elderly residents. Eleven jurisdictions with poverty rates of 13 percent or greater for their elderly populations over the period 1998 to 2000 are Mississippi (18 percent); Louisiana (17 percent); District of Columbia (17 percent); Alabama (15 percent);

TABLE 7.12
Percent of Oldest-Old Living with Incomes below 125 Percent of the Poverty Level
by Sex: 2002

	Total	Men	Women
	%	%	%
All Races	23	13	28
White	21	12	26
Black	42	29	47
Asian	32	---	---
Hispanic	33	---	34

Note: All race and Hispanic statistics refer to "alone or in combination."
Source: Bureau of the Census, *Poverty in the United States: 2002*.

Tennessee (15 percent); Arkansas (15 percent); New Mexico (15 percent); Kentucky (13 percent); West Virginia (13 percent); New York (13 percent); and Texas (13 percent).[3]

NOTES

1. Social Security Administration. *Income of the Population 55 or Older, 2000.* Available online at http://www.ssa.gov.
2. Bureau of the Census. *Poverty in the United States: 2002.* Available online at http://census.gov.
3. Administration on Aging. (2002). *Profile of Older Americans.* Available online at http://aoa.gov.

CHAPTER 8

Finances—Assets, Savings, Debt, and Attitudes

Who is rich? He that is content. Who is that? Nobody.

—Benjamin Franklin

Creditors have better memories than debtors.

—Benjamin Franklin

This chapter is primarily based on data from the Federal Reserve Board's Survey of Consumer Finances (SCF),[1] which is conducted every three years. Data from 1992, 1995, 1998, and 2001 are included. Also included are data from NOP World and Mediamark Research.

The primary unit of analysis with the SCF is the "family." Unlike the Census Bureau definition, a **family** can consist of an individual. The family consists of the economically dominant single individual or couple in the household and all other people in the household who are financially interdependent with that person or persons. If a single individual is economically dominant, this person is designated as the family "head." If a couple is economically dominant, in a mixed-sex couple, the male is chosen as the family head; in a same-sex couple, the older person is so designated.

In this chapter, those in the 65 to 74 age group are referred to as **younger elderly-headed families** or the **younger elderly**. Those in the 75+ age group are referred to as **older elderly-headed families** or the **older elderly**.

Chapter highlights include:

- Elderly families are among the wealthiest.

- Elderly families are the least likely to have retirement accounts but the most likely to have certificates of deposit.

- Stocks and mutual funds are among the least likely type of asset held by the elderly. However, when they do hold these equity assets, the value of those holdings are the most substantial of any assets they own.

- Homes are a significant asset for the elderly, only surpassed in value by stock holdings.

- The elderly are just as likely as most younger families to save, but are less likely to carry debt.

- The elderly are more likely to hold mortgage debt than in the past.

- Compared with younger people, the elderly are more confident of their financial knowledge.

FINANCIAL ASSETS

Elderly families are among the wealthiest

In 2001, median **net worth** (the difference between gross assets and liabilities) peaked at $181,500 in the 55 to 64 age group, with net worth among the younger elderly about 3 percent lower ($176,300; see Chart 8.1). While median net worth

CHART 8.1

Median Family Net Worth (in Thousands of 2001 Dollars), by Age of Family Head: 1992, 1995, 1998, 2001

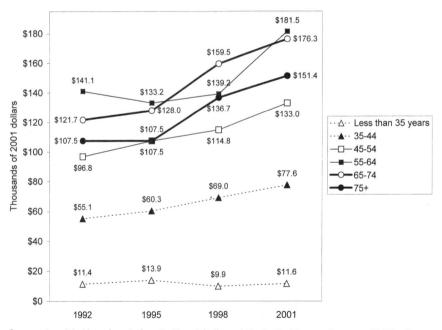

Source: Ana M. Aizcorbe, Arthur B. Kennickell, and Kevin B. Moore. (January 2003). "Recent Changes in U.S. Family Finances: Evidence from the 1998 and 2001 Survey of Consumer Finances." *Federal Reserve Bulletin*, vol. 89, 1–32, and Updated Tables at www.federalreserve.gov/pubs/oss/oss2/2001/scf2001home.htm.

among the older elderly is 17 percent lower than for those in the peak age group of 55 to 64, it is still higher than for those in the 45 to 54 age group.

Net worth among elderly-headed families increased 11 percent between 1998 and 2001 and more than 40 percent between 1992 and 2001; the latter increase was the highest of any age group.

■ The elderly have a variety of assets

Virtually all elderly-headed families (95 percent) have some financial assets (such as transaction accounts, certificates of deposit, stocks, bonds, mutual funds, retirement accounts, and life insurance). **Transaction accounts** (such as checking, savings, money market deposit, and money market mutual funds) constitute the most common type of financial asset, being held by 94 percent of elderly-headed families (see Chart 8.2).

Retirement accounts, life insurance, and certificates of deposits are the next most likely financial asset the elderly hold. Between one-quarter and nearly one-half of the elderly have such assets (see Chart 8.2). About 1 in 5 elderly holds stocks or mutual funds. Bonds are among the least commonly held assets, with savings bonds more common than other types of bonds.

CHART 8.2
Percent of Elderly-Headed Families Holding Specific Type of Financial Asset, by Age of Family Head: 2001

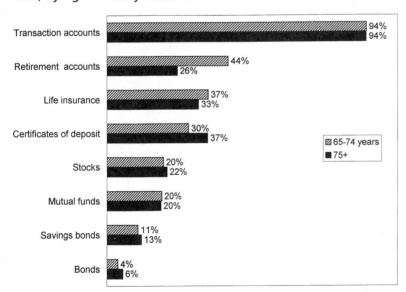

Source: Ana M. Aizcorbe, Arthur B. Kennickell, and Kevin B. Moore. (January 2003). "Recent Changes in U.S. Family Finances: Evidence from the 1998 and 2001 Survey of Consumer Finances." *Federal Reserve Bulletin*, vol. 89, 1–32, and Updated Tables at www.federalreserve.gov/pubs/oss/oss2/2001/scf2001home.htm.

▓ Transaction accounts have low balances

Not surprisingly, transaction accounts, though widely held by all ages, typically do not have large balances, with median values under $10,000 for all ages (see Chart 8.3). However, the elderly typically carry higher balances than do younger people.

▓ Elderly families are the least likely to have retirement accounts

Tax-deferred retirement accounts (such as IRAs, Keough's, 401(k), and 403(b) accounts) are held by 44 percent of the younger elderly and 26 percent of the older elderly (see Chart 8.4). These figures are substantially lower than for most younger families. In part, this may be due to elderly-headed families having fewer working years to take advantage of these types of accounts, as they have only existed for about 20 years. Also, if they did establish such accounts, the funds may be exhausted or may have been converted to an annuity, which the SCF categorizes as a different type of managed asset. Nonetheless, among those who hold such assets, elderly-headed families in the 65 to 74 age group have the highest median holdings in retirement accounts, $60,000 in 2001.

Retirement accounts have become much more common among elderly-headed families in the 75+ age group. In 1992, only 6 percent of families in this age group held these accounts, versus 26 percent in 2001. Among younger elderly families, the

CHART 8.3

Percent of Families Holding Transaction Accounts and Median Value of the Accounts (in Thousands of Dollars), by Age of Family Head: 2001

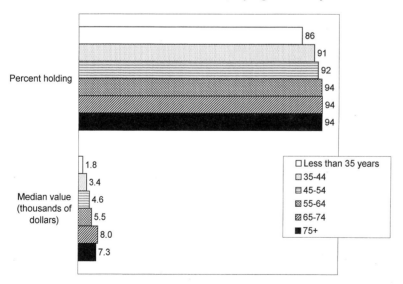

Source: Ana M. Aizcorbe, Arthur B. Kennickell, and Kevin B. Moore. (January 2003). "Recent Changes in U.S. Family Finances: Evidence from the 1998 and 2001 Survey of Consumer Finances." *Federal Reserve Bulletin*, vol. 89, 1–32, and Updated Tables at www.federalreserve.gov/pubs/oss/oss2/2001/scf2001home.htm.

CHART 8.4
Percent of Families Holding Retirement Accounts and Median Value of
the Accounts (in Thousands of Dollars), by Age of Family Head: 2001

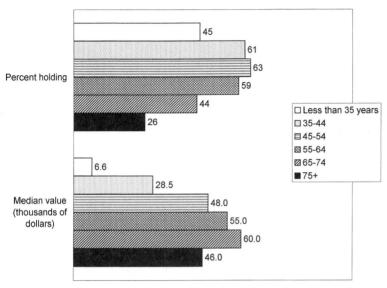

Source: Ana M. Aizcorbe, Arthur B. Kennickell, and Kevin B. Moore. (January 2003).
"Recent Changes in U.S. Family Finances: Evidence from the 1998 and 2001 Survey
of Consumer Finances." *Federal Reserve Bulletin*, vol. 89, 1–32, and Updated Tables
at www.federalreserve.gov/pubs/oss/oss2/2001/scf2001home.htm.

likelihood of having these assets increased from 35 percent to 44 percent over the
same period.

> Both the elderly and younger people have favorable opinions of the life insur-
> ance industry, with 67 percent of the former, and 63 percent of the latter, ex-
> pressing favorable attitudes.[2]

■ One-third of the elderly have cash-value life insurance policies

About 1 in 3 elderly-headed families has **cash value life insurance** (life insurance
which includes an investment vehicle). This level is somewhat lower than in 1992
and quite similar to the propensity among those in the 45 to 64 year age groups (see
Chart 8.5). The median current value of cash-value life insurance policies for elderly
families is less than $10,000.

■ CDs are the province of the elderly, with about one-third holding them

Elderly-headed families are the most likely to hold certificates of deposit (CDs); 30
percent of the younger elderly and 37 percent of the older elderly have CDs (see Chart
8.6). These levels are relatively unchanged from 1992 and are at least twice the level

CHART 8.5
Percent of Families Holding Cash-Value Insurance Policies and Median
Value of the Accounts (in Thousands of Dollars), by Age of Family
Head: 2001

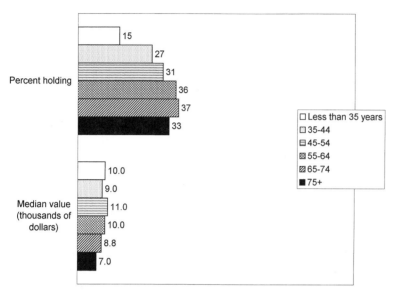

Source: Ana M. Aizcorbe, Arthur B. Kennickell, and Kevin B. Moore. (January 2003).
"Recent Changes in U.S. Family Finances: Evidence from the 1998 and 2001 Survey
of Consumer Finances." *Federal Reserve Bulletin*, vol. 89, 1–32, and Updated Tables
at www.federalreserve.gov/pubs/oss/oss2/2001/scf2001home.htm.

of younger families. Elderly families have median CD holdings of between $20,000
and $25,000, the highest of any age group.

The elderly are more than twice as likely to bank in-person than to use an ATM

In the past year, slightly more than half of the elderly have conducted in-person banking, similar to younger people (see Table 8.1). However, they are much less likely
to have used an ATM machine, phone, or online banking services.[3]

TABLE 8.1
Banking Services Used in the Past 12 Months, by Age: 2003

	18-64 Years	65+ Years	Ratio of 65+ to 18-64
	%	%	
Bank in-person	56	54	0.96
ATM machine	52	24	0.46
Phone	21	8	0.37
Online	15	3	0.20

Source: Mediamark Research Inc., 2003.

CHART 8.6
Percent of Families Holding Certificates of Deposit and Median Value
of the Accounts (in Thousands of Dollars), by Age of Family Head: 2001

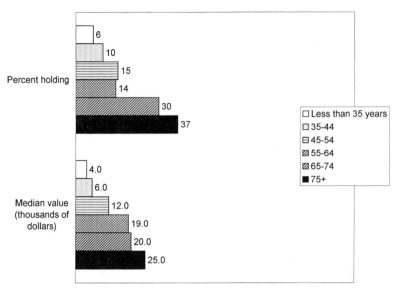

Source: Ana M. Aizcorbe, Arthur B. Kennickell, and Kevin B. Moore. (January 2003). "Recent Changes in U.S. Family Finances: Evidence from the 1998 and 2001 Survey of Consumer Finances." *Federal Reserve Bulletin*, vol. 89, 1–32, and Updated Tables at www.federalreserve.gov/pubs/oss/oss2/2001/scf2001home.htm.

Equity assets contribute substantial funds to the elderly who own them

Although stocks or mutual funds are among the assets least likely to be owned by the elderly, for those who do own them, median holdings in these assets are the most substantial of any assets they hold, separately ranging between $60,000 and $85,000 (see Chart 8.7). The elderly's likelihood of owning these assets is relatively similar to all but the youngest families. However, the median value of these equity assets among the elderly is the highest of any age group.

More than 1 in 3 elderly own some type of stock

When all direct and indirect forms of publicly traded stock ownership are considered (such as in mutual funds and retirement accounts), more than one-third of elderly-headed families had stock holdings in 2001, an increase of more than 30 percent from 1992 (see Chart 8.8).

Over this same period, the median value of stock holdings (among those with holdings) increased about eight times for the younger elderly and four times for the older elderly. Between 1998 and 2001, the figure had doubled for both age groups (see Chart 8.8).

CHART 8.7

Percent of Families Holding Stocks or Mutual Funds and
Median Value of the Accounts (in Thousands of Dollars),
by Age of Family Head: 2001

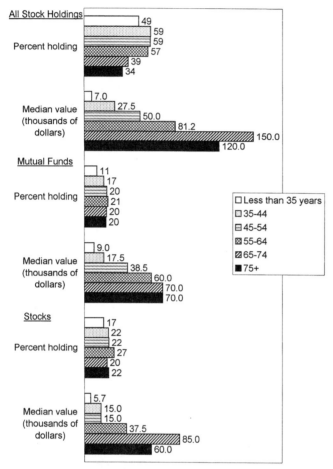

Source: Ana M. Aizcorbe, Arthur B. Kennickell, and Kevin B. Moore.
(January 2003). "Recent Changes in U.S. Family Finances: Evidence
from the 1998 and 2001 Survey of Consumer Finances." *Federal Reserve
Bulletin*, vol. 89, 1–32, and Updated Tables at www.federalreserve.gov/
pubs/oss/oss2/2001/scf2001home.htm.

As the median value of stocks has risen, so too has the relative importance of stocks
to the whole financial assets portfolio. Between 1992 and 2002, stock holdings
doubled in importance among the oldest elderly age group, and nearly doubled among
the younger elderly age group (see Chart 8.8), such that stocks now account for half
of the financial assets of the elderly who own such assets. These figures and trends
are quite similar to those of younger people.

CHART 8.8

Percent of Elderly Families Holding Stock (Directly or Indirectly), Median Value of the Stock Holdings (in Thousands of 2001 Dollars), and Share of Assets Attributable to Stock Holdings, by Age of Family Head: 1992, 1995, 1998, 2001

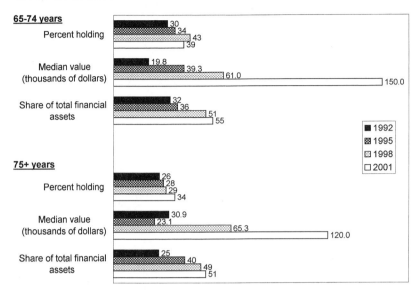

Source: Ana M. Aizcorbe, Arthur B. Kennickell, and Kevin B. Moore. (January 2003). "Recent Changes in U.S. Family Finances: Evidence from the 1998 and 2001 Survey of Consumer Finances." *Federal Reserve Bulletin*, vol. 89, 1–32, and Updated Tables at www.federalreserve.gov/pubs/oss/oss2/2001/scf2001home.htm.

Like their younger counterparts, the elderly's opinions of the Internal Revenue Service are tipped toward the negative end, with slightly more than half having unfavorable opinions of this taxing authority (54 percent versus 53 percent among younger people aged 18–64).[4] The elderly hold the stock brokerage industry in as high disfavor as the IRS. Six in 10 elderly (59 percent) express unfavorable opinions of the stock brokerage industry and they are somewhat stronger in their opinions than are younger people (53 percent).

About 1 in 10 elderly families has savings bonds

Bonds are among the least commonly held assets, with savings bonds more common than other types of bonds. The median value of savings bonds is relatively minuscule among the elderly, ranging between $2,000 and $3,000 (see Chart 8.9). As for other bonds, the younger elderly have the highest median bond holdings of any age group (more than $70,000). The median value of bond holdings among the older elderly is substantially lower, about half that of their younger elderly counterparts.

CHART 8.9
Percent of Families Holding Bonds and Median Value of the Accounts
(in Thousands of Dollars), by Age of Family Head: 2001

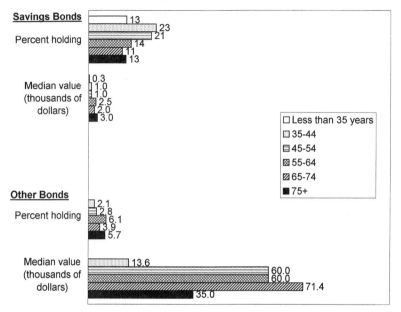

Source: Ana M. Aizcorbe, Arthur B. Kennickell, and Kevin B. Moore. (January 2003).
"Recent Changes in U.S. Family Finances: Evidence from the 1998 and 2001 Survey
of Consumer Finances." *Federal Reserve Bulletin*, vol. 89, 1–32, and Updated Tables
at www.federalreserve.gov/pubs/oss/oss2/2001/scf2001home.htm.

NONFINANCIAL ASSETS

At least three-quarters of elderly families own a vehicle or home

Virtually all elderly-headed families own some type of nonfinancial asset, with
vehicles and primary residences being the predominant asset; about three-quarters
own these particular assets (see Chart 8.10).

Homeownership is high among the elderly, with younger elderly families just as
likely as the next younger cohort (aged 55 to 64) to own a home. Homeownership is
slightly lower among the older elderly.

Vehicle ownership peaks in the 35 to 64 age range and then declines in the elderly years, with the older elderly the least likely to own a vehicle.

Homes are a significant asset for the elderly

Home values are substantial for the elderly, with a median value of $129,000 for
the younger elderly and $111,000 for the older elderly (see Chart 8.11). These home
values exceed the median value of all individual financial assets except total stock

CHART 8.10
Percent of Families Owning Specific Type of
Nonfinancial Asset, by Age of Family Head: 2001

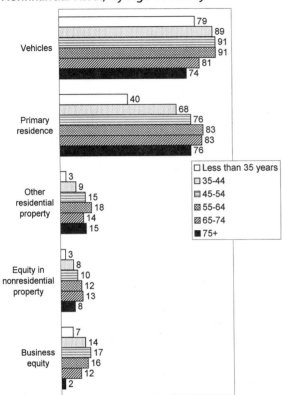

Source: Ana M. Aizcorbe, Arthur B. Kennickell, and Kevin B.
Moore. (January 2003). "Recent Changes in U.S. Family
Finances: Evidence from the 1998 and 2001 Survey of
Consumer Finances." *Federal Reserve Bulletin*, vol. 89, 1–32,
and Updated Tables at www.federalreserve.gov/pubs/oss/
oss2/2001/scf2001home.htm.

holdings. Between 1992 and 2001, the median home value increased 51 percent
among younger elderly-headed families and 28 percent among older elderly-headed
families.

Four percent of elderly households own a vacation or weekend home, 1 percent have investments in gold or other precious metals, and 1 percent have
investment collections such as antiques or books.[5]

▪ Fewer than 1 in 5 elderly families own other types of real estate

Fewer than 1 in 5 elderly-headed families own other types of residential property
outside their residence (such as second homes, time shares, and multi-family rental

CHART 8.11

Median Value of Specific Nonfinancial Asset (in Thousands of Dollars), by Age of Family Head: 2001

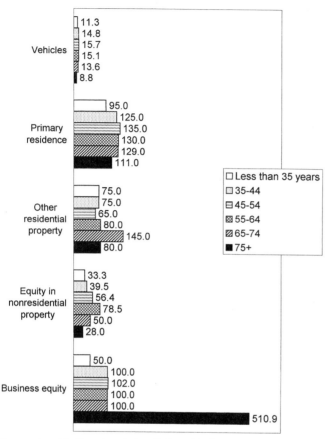

Source: Ana M. Aizcorbe, Arthur B. Kennickell, and Kevin B. Moore. (January 2003). "Recent Changes in U.S. Family Finances: Evidence from the 1998 and 2001 Survey of Consumer Finances." *Federal Reserve Bulletin*, vol. 89, 1–32, and Updated Tables at www.federalreserve.gov/pubs/oss/oss2/2001/scf2001home.htm.

properties; see Chart 8.10). However, the younger elderly-headed families have the highest median value of such property of any age group (see Chart 8.11).

Fewer than 1 in 10 elderly families own nonresidential properties (see Chart 8.10). Median values for this type property are substantially lower among elderly families than for those in the most common ownership age group of 55 to 64 (see Chart 8.11).

While the oldest elderly age group is the least likely group to have privately held business equity (only 2 percent of them do), they by far have the highest median value of those assets, more than half a million dollars versus $100,000 for younger age groups (see Charts 8.10 and 8.11).

SAVINGS AND DEBT

Six percent of the elderly used financial planning or money management counsel in the past 12 months.[6] Thirteen percent of the elderly have conducted some type of investment transaction (stocks, bonds, mutual funds) in the past 12 months and have done so an average of 6.4 times.[7]

■ Younger elderly families are as likely to save as most younger families

The SCF asks if family spending over the preceding year was less than, more than, or about equal to their income. In 2001, 62 percent of younger elderly families reported that they saved in the preceding year, the same level reported by all but the youngest and oldest families (53 percent of those less than 35 years, and 56 percent of those aged 75+).

Over a three-year period (2001 versus 1998), the proportion of younger elderly families reporting that they saved increased 6 percentage points; for the older elderly the increase was 7 percentage points.

■ The elderly are the least likely to carry debt, but the younger elderly are twice as likely as the older elderly to do so

The elderly are the least likely age group to be in debt, and the median value of that debt is lower than for any other age group as well (see Chart 8.12). Nonetheless, 57 percent of younger elderly families and 29 percent of older elderly families held some debt in 2001, with a median value of $13,100 and $5,000, respectively. The younger elderly are about 10 percent more likely to be holding debt than their counterparts were in 1992, while the older elderly are about 10 percent less likely.

■ Credit-card debt is the most common type of debt among older elderly families

Home-secured loans and credit cards represent the most common types of debt the elderly have (see Chart 8.13). Younger elderly families are about as likely to have credit-card debt as they are to have a home mortgage (30 percent versus 32 percent). For older elderly families, credit-card debt is the most likely type of debt held and is twice as likely as home-secured debt.

Median credit-card balances for elderly families are $1,000 or less and are relatively unchanged from 1992.

■ The younger elderly are now more likely to have mortgage debt and more of it

For the younger elderly, the likelihood of mortgage debt increased substantially between 1992 and 2001, from 19 percent to 32 percent, while that for older elderly families remained basically unchanged. The median value of mortgage debt nearly doubled among younger elderly families during this period (from $21,000

CHART 8.12
Percent of Families with Debt and the Median Value of the Debt, by Age of Family Head: 2001

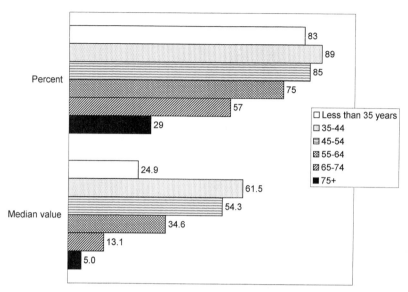

Source: Ana M. Aizcorbe, Arthur B. Kennickell, and Kevin B. Moore. (January 2003). "Recent Changes in U.S. Family Finances: Evidence from the 1998 and 2001 Survey of Consumer Finances." *Federal Reserve Bulletin*, vol. 89, 1–32, and Updated Tables at www.federalreserve.gov/pubs/oss/oss2/2001/scf2001home.htm.

to $39,000), while that for older elderly families rose 28 percent (from $35,000 to $45,000).

FINANCIAL ATTITUDES

■ Older = wiser (at least as far as money goes), but perhaps not wise enough

The elderly are more confident of their financial knowledge than are younger people, with the elderly nearly twice as likely as younger people to state that they are knowledgeable investors (see Table 8.2). However, despite their years, nearly half of the elderly (44 percent) classify themselves as beginner investors, and fewer than 20 percent think they are knowledgeable investors.

■ The elderly are more confident than younger people with many financial decisions

The elderly are most confident of their competency in saving and in managing their debts; about half of the elderly feel quite competent in doing so (see Table 8.3).

CHART 8.13
Percent of Elderly-Headed Families Holding Specific Type of Debt, by
Age of Family Head: 2001

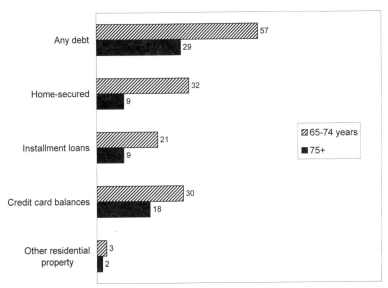

Source: Ana M. Aizcorbe, Arthur B. Kennickell, and Kevin B. Moore. (January 2003).
"Recent Changes in U.S. Family Finances: Evidence from the 1998 and 2001
Survey of Consumer Finances." *Federal Reserve Bulletin*, vol. 89, 1–32, and Updated
Tables at www.federalreserve.gov/pubs/oss/oss2/2001/scf2001home.htm.

The elderly feel more competent than do younger adults in dealing with many types
of financial decisions and processes. Not surprisingly, estate planning is an area where
the age differences are greatest, perhaps because the elderly are more firmly in that lifecycle stage. Nevertheless, this is an area where the elderly feel relatively less competent, with less than 1 in 3 stating they are quite competent in estate planning. In fact,
14 percent of the elderly feel at a total loss when it comes to this planning.

TABLE 8.2
Self-Impressions of Level of Investment Knowledge among Those Expressing an Opinion:
2003

	18-64 Years	65+ Years	Ratio of 65+ to 18-64
	%	%	
Beginner investor	62	44	0.71
Intermediate investor	28	39	1.41
Knowledgeable investor	9	17	1.84

Source: NOP World, 2003.

TABLE 8.3
Level of Competency with Various Financial Processes, by Age: 2003

	Percent Stating "Quite Competent"		Ratio of 65+ to 18-64
	18-64 Years	65+ Years	
Knowing how to save money	38	52	1.37
Buying, home, auto, or liability insurance	40	49	1.23
Managing debts	31	49	1.58
Financing a home	30	43	1.43
Retirement planning	21	40	1.90
Buying life insurance	30	39	1.30
Planning financial future	23	39	1.70
Getting a line of credit or large loan	25	35	1.40
Estate planning	13	31	2.38
Minimizing tax liability	16	25	1.56
Making money in the stock market	9	15	1.67
Making financial transactions or investments on-line	14	14	1.00

Source: NOP World, 2003.

The elderly are least confident about their ability to make money in the stock market and in making online financial transactions or investments (see Table 8.3). Predictably, the elderly are more likely than younger people to feel they are at a total loss when it comes to conducting online financial transactions (46 percent versus 32 percent). However, it is interesting to note that younger people, who generally have more hands-on computer expertise, express no more competency in online transactions than the elderly (only 14 percent of both groups express being "quite competent").

One-quarter of the elderly (25 percent) are concerned about their ability to provide financial support to an adult child who needs such support.[8]

■ Ability to pay medical bills for a serious illness is a substantial concern for the elderly

The elderly, like younger adults, are most concerned about their ability to pay medical bills for serious and extended illnesses—more than one-third (for whom this is an applicable concern) express this as a major concern of theirs (see Table 8.4). A slightly smaller group, about one-quarter of the applicable elderly, indicate paying ordinary medical bills as a major concern. Among those for whom it is an applicable concern, the elderly are less concerned about having enough funds in retirement than are younger people.

TABLE 8.4
Selected Financial Concerns, by Age: 2003

	Concern is Applicable		Those Stating it as a "Major Concern"*		
	18-64 Years	65+ Years	18-64 Years	65+ Years	Ratio of 65+ to 18-64
	%	%	%	%	
Ability to pay medical bills for prolonged and serious illness	92	91	37	38	1.04
Ability to pay for major household repairs	81	83	25	24	0.98
Ability to pay ordinary medical bills	92	93	20	23	1.15
Having enough money to live on in retirement	95	85	38	22	0.59

*Among those for whom it is an applicable concern.
Source: NOP World, 2003.

▪ More than one-quarter of the elderly rely solely on themselves for financial advice

The elderly most commonly turn to friends or relatives, a bank officer, or just themselves for financial advice (see Table 8.5). The elderly are 21 percent more likely than younger people to rely totally on themselves for financial advice. Among those who rely on others, more than 4 in 10 elderly rely on friends, relatives, or a bank officer.

TABLE 8.5
People Whom Household Members Turn to for Financial Advice, by Age: 2003

	Total			Those Who Rely on Someone Else		
	18-64 Years	65+ Years	Ratio of 65+ to 18-64	18-64 Years	65+ Years	Ratio of 65+ to 18-64
	%	%		%	%	
No one, rely only on self	24	29	1.21	NA	NA	NA
Friends or relatives	39	32	0.82	51	45	0.88
Bank officer	26	29	1.12	34	41	1.19
Accountant	21	20	0.95	28	28	1.02
Financial planner	18	15	0.83	24	21	0.89
Lawyer	13	12	0.92	17	17	0.99
Full service stock broker	7	8	1.14	9	11	1.22

Source: NOP World, 2003.

TABLE 8.6
Credit-Card Incidence and Reasons for Using or Not Using a Credit Card: 2002

	18-64 Years	65+ Years	Ratio of 65+ to 18-64
	%	%	
Use a credit card	60	67	1.12
Major Reasons for using a credit card			
Emergency use	84	80	0.95
Convenience	72	71	0.99
Safer than cash	51	54	1.06
Do not use a credit card	40	33	0.83
Major Reasons for not using a credit card			
Easy to get into debt	79	74	0.94
High interest rates	72	65	0.90
Annual fees too high	52	53	1.02

Source: NOP World, 2002.

Credit-card debt is less common with the elderly

Two-thirds of the elderly (67 percent) have a credit card, quite comparable to the 60 percent level among younger people (see Table 8.6). On average, the elderly who have credit cards carry 3.4 credit cards and have an average monthly expenditure of $339, comparable to the 3.6 cards carried by younger people and their $358 monthly expenditures.[9]

However, the elderly are twice as likely as younger people to pay off their credit-card balances (51 percent do so versus 25 percent, respectively).[10]

The elderly and younger people are similarly motivated for having or not having a credit card. Emergency use, convenience, and safety are the major reasons credit cards are used. On the other hand, concerns about getting into debt, high interest rates, and annual fees haunt those who do not have credit cards.

One in five elderly have a debit card

One-quarter of the elderly (26 percent) have not heard of a debit card compared with 9 percent of younger people.[11] Among the aware elderly, 30 percent have a debit card, for a net incidence of 22 percent, half the level of younger people (45 percent).

NOTES

1. Unless otherwise noted, all data in this chapter are from the Updated Tables from Internal Data available at www.federalreserve.gov/pubs/oss/oss2/2001/scf2001home.html and based on Ana M. Aizcorbe, Arthur B. Kennickell, and Kevin B. Moore. (January 2003).

"Recent Changes in U.S. Family Finances: Evidence from the 1998 and 2001 Survey of Consumer Finances." *Federal Reserve Bulletin*, vol. 89, 1–32.

2. NOP World, 2002.
3. Mediamark Research Inc., 2003.
4. NOP World, 2002.
5. Mediamark Research Inc., 2003.
6. Ibid.
7. Ibid.
8. NOP World, 2003.
9. Mediamark Research Inc., 2003.
10. NOP World, 2003.
11. NOP World, 2002.

CHAPTER 9

Consumer Spending

The greatest use of life is to spend it for something that will outlast it.

—*William James*

Every time you spend money, you're casting a vote for the kind of world you want.

—*Anna Lappe*

In this chapter, the authors analyze the Bureau of Labor Statistics' 2001 Consumer Expenditure Survey (CE) data to better understand the elderly's spending patterns.[1] More specifically, the elderly's spending behavior is compared with that of younger households, and interesting spending differences among the elderly are noted by region and income. Specific spending categories included in this chapter are housing, transportation, health care, food (at home and away from home), cash contributions, pensions and social security, life insurance and other personal insurance, entertainment, and apparel.

The Consumer Expenditure Survey, conducted annually, reports the purchasing behavior of the total civilian noninstitutionalized population. CE data are based on the "consumer unit." Technically, a **consumer unit** comprises either: (1) all members of a particular household who are related by blood, marriage, adoption, or other legal arrangements; (2) a person living alone or sharing a household with others or living as a roomer in a private home or lodging house or in permanent living quarters in a hotel or motel, but who is financially independent; or (3) two or more persons living together who use their income to make joint expenditure decisions. Financial independence is determined by the three major expense categories: housing, food, and other living expenses. To be considered financially independent, at least two of the three major expense categories have to be provided entirely, or in part, by the respondent. **In this chapter, the term *household* is used interchangeably with *consumer unit*.**

The data in this chapter are analyzed by age. However, age is a characteristic of an individual, while the CE household/consumer unit refers to a group of individuals. The "age" of a household/consumer unit is determined by that person designated as the "reference person"—the first member mentioned by the respondent when asked to "Start with the name of the person or one of the persons who owns or rents the home." For ease of discussion, **when this chapter refers to people or households of a certain age, that age is the age of the household's reference person.**

Household size and composition vary dramatically with the age of the householder. Elderly households are smaller, on average, than most other households and more likely to be composed of just one person. The CE sample reflects this (see Table 9.1).

Also, as might be expected, household spending increases with household size. On average, the CE data indicate that overall spending for two-person households is 70 percent higher than for one-person households, and three-person households spend 15 percent more than do two-person households.

Given that elderly households are smaller, it would be expected that their spending would be less. Thus, to compensate for this household size factor, the author's provide an additional measure referred to as a **per-person per-household** consumption statistic. Specifically, average annual expenditures are divided by the average household size. This statistic reflects the average consumption of a person in a household whose reference person is of the prescribed age. While not a perfect measure, it does help to compensate for household size factors.

Chapter highlights include:

- The elderly in the South are the most frugal with their money.

- Housing accounts for the largest share of the elderly's spending, 1 of every 3 dollars.

- People in the oldest households spend more than eight times as much, on a per-person per-household basis, on health care than do those in the youngest households.

- Elderly-headed households are the most generous with their money, contributing more, per-person per-household, than any other age group.

TABLE 9.1
Household Size by Age of Reference Person: 2001

	Under 25 Years	25-34 Years	35-44 Years	45-54 Years	55-64 Years	65-74 Years	75+ Years
	%	%	%	%	%	%	%
Household size:							
1 person	54	23	16	23	28	38	59
2 person	21	23	17	30	48	49	35
3+ person	25	54	67	47	24	13	5
1 or 2 persons	75	46	33	53	76	87	95
Average household size	1.9	2.9	3.3	2.7	2.1	1.9	1.5

Source: U.S. Department of Labor, Bureau of Labor Statistics. "2001 Consumer Expenditure Survey." www.bls.gov/cex/home.htm.

Definition: *Expenditures* consist of the transaction costs, including excise and sales taxes, of goods and services acquired during the interview or record-keeping period. Expenditure estimates include expenditures for gifts, but exclude purchases or portions of purchases directly assignable to business purposes. Also excluded are periodic credit or installment payments on goods or services already acquired. The full cost of each purchase is recorded, even though full payment may not have been made at the date of purchase.

SPENDING OVERVIEW

Elderly households spend more than half a trillion dollars each year

Elderly households accounted for 14 percent of all consumer spending in 2001, or $608 billion (see Chart 9.1). The average elderly household spent $27,714 in 2001, substantially less than the $42,432 spent by non-elderly households. On a household basis, spending is highest among those with a reference person aged 45–54 and lowest among the oldest households (those with a reference person aged 75+; see Chart 9.2). As mentioned, elderly households are, on average, smaller than younger households, thus contributing to some of the differential. When annual household expen-

CHART 9.1

Aggregate Annual Expenditures (in Thousands of Dollars), by Age of Reference Person in Household: 2001

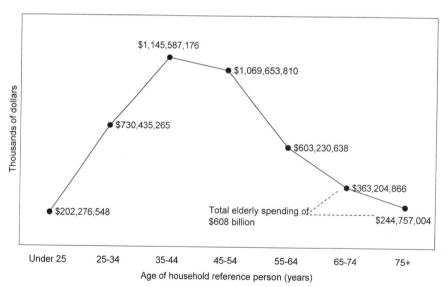

Source: Author calculations based on data from U.S. Department of Labor, Bureau of Labor Statistics, "2001 Consumer Expenditure Survey," www.bls.gov/cex/home.htm.

CHART 9.2
Average Annual Expenditures, by Age of Reference Person in Household: 2001

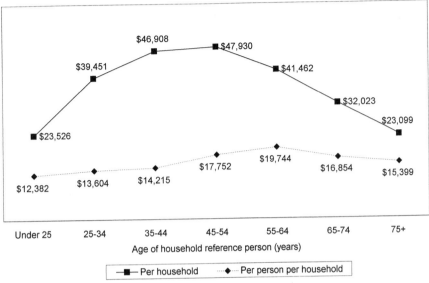

Source: U.S. Department of Labor, Bureau of Labor Statistics. "2001 Consumer Expenditure Survey." www.bls.gov/cex/home.htm.

ditures are reconfigured on a per-person per-household basis,* a very different, less drastic, spending pattern arises by age; per-person per-household spending peaks among households aged 55–64 and then declines somewhat among elderly households, yet remains higher than households aged 44 and younger (see Chart 9.2).

■ Southern elderly are most frugal

On a per-person per-household basis, elderly households in the South spend the least amount of money, about 15 percent less than their highest spending counterparts in the Midwest (see Table 9.2). Spending patterns vary much more drastically by income, with the highest income elderly households spending more than twice as much, on a per-person per-household basis, as the lowest income elderly (see Table 9.3).

■ One in 3 dollars that the elderly spend goes toward housing

Housing is the elderly's single largest expense, accounting for 1 in every 3 dollars they spend (see Chart 9.3). Transportation is the second largest expenditure, account-

---

*Per-person per-household statistics are generated by dividing the average annual expenditures by the average household size.

TABLE 9.2

Average Annual Expenditures and Average Household Size among Households with an Elderly Reference Person, by Region: 2000–2001

	Northeast	Midwest	South	West
Average number of persons per consumer unit	1.7	1.6	1.7	1.8
Expenditures per consumer unit	$27,963	$27,543	$24,900	$29,594
Expenditures per person per household	$16,449	$17,214	$14,647	$16,441

Source: U.S. Department of Labor, Bureau of Labor Statistics. "2001 Consumer Expenditure Survey." www.bls.gov/cex/home.htm.

TABLE 9.3

Average Annual Expenditures and Average Household Size among Households with an Elderly Reference Person, by Income: 2000–2001

	Average Annual Income								
	Less than $5,000	$5,000 to $9,999	$10,000 to $14,999	$15,000 to $19,999	$20,000 to $29,999	$30,000 to $39,999	$40,000 to $49,999	$50,000 to $69,999	$70,000 and over
Average number of persons per consumer unit	1.4	1.2	1.4	1.7	1.8	2.0	2.0	2.1	2.4
Expenditures per consumer unit	$17,993	$14,274	$19,236	$24,057	$29,570	$32,962	$41,403	$48,213	$70,531
Expenditures per person per household	$12,852	$11,895	$13,740	$14,151	$16,428	$16,481	$20,702	$22,959	$29,388

Source: U.S. Department of Labor, Bureau of Labor Statistics. "2001 Consumer Expenditure Survey." www.bls.gov/cex/home.htm.

ing for 16 percent of elderly household spending. Together, housing and transportation account for half of what elderly households spend. Health care and food expenditures (both at home and away from home) together account for 1 in 4 dollars spent. Six percent of all elderly expenses go toward cash contributions.

HOUSING

Housing expenditures, as defined by the CE, include:

Shelter:

Owned dwellings: interest on mortgages, interest on home equity loans and lines of credit, property taxes and insurance, refinancing and prepayment charges, ground rent, expenses for property management and security, homeowners' insurance, fire insurance and extended coverage, expenses for repairs and maintenance contracted out, and expenses of materials for owner-performed repairs and maintenance for dwellings used or maintained by the

CHART 9.3
Share of Spending among Households with an Elderly Reference
Person: 2001

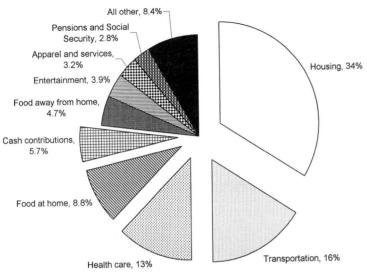

Source: U.S. Department of Labor, Bureau of Labor Statistics. "2001 Consumer Expenditure Survey." www.bls.gov/cex/home.htm.

consumer unit. Mortgage principal repayments are payments of loans and not considered as shelter costs.

Rented dwellings: rent paid for dwellings, rent received as pay, parking fees, maintenance, and other expenses.

Other lodging: all expenses for vacation homes, school, college, hotels, motels, and other lodging while out of town.

Utilities, fuels, and public services: natural gas; electricity; fuel oil and other fuels, such as wood, kerosene, coal, and bottled gas; water and other public services, such as garbage and trash collection, sewerage maintenance, septic tank cleaning; and telephone charges.

Household operations:

Personal services: baby-sitting; day care, nursery school, and preschool tuition; care of the elderly, invalids and handicapped; adult day care; and domestic and other duties.

Other household expenses: housekeeping services, gardening and lawn care services, coin-operated laundry and dry-cleaning (non-clothing), termite and pest control products and services, home security systems service fees, moving, storage, and freight expenses, repair of household appliances and other household equipment, repair of computer systems for home use, computer information services, reupholstering and furniture repair, rental and repair of lawn and gardening tools, and rental of other household equipment.

Housekeeping supplies: laundry and cleaning supplies, cleaning and toilet tissues, stationery supplies, postage, delivery services, miscellaneous household products, and lawn and garden supplies.

Household furnishings and equipment:

Household textiles: bathroom, bedroom, kitchen and dining room, other linens, curtains and drapes, slipcovers and decorative pillows, and sewing materials.

Furniture: living room; dining room; kitchen; bedroom; nursery; porch, lawn, and other outdoor furniture.

Floor covering: new and replacement wall-to-wall carpets, room-size rugs, and other non-permanent floor coverings.

Major appliances: refrigerators and freezers, dishwashers and garbage disposals, stoves and ovens, vacuum cleaners, microwaves, air-conditioners, sewing machines, washing machines and dryers, and floor cleaning equipment.

Small appliances/miscellaneous housewares: small electrical kitchen appliances, portable heating and cooling equipment, china and other dinnerware, flatware, glassware, silver and other serving pieces, non-electric cookware, and plastic dinnerware (excludes personal care appliances).

Miscellaneous household equipment: typewriters, luggage, lamps and light fixtures, window coverings, clocks, lawnmowers and gardening equipment, other hand and power tools, telephone answering devices, telephones and accessories, computers and computer hardware for home use, computer software and accessories for home use, calculators, business equipment for home use, floral arrangements and house plants, rental of furniture, closet and storage items, other household decorative items, infants' equipment, outdoor equipment, smoke alarms, other household appliances, and other small miscellaneous furnishings.

■ Households of all ages appropriate about the same share of spending on housing

As a share of all expenditures, housing-related spending does not vary considerably by age, accounting for about 1 in 3 dollars spent by households of all ages (see Chart 9.4).

Housing accounts for somewhat more of an elderly household's total spending in the West and Northeast (35 percent and 37 percent, respectively) than in the South and Midwest (33 percent and 31 percent). This is reflected in the fact that the elderly households in these two regions spend more of their housing dollars on their basic shelter than do their counterparts in the other regions (see Table 9.4).

■ Housing costs account for a higher share of spending among lower-income elderly

Higher-income elderly appropriate less of their total spending on housing than do lower-income elderly; about 30 percent among elderly households with annual incomes above $20,000, versus nearly 40 percent among those with the lowest incomes.

CHART 9.4

Average Annual Housing Expenditures and Share of Total Expenditures, by Age of Reference Person in Household: 2001

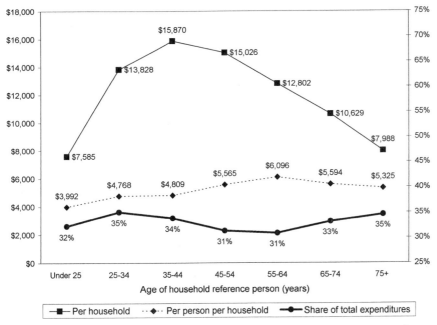

Source: U.S. Department of Labor, Bureau of Labor Statistics. "2001 Consumer Expenditure Survey." www.bls.gov/cex/home.htm.

◼ The elderly's housing costs are not dramatically different than younger people's

On a per-person per-household basis, housing related spending rises steadily with age, peaking among the 55- to 64-year-old households and then declining only slightly among elderly households (see Chart 9.4).

TABLE 9.4

Share of Housing Expenditures among Households with an Elderly Reference Person, by Region: 2000–2001

	Northeast	Midwest	South	West
	%	%	%	%
Total housing spending	100	100	100	100
Shelter	57	52	47	55
Utilities, fuels, and public services	23	27	30	22
Household furnishings and equipment	8	11	10	10
Household operations	7	6	8	8

Source: Author calculations based on data from U.S. Department of Labor, Bureau of Labor Statistics, "2001 Consumer Expenditure Survey," www.bls.gov/cex/home.htm.

More than half of elderly households own a home with no mortgage

Shelter accounts for the majority of housing-related spending among all households (see Chart 9.5). However, with age, paying for the roof over one's head consumes less and less of housing related expenses; half of the housing costs of elderly households are for shelter compared with 64 percent among the youngest households. In part, this is due to substantial variations in homeownership dynamics by age.

Homeownership, and especially mortgage-free homeownership, increases with age (see Charts 9.6 and 9.7). Eight in 10 elderly households own a home, with 70 percent of elderly homeowners aged 65–74, and 87 percent of those aged 75+, living in their home mortgage-free. Overall, this means that 57 percent of the younger elderly households and 68 percent of the older elderly households own a home that is free and clear of any mortgage.

Higher-income elderly are less likely to live mortgage-free

Mortgage-free home ownership among the elderly declines with income. Fewer than 1 in 4 elderly households with incomes below $40,000 have a mortgage, compared to 40 percent with incomes $70,000+ (see Chart 9.8). In part, this could be driven by home values, which tend to increase with income. As well, higher-income elderly households are younger (and thus more likely to have a mortgage) and have

CHART 9.5
Share of Housing Expenditures, by Age of the Household Reference Person: 2001

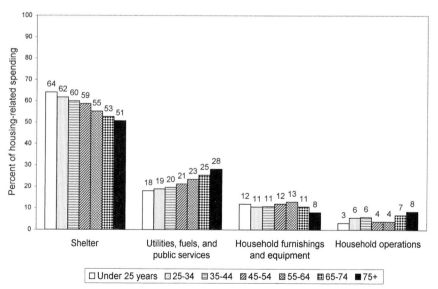

Source: Author calculations based on data from U.S. Department of Labor, Bureau of Labor Statistics, "2001 Consumer Expenditure Survey," www.bls.gov/cex/home.htm.

CHART 9.6
Homeownership, by Age of the Household Reference Person: 2001

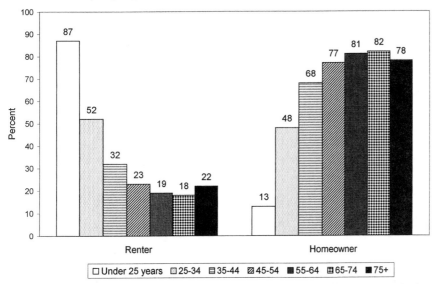

Source: Author calculations based on data from U.S. Department of Labor, Bureau of Labor Statistics, "2001 Consumer Expenditure Survey," www.bls.gov/cex/home.htm.

CHART 9.7
Mortgage Status among Homeowners, by Age of the Household Reference Person: 2001

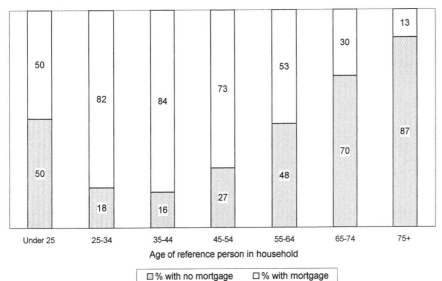

Source: Author calculations based on data from U.S. Department of Labor, Bureau of Labor Statistics, "2001 Consumer Expenditure Survey," www.bls.gov/cex/home.htm.

CHART 9.8

Mortgage Status and Home Market Value among Households with an Elderly Reference Person, by Income: 2000–2001

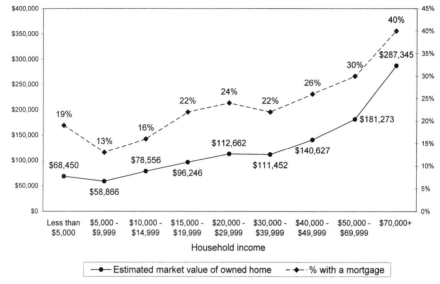

Source: U.S. Department of Labor, Bureau of Labor Statistics. "2001 Consumer Expenditure Survey." www.bls.gov/cex/home.htm.

a higher likelihood of a member who works (thus increasing the ability to support a mortgage; see the discussion in this chapter under Pensions and Social Security, page 176).

Regionally, elderly households in the Northeast and West have the highest home values, about twice that of their Midwest and Southern counterparts (see Table 9.5). However, those in the West are the most likely to have a mortgage.

Interestingly, shelter accounts for the same percent of housing costs regardless of the elderly household's income (see Table 9.6). With higher incomes, though, hous-

TABLE 9.5

Mortgage Status and Home Market Value in Households with an Elderly Reference Person, by Region: 2000–2001

	Northeast	Midwest	South	West
Without a mortgage	84%	81%	77%	72%
With a mortgage	16%	19%	23%	28%
Estimated market value of owned home	$161,001	$84,710	$86,276	$164,073

Source: U.S. Department of Labor, Bureau of Labor Statistics. "2001 Consumer Expenditure Survey." www.bls.gov/cex/home.htm.

TABLE 9.6

Share of Housing Expenditures in Households with an Elderly Reference Person, by Income: 2000–2001

	Average Annual Income								
	Less than $5,000	$5,000 to $9,999	$10,000 to $14,999	$15,000 to $19,999	$20,000 to $29,999	$30,000 to $39,999	$40,000 to $49,999	$50,000 to $69,999	$70,000 and over
	%	%	%	%	%	%	%	%	%
Total housing spending	100	100	100	100	100	100	100	100	100
Shelter	51	52	50	52	51	50	52	50	52
Utilities, fuels, and public services	28	30	29	28	27	26	23	23	17
Household furnishings and equipment	6	8	9	9	10	11	13	13	14
Household operations	10	5	7	5	6	7	6	8	12
House-keeping supplies	4	6	5	5	5	5	6	7	4

Source: U.S. Department of Labor, Bureau of Labor Statistics. "2001 Consumer Expenditure Survey." www.bls.gov/cex/home.htm.

ing-related spending shifts away from utilities and toward furnishings and equipment, not a surprising development given the more discretionary nature of the latter.

■ Utilities consume more of the elderly's housing dollars, especially those in the South

Utilities consume an increasing share of housing dollars with age, rising from 18 percent of the youngest households' housing expenses to 28 percent of the oldest households' (see Chart 9.5). Elderly households in the South spend a greater share of their housing dollars on utilities, but less on shelter, than do their counterparts in the rest of the United States (see Table 9.4).

Household operations consume more of the elderly's housing dollars closely followed by 25- to 44-year-old households (see Chart 9.5). This is not surprising given that this spending category includes baby-sitting, day care, and nursery school tuition as well as adult day care and other care of the elderly (but not nursing home care). Among elderly households, household operations spending skews the most toward those with the highest and lowest incomes (see Table 9.6).

TRANSPORTATION

Transportation expenditures, as defined by the CE, include:

Vehicle purchases (net outlay): the net outlay (purchase price minus trade-in value) on new and used domestic and imported cars and trucks and other vehicles, including motorcycles and private planes.

Vehicle rental, leases, licenses, and other charges: leased and rented cars, trucks, motorcycles, and aircraft; inspection fees; state and local registration; driver's license fees; parking fees; towing charges; tolls; and automobile service clubs.

Vehicle finance charges: the dollar amount of interest paid for a loan contracted for the purchase of vehicles described above.

Gasoline and motor oil: gasoline, diesel fuel, and motor oil.

Maintenance and repairs: tires, batteries, tubes, lubrication, filters, coolant, additives, brake and transmission fluids, oil change, brake work including adjustment, front-end alignment, wheel balancing, steering repair, shock absorber replacement, clutch and transmission repair, electrical system repair, exhaust system repair, body work and painting, motor repair, repair to cooling system, drive train repair, drive shaft and rear-end repair, tire repair, audio equipment, other maintenance and services, and auto repair policies.

Vehicle insurance: the premium paid for insuring cars, trucks, and other vehicles.

Public transportation: fares for mass transit, buses, trains, airlines, taxis, school buses for which a fee is charged, and boats.

▮ Elderly households appropriate less of their spending toward transportation

Transportation expenditures account for about 1 in 5 dollars spent by non-elderly households, but this proportion declines among elderly households (see Chart 9.9). On a per-person per-household basis, it is the oldest elderly households (aged 75+) that spend the least on transportation. Younger elderly households (aged 65–74) spend less, per-person per-household, than their next-in-line cohorts, aged 45 to 64, but more than those households younger than 45 years.

Vehicle purchases account for the lion's share of transportation spending among all households (see Table 9.7). Despite the fact that the elderly households have vehicle ownership characteristics similar to the youngest households (see Table 9.8), elderly households spend less of their transportation dollars on vehicles than do younger households. Less than 40 percent of elderly household's transportation spending is for vehicle purchases, versus about half that for younger households.

CHART 9.9

Average Annual Transportation Expenditures and Share of Total Expenditures, by Age of the Household Reference Person: 2001

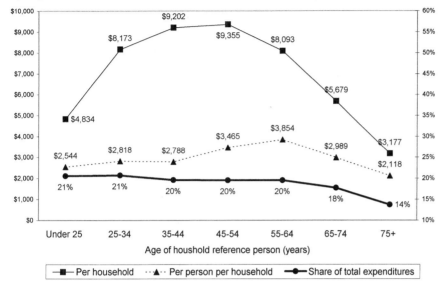

Source: U.S. Department of Labor, Bureau of Labor Statistics. "2001 Consumer Expenditure Survey." www.bls.gov/cex/home.htm.

TABLE 9.7

Share of Transportation Expenditures, by Age of the Household Reference Person: 2001

	Age (Years)						
	Under 25 %	25-34 %	35-44 %	45-54 %	55-64 %	65-74 %	75+ %
Total transportation spending	100	100	100	100	100	100	100
Vehicle purchases (net outlay)	51	48	49	46	47	44	38
Gasoline and motor oil	18	16	16	17	17	18	18
Vehicle insurance	9	10	10	11	11	12	17
Maintenance and repairs	7	7	9	9	8	9	13
Vehicle rental, leases, licenses, finance, and other charges	10	14	12	12	11	9	8
Public transportation	5	4	5	5	6	8	8

Source: Author calculations based on data from U.S. Department of Labor, Bureau of Labor Statistics, "2001 Consumer Expenditure Survey," www.bls.gov/cex/home.htm.

TABLE 9.8

Vehicle Ownership Characteristics, by Age of the Household Reference Person: 2001

	Age (Years)						
	Under 25	25-34	35-44	45-54	55-64	65-74	75+
Average number of vehicles	1.2	1.8	2.1	2.4	2.3	1.8	1.2
At least one vehicle owned or leased	72%	89%	92%	92%	92%	87%	76%

Source: U.S. Department of Labor, Bureau of Labor Statistics. "2001 Consumer Expenditure Survey." www.bls.gov/cex/home.htm.

HEALTH CARE

Health care expenditures, as defined by the CE, include:

Health insurance: traditional fee-for-service health plans, preferred-provider health plans, health maintenance organizations (HMOs), commercial Medicare supplements, and other health insurance.

Medical services: hospital room and services, physicians' services, service by a professional other than a physician, eye and dental care, lab tests and X-rays, medical care in a retirement community, care in convalescent or nursing home, and other medical care service.

Drugs: nonprescription drugs and vitamins and prescription drugs.

Medical supplies: topicals and dressings, antiseptics, bandages, cotton, first aid kits, contraceptives, syringes, ice bags, thermometers, sun lamps, vaporizers, heating pads, medical appliances (such as braces, canes, crutches, walkers, eyeglasses, and hearing aids), and rental and repair of medical equipment.

Health care spending increases dramatically with age

Health care spending rises precipitously with age. With every 10-year age increment, per-person per-household health care spending rises between 20 and 59 percent from the prior age category. As a result, people in the oldest households spend more than eight times as much, per-person per-household, on health care than do those in the youngest households, and 1.8 times more than those aged 55 to 64 (see Chart 9.10).

Predictably, health care accounts for a greater share of the elderly's household spending than it does for younger households; the differential is more than six times higher among the oldest elderly households than the youngest (14.7 percent for aged 75+ households versus 2.3 percent for households younger than 25 years old; see Chart 9.10).

CHART 9.10

Health Care Expenditures and Share of Total Expenditures, by Age of Reference Person in Household: 2001

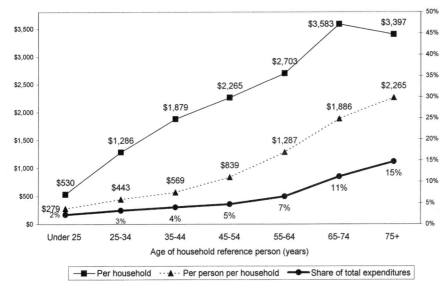

Source: U.S. Department of Labor, Bureau of Labor Statistics. "2001 Consumer Expenditure Survey." www.bls.gov/cex/home.htm.

■ Health insurance consumes the greatest part of health care spending

Despite enrollment in Medicare, health insurance accounts for about 1 in 2 health care dollars spent by elderly households, quite similar to that spent by younger households (see Table 9.9). Interestingly, elderly households spend proportionately less of their health care dollars on medical services and supplies than do younger households.

■ Drugs account for about 1 in 4 of the elderly's health care dollars

Drug spending patterns differ somewhat by age (see Table 9.9). The oldest households (aged 75+) allocate the larger share of their health care spending on drugs, while households aged 25–34 allocate the smaller share (28 percent and 14 percent, respectively). Drugs compose 23 percent of younger elderly household health care spending, similar to that of their next younger cohort (aged 55–64).

Elderly households in the Northeast spend the largest share of their health care dollars on health insurance and those in the West spend the least (see Table 9.10). Drug spending is a disproportionately larger share of health care spending among midwestern and southern elderly households, while medical services consume the larger share of health care spending among those in the West.

The highest-income elderly households spend fewer health care dollars on insurance and drugs and more on medical services than do lower-income elderly households (see Table 9.11).

TABLE 9.9

Share of Health Care Expenditures, by Age of the Household Reference Person: 2001

	Age (Years)						
	Under 25	25-34	35-44	45-54	55-64	65-74	75+
	%	%	%	%	%	%	%
Total health care spending	100	100	100	100	100	100	100
Health insurance	47	54	49	46	44	49	53
Medical services	25	28	30	30	28	24	15
Drugs	20	14	16	19	22	23	28
Medical supplies	7	4	4	5	5	4	4

Source: Author calculations based on data from U.S. Department of Labor, Bureau of Labor Statistics, "2001 Consumer Expenditure Survey," www.bls.gov/cex/home.htm.

TABLE 9.10

Share of Health Care Expenditures among Households with an Elderly Reference Person, by Region: 2000–2001

	Northeast	Midwest	South	West
	%	%	%	%
Total health care spending	100	100	100	100
Health insurance	55	50	50	47
Medical services	18	21	19	25
Drugs	22	26	28	23
Medical supplies	5	4	3	6

Source: Author calculations based on data from U.S. Department of Labor, Bureau of Labor Statistics, "2001 Consumer Expenditure Survey," www.bls.gov/cex/home.htm.

FOOD

Food expenditures, as defined by the CE, include:

Food-at-home: total expenditures for food at grocery stores (or other food stores) and food prepared by the consumer unit on trips. It excludes the purchase of nonfood items.

Food-away-from-home: all meals (breakfast and brunch, lunch, dinner and snacks and nonalcoholic beverages), including tips at fast food, take-out, delivery, concession stands, buffet and cafeteria, at full-service restaurants, and at vending machines and mobile vendors. Also included are board (including at school), meals as pay, special catered affairs, such as weddings, bar mitzvahs, and confirmations, school lunches, and meals away from home on trips.

TABLE 9.11

Share of Health Care Expenditures among Households with an Elderly Reference Person, by Income: 2000–2001

	Average Annual Income								
	Less than $5,000	$5,000 to $9,999	$10,000 to $14,999	$15,000 to $19,999	$20,000 to $29,999	$30,000 to $39,999	$40,000 to $49,999	$50,000 to $69,999	$70,000 and over
	%	%	%	%	%	%	%	%	%
Total health care spending	100	100	100	100	100	100	100	100	100
Health insurance	51	52	51	48	52	50	51	44	45
Medical services	21	14	17	19	17	23	21	33	29
Drugs	24	29	29	29	27	22	22	19	21
Medical supplies	4	4	3	4	4	4	6	4	5

Source: Author calculations based on data from U.S. Department of Labor, Bureau of Labor Statistics, "2001 Consumer Expenditure Survey," www.bls.gov/cex/home.htm.

■ The elderly's food-at-home spending is among the highest

Per-person per-household food-at-home expenditures peak among households aged 55 to 64 but decline 11 percent among households aged 65 to 74 and then increase among those aged 75+ (see Chart 9.11).

The proportion of total spending allocated to food-at-home remains rather stable across age groups, with a substantial increase, though, among the oldest households (see Chart 9.11).

Households of all ages spend their food dollars similarly (see Table 9.12). Spending for meat, poultry, fish, and eggs constitutes the largest component of food-at-home expenditures—about 1 in 4 food-at-home dollars.

■ The oldest households have the lowest food-away-from-home spending

Food-away-from-home composes a larger share of the youngest households' spending, with a precipitous drop at age 25, and then declining again after age 55 (see Chart 9.12). The oldest households allocate about half as much of their total spending on food-away-from-home as do the youngest households (4.3 percent versus 7.9 percent).

Per-person per-household food-away-from-home expenditures peak among the 45- to 64-year-old households, and then decline about 20 percent among 65- to 74-year-old households and a further 20 percent among those aged 75+ (see Chart 9.12). In fact, the oldest households have the lowest per-person per-household food-away-from-home consumption.

CHART 9.11
Food at Home Expenditures and Share of Total Expenditures, by Age of the Household Reference Person: 2001

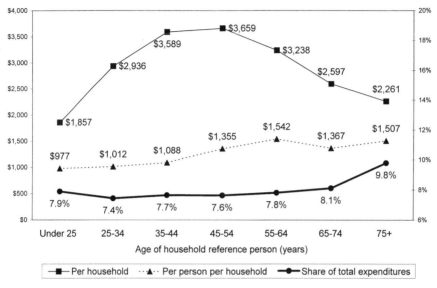

—■— Per household   ⋯▲⋯ Per person per household   —●— Share of total expenditures

Source: U.S. Department of Labor, Bureau of Labor Statistics. "2001 Consumer Expenditure Survey." www.bls.gov/cex/home.htm.

▤ The highest-income elderly households spend more on food-away-from-home than at-home

Elderly households tend to spend similar amounts for food-at-home, regardless of their income. However, food away-from-home spending dramatically increases with income—so much so, in fact, that the elderly households with the highest incomes ($70,000+) spend more on away-from-home food than they do on food-at-home (see Chart 9.13).

TABLE 9.12
Share of Food at Home Expenditures, by Age of the Household Reference Person: 2001

	Age (Years)						
	Under 25	25-34	35-44	45-54	55-64	65-74	75+
	%	%	%	%	%	%	%
Total food at home spending	100	100	100	100	100	100	100
Meats, poultry, fish, and eggs	25	27	26	27	28	27	26
Fruits and vegetables	16	16	16	17	17	19	19
Cereals and bakery products	15	14	15	14	14	15	16
Dairy products	10	11	11	11	11	11	11

Source: Author calculations based on data from U.S. Department of Labor, Bureau of Labor Statistics, "2001 Consumer Expenditure Survey," www.bls.gov/cex/home.htm.

CHART 9.12

Food Away from Home Expenditures and Share of Total Expenditures, by Age of the Household Reference Person: 2001

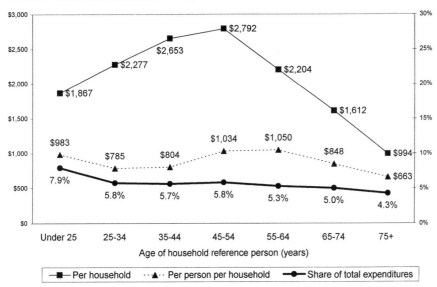

Source: U.S. Department of Labor, Bureau of Labor Statistics. "2001 Consumer Expenditure Survey." www.bls.gov/cex/home.htm.

CHART 9.13

Per Person per Household Food Expenditures in Households with an Elderly Reference Person, by Income: 2000–2001

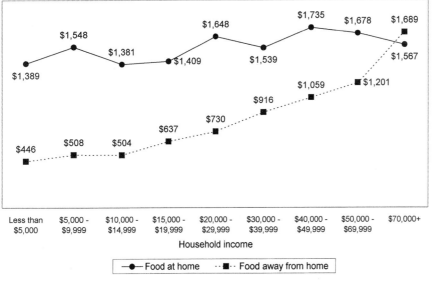

Source: Author calculations based on data from U.S. Department of Labor, Bureau of Labor Statistics, "2001 Consumer Expenditure Survey," www.bls.gov/cex/home.htm.

CASH CONTRIBUTIONS

Cash contribution expenditures, as defined by the CE, include: cash contributed to persons or organizations outside the consumer unit, including alimony and child support payments; care of students away from home; and contributions to religious, educational, charitable, or political organizations.

■ Elderly households are the most generous with their money

Cash contributions increase substantially with age, with the oldest households (aged 75+) contributing the most; more than eight times as much, per-person per-household, as the youngest households do, and 1.5 times as much as their next younger cohort, those aged 65 to 74 (see Chart 9.14). In part, this may reflect asset disposition among the elderly as they near the end of their lives.

Cash contributions also account for more of the spending of older than younger households—7.5 percent of the oldest households' total spending versus 1.1 percent of the youngest households' spending.

CHART 9.14
Cash Contribution Expenditures and Share of Total Expenditures, by Age of the Household Reference Person: 2001

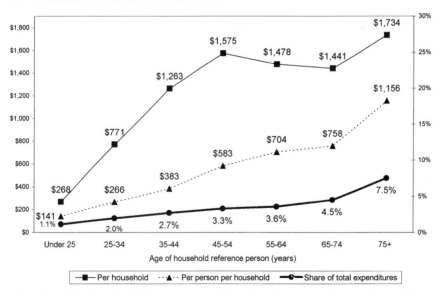

Source: U.S. Department of Labor, Bureau of Labor Statistics. "2001 Consumer Expenditure Survey." www.bls.gov/cex/home.htm.

In the past month, 33 percent of the elderly made a charitable contribution com-pared with 22 percent of younger people, aged 18–64 years.[2]

Midwestern elderly are even more generous

Elderly households in the Midwest are the most generous with their money, con-tributing nearly three times more, per-person per-household, than their least gener-ous counterparts in the North ($1,903 versus $681; see Chart 9.15).

Predictably, elderly households with higher incomes contribute more than do those with lower incomes (see Chart 9.15). Those with the highest incomes (of at least $70,000) contribute more than 1.5 times as much, on a per-person per-household basis, as those in the next lower income level (incomes between $50,000 and $70,000); $2,729 per-person per-household versus $1,771 respec-tively. The differential between the highest and lowest incomes is more than five times.

CHART 9.15
Cash Contribution Expenditures in Households with an Elderly Reference Person, by Income and Region: 2000–2001

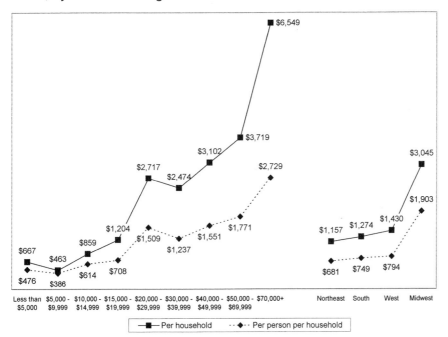

Source: U.S. Department of Labor, Bureau of Labor Statistics. "2001 Consumer Expenditure Survey." www.bls.gov/cex/home.htm.

ENTERTAINMENT

Entertainment expenditures, as defined by the CE, include: fees and admissions, television, radio, and sound equipment, pets, toys, hobbies, and playground equipment, and other entertainment equipment and services (such as indoor exercise equipment, athletic shoes, bicycles, trailers, purchase and rental of motorized campers and other recreational vehicles, camping equipment, hunting and fishing equipment, sports equipment boats, boat motors and boat trailers, rental of boats, landing and docking fees, rental and repair of sports equipment, photographic equipment and supplies (film and film processing), photographer fees, repair and rental of photo equipment, fireworks, and pinball and electronic video games.

■ The oldest-elderly spend the least on entertainment

Entertainment spending declines in importance with age, with elderly households allocating the smallest share of their total spending toward these items (see Chart 16).

On a per-person per-household basis, entertainment spending increases up through age 64 but then drops precipitously, with people in 65–74 aged households spending nearly 40 percent less per-person per-household than their 55- to-64-year old counterparts. Per-person per-household spending in households aged 75+ is about 20 percent less than their younger elderly counterparts.

CHART 9.16
Entertainment Expenditures, by Age of the Household Reference Person: 2001

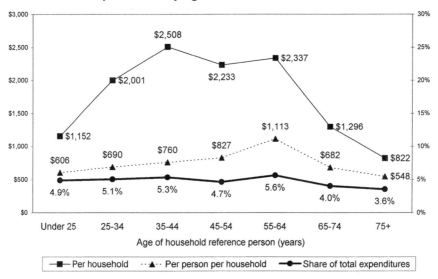

Source: U.S. Department of Labor, Bureau of Labor Statistics. "2001 Consumer Expenditure Survey." www.bls.gov/cex/home.htm.

The elderly prefer to shop in a store more so than do younger people

The elderly most commonly rely on personally shopping in a store when making a purchase, and do so to a somewhat higher degree than do younger people (70 percent versus 63 percent; see Table 9.13). The elderly are about half as likely to use catalog purchasing as in-store purchasing.

All age groups equally rely upon mail or delivery services, while other purchasing vehicles are much more the province of younger people.

TABLE 9.13
Sources Used When Trying to Purchase Products: 2003

	18-64 Years	65+ Years	Ratio of 65+ to 18-64
	%	%	
In-person	63	70	1.11
Catalogs	45	38	0.84
Mail or delivery service	19	20	1.05
Telephone	23	18	0.78
Newspapers	14	12	0.86
Television	11	9	0.82
Online service/internet	23	8	0.35
Computer	21	8	0.38
Magazines	11	5	0.45

Source: NOP World, 2003.

APPAREL AND SERVICES

Apparel and services expenditures, as defined by the CE, include apparel for all aged people, footwear (but not for sports such as bowling or golf shoes), material for making clothes, shoe repair, alterations and repairs, sewing patterns and notions, clothing rental, clothing storage, dry cleaning and sent-out laundry, watches, jewelry, and repairs to watches and jewelry.

■ Elderly households spend the least amount on apparel and related services

With age, apparel-related products and services progressively account for a smaller portion of total spending, from a high of 5.1 percent among the youngest households to less than 3 percent of the oldest households (see Chart 9.17). On a per-person per-household basis, apparel spending peaks at age 45 to 54 and then progressively declines to less than half the amount among the oldest households.

CHART 9.17
Apparel and Services Expenditures, by Age of the Household Reference Person: 2001

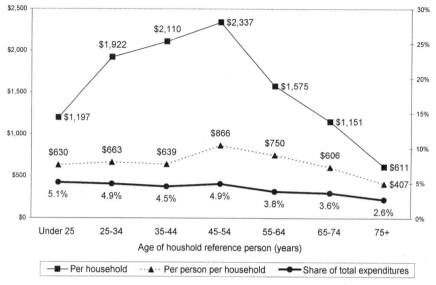

Source: U.S. Department of Labor, Bureau of Labor Statistics. "2001 Consumer Expenditure Survey." www.bls.gov/cex/home.htm.

PENSIONS AND SOCIAL SECURITY

Pension and Social Security expenditures, as defined by the CE, include all Social Security contributions paid by employees; employee contributions to railroad retirement, government retirement, and private pension programs; and retirement programs for the self-employed.

As covered in Chapter 10 (Work and Retirement), the elderly are the least likely to work. Predictably, their pension-related expenditures are substantially lower than that for younger households (see Chart 9.18). Elderly households allocate less than 4 percent of their spending to pension and Social Security contributions, versus about 9 percent among most younger households.

Among elderly households, pension-related expenditures are one of the spending categories that most differs by income (see Table 9.14). Pensions and Social Security account for less than 1 percent of the total spending of elderly households, with the lowest nearly 10 percent less than among those with incomes above $70,000. This substantial difference is mirrored in the age and employment statistics collected in the CE, and reflect the fact that younger people are more likely to work than older people.

More specifically, the average age of the household reference person in elderly-headed households generally declines with income—it is four years younger in the highest-income elderly households than in the lowest-income elderly households (see Table 9.14). Also, on average, 58 percent of the household members in the highest-

CHART 9.18

Pension and Social Security Expenditures, by Age of the Household Reference Person: 2001

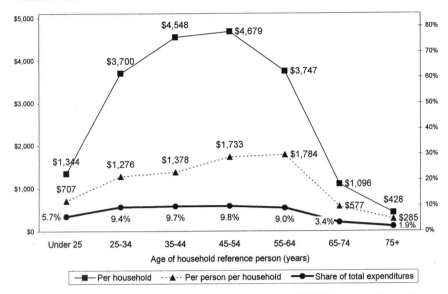

Source: U.S. Department of Labor, Bureau of Labor Statistics. "2001 Consumer Expenditure Survey." www.bls.gov/cex/home.htm.

TABLE 9.14

Pension and Social Security Payments, Age, Household Size, and Work Force Statistics in Households with an Elderly Reference Person, by Income: 2000–2001 (Average Annual Income)

	Average Annual Income								
	Less than $5,000	$5,000 to $9,999	$10,000 to $14,999	$15,000 to $19,999	$20,000 to $29,999	$30,000 to $39,999	$40,000 to $49,999	$50,000 to $69,999	$70,000 and over
Pensions and Social Security payments as % of total spending	0.6%	0.1%	0.4%	0.8%	1.2%	2.8%	3.6%	5.7%	9.6%
Average age of reference person (years)	75.5	76.6	76.9	75.1	74.3	73.3	72.5	72.1	71.5
Average number in consumer unit:									
Persons	1.4	1.2	1.4	1.7	1.8	2	2	2.1	2.4
Earners	0.3	0.1	0.2	0.3	0.4	0.7	0.7	1	1.4
Persons under age 65	0.3	0.1	0.2	0.3	0.3	0.5	0.5	0.6	0.9
Household members that are:									
Earners	21%	8%	14%	18%	22%	35%	35%	48%	58%
Under age 65	21%	8%	14%	18%	17%	25%	25%	29%	38%

Source: Author calculations based on data from U.S. Department of Labor, Bureau of Labor Statistics, "2001 Consumer Expenditure Survey," www.bls.gov/cex/home.htm.

income elderly households are working, compared with less than 20 percent of those in households with incomes under $20,000. While some of the household members who are actually elderly may be working, given the low labor force participation rates of the elderly (see Chapter 10 Work and Retirement), it is more likely the non-elderly members who are working. In fact, non-elderly household members are more than twice as prevalent in the highest income elderly households as they are in the lowest (38 percent in households with incomes above $70,000 versus less than 20 percent among those with incomes less than $30,000).

LIFE AND OTHER PERSONAL INSURANCE

Life and other personal insurance, as defined by the CE, includes: premiums for whole life and term insurance; endowments; income and other life insurance; mortgage guarantee insurance; mortgage life insurance; premiums for personal liability, accident and disability, and other non-health insurance other than for homes and vehicles.

■ Personal insurance spending by elderly households is quite robust

While 55- to 64-year-olds are in the peak years for personal insurance expenses, elderly households still spend about as much per-person per-household, if not more, than do people in households with a reference person aged 45 to 54 years (see Chart 9.19).

CHART 9.19
Life and Other Personal Insurance Expenditures, by Age of the Household Reference Person: 2001

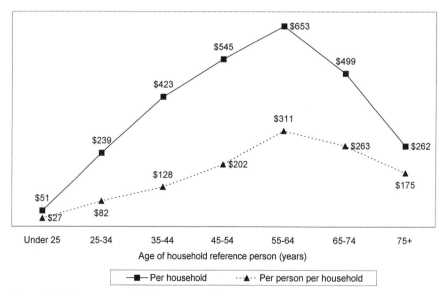

Source: U.S. Department of Labor, Bureau of Labor Statistics. "2001 Consumer Expenditure Survey." www.bls.gov/cex/home.htm.

NOTES

1. Unless otherwise noted, all data is sourced from the Bureau of Labor Statistics, "2001 Consumer Expenditure Survey." Available at www.bls.gov/cex/home.htm.
2. NOP World, 2002.

CHAPTER 10

Work and Retirement

Hard work never killed anybody, but why take a chance?

—*Edgar Bergen*

Retirement kills more people than hard work ever did.

—*Malcolm S. Forbes*

This chapter covers the related topics of work and retirement. At the beginning of the 20th century, people worked for as long as they were able, and employer-provided retirement benefits were rare.[1] Those who left the workforce, often due to illness or disability, survived on the generosity of friends, neighbors, and various charitable organizations.[2]

Work is easily measured by **labor force participation rates**—the percentage of a given population that is either working or is actively seeking work (i.e., unemployed). Measuring retirement, however, is less straightforward, as retirement can be more of a process than an event.[3] Recent analysis finds that at least one-third of older men and nearly one-half of older women used transitionary "bridge" jobs before completely leaving the job market.[4] In such instances, people transition from full-time work to part-time work before retiring. People can also receive Social Security retirement benefits or other pension/retirement income yet still be employed. In fact, the Current Population Survey indicates that 12 percent of elderly men and 7 percent of elderly women report that in 2000 they worked yet still received pension income.[5]

This leads to a variety of ways to measure retirement. Labor force participation rates provide one measure of potential retirement behavior. More precisely, it is the change in rates which indicate changes in retirement behavior. One definition of the average age of retirement is the age at which half of the population is in the labor force and the other half is out.[6] Another indicator is receipt of Social Security retirement benefits or other pension/retirement income. As mentioned, though, receipt of such payments does not preclude continued employment. Economists typically classify someone as retired if the majority of their income is from Social Security, pensions, and/or savings even if they still are in the paid workforce.[7] Many retirement-based surveys rely on how a respondent defines his or her retirement status.[8]

Highlights from this chapter include:

- The elderly constitute 3 percent of the civilian labor force.

- Labor force participation rates vary dramatically with age.

- Labor force participation rates for the elderly declined dramatically through 1985. Since then, the rates have been slowly but steadily increasing.

- At the 1985 low point, elderly male labor force participation rates were one-third of the 1950 level.

- Many factors have affected work and retirement, including increasing wealth and policies such as Social Security and private-sector benefit plans.

- Most retirees have found their retirement life to be the same or better than those years just prior to retirement.

- Retirees with defined benefit pensions are happier in retirement and maintain that happiness longer than their counterparts who do not have such benefits.

- About half of retirees who are working are doing so in a job that is entirely different from what they had in pre-retirement.

LABOR FORCE STATISTICS

One in 33 workers is elderly

In 2002, 2.54 million elderly men and 1.93 million elderly women were in the civilian labor force.[9] Respectively, these elderly workers account for 1.8 percent and 1.3 percent of the total civilian labor force aged 16+.

The elderly male workforce grew 2.2 percent annually during the 1990s, while the elderly female workforce grew 1.7 percent.[10] Projections to 2010 indicate that the elderly workforce will grow at a rate higher than that for the total workforce.[11] Between 2000 and 2010, the elderly male workforce is expected to increase 2.5 percent annually (versus 0.9 percent for all male workers). The elderly female workforce is expected to increase 2.8 percent annually over the same period (versus 1.4 percent for all female workers).

Labor force participation varies dramatically by age

Labor force participation rates vary dramatically by age. In 2002, about two-thirds of young adults aged 16 to 24 years were in the workforce (see Chart 10.1). This increases to more than 90 percent of men and 75 percent of women in the key working ages of 25 to 54 years. Participation rates then decline dramatically among those aged 55 to 64, with 7 in 10 men and slightly more than half of women in the

CHART 10.1
Civilian Labor Force Participation Rates, by Age and Sex: 2002

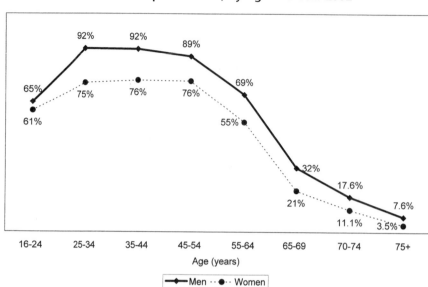

Source: Bureau of Labor Statistics. "Employment Status of the Civilian Noninstitutional Population by Age, Sex, and Race," Available online at www.bls.gov/cps.

workforce. Among the elderly, about 1 in 6 men (17.9 percent) and 1 in 10 women (9.8 percent) were in the workforce in 2002. However, labor force participation skews decidedly toward the younger elderly; those aged 65–69 are 4 to 6 times more likely to be in the workforce than those aged 75+.

■ Elderly Hispanics are less likely to be in the labor force

Among the elderly, male labor force participation rates range from a low of 16.3 percent among Hispanics to 17.8 percent among whites (see Table 10.1). Among elderly women, labor force participation is also lowest among Hispanics.

■ Elderly male workers more likely to be working full-time

Older people who work often transition from full-time to part-time work.[12] This trend is evident with both men and women. More than 90 percent of employed men aged 55 to 61 are employed full-time, compared with half of those aged 70+ (see Chart 10.2).[13] Employed men aged 65 to 69 are still more likely to be employed full-time; 6 in 10 are employed full-time. Among older employed men aged 70+, full-time and part-time employment are equally as likely.

■ Elderly female workers more likely to be working part-time

Employed women aged 55+ are more likely than their male counterparts to be employed part-time; part-time employment is about 15 percentage points higher

TABLE 10.1
Labor Force Participation Rates among the Elderly,
by Sex and Race: 2002

	Men	Women
	%	%
All Races	17.9	9.8
White	17.8	9.9
Black	16.9	9.8
Hispanic	16.3	8.5

Source: Bureau of Labor Statistics. "Employment Status of
the Civilian Noninstitutional Population by Age, Sex, and
Race," Available online at www.bls.gov/cps.

among women in this age group than men. The trend toward increasing part-time
employment is evident among women as well; about three-quarters of women aged
55 to 61 are employed full-time, versus about one-third of those aged 70+ (see Chart
10.2). In fact, among all elderly women, part-time employment is more likely than
full-time.

CHART 10.2
Full-Time and Part-Time Working Status among Employed Persons, by Age and
Sex: 2000

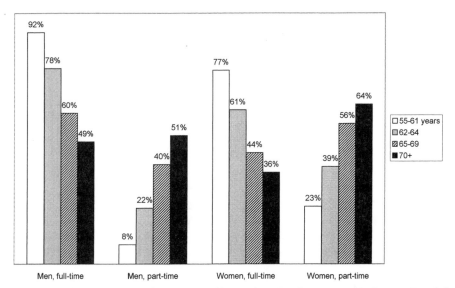

Source: Patrick J. Purcell. (October 2000). "Older Workers: Employment and Retirement Trends."
Monthly Labor Review Online. 19–30. Available online at www.bls.gov/opub/mlr/archive.htm.

■ Elderly workers work fewer weeks and fewer hours per week than do younger workers

Older workers work fewer weeks and hours than do younger workers.[14] On average, workers aged 62 to 64 work 43.4 weeks a year, while those aged 65 to 69 work 40.5 weeks and those aged 80+ work 38.1 weeks. Hours worked per week similarly decline, from 35.5 hours to 29.9 hours and 25.2 hours, among these respective workers.

■ Older workers have lower wages than younger people

Among working men, wages diminish greatly with age.[15] According to the 1998 Health and Retirement Survey, economists Steven Haider and David Loughran report that 33 percent of working men aged 62 to 64 had wages that were comparable to the bottom one-fifth of male workers aged 50 to 61. This increases to 51 percent of working men aged 65 to 67 and ultimately to 76 percent of those aged 80+.

■ Older workers more likely to be healthy . . .

Haider and Loughran also find that the elderly labor supply is concentrated among the healthiest, wealthiest and most educated individuals, but, as previously stated, they earn very low wages.[16] Among the elderly, those who are working are less disabled and are healthier than those who do not work. For example, ADL (activities of daily living) limitations are 1.5 to nearly 2 times more prevalent among the non-working elderly than among those who are employed. As well, labor force participation rates decline dramatically with added ADL limitations.

■ . . . wealthy . . .

Median bequeathable wealth is higher among the working elderly than among those not working.[17] The differences are most noticeable among those older than age 70 where bequeathable wealth for those not working declines with age while that for workers increases. Labor force participation becomes increasingly concentrated among the wealthier at older ages. At ages 65 to 67, labor force participation among men is 24 percent among those in the bottom one-fifth of bequeathable wealth but 34 percent among those in the top one-fifth of bequeathable wealth. At ages 77 to 79, the comparable figures are 5 percent and 15 percent, and at age 80+ they are 3 percent and 7 percent.

■ . . . and wise

At all ages, labor force participation is higher among those with more education.[18] Among people aged 65 to 67, those with advanced degrees are twice as likely to be working as those who have a high school degree (42 percent versus 22 percent). By the ages of 77 to 79, there is a threefold difference (14 percent versus 5 percent).

■ Elderly men in 1985 were one-third as likely as their 1950 counterparts to be working

Retirement was the province of the few at the beginning of the 20th century, when two-thirds of elderly men were employed.[19] At mid-century, this had declined to less than 50 percent, and by the end of the century fewer than 1 in 5 were in the workforce (see Chart 10.3). More specifically, 46 percent of men aged 65+ were in the workforce in 1950, declining to a low of 15.8 percent in 1985. Since then, the rates increased two percentage points to 17.9 percent in 2002. Men in the 55–64 age group have also experienced declining labor force participation rates, though not as dramatically (see Chart 10.3).

Longitudinal data show that successive cohorts of men experienced similar labor force participation patterns during their lifecycle, with rates declining after age 50.[20] However, successively younger cohorts have experienced lower labor force participation rates

CHART 10.3
Labor Force Participation Rates among Those Aged 55 to 64 and the Elderly, by Sex: 1950–2002

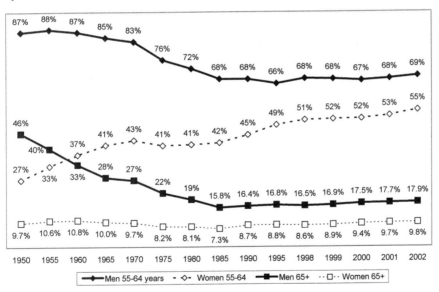

Sources: Howard N. Fullerton, Jr., and Mitra Toossi. (November 2001). "Labor Force Projections to 2010: Steady Growth and Changing Composition." *Monthly Labor Review Online.* 21–38. Available online at www.bls/gov/opub/mlr/archive.htm; Patrick J. Purcell. (October 2000). "Older Workers: Employment and Retirement Trends." *Monthly Labor Review Online.* 19–30. Available online at www.bls.gov/opub/mlr/archive.htm; Bureau of Labor Statistics. "Employment Status of the Civilian Noninstitutional Population by Age, Sex, and Race," Available online at www.bls.gov/cps; and Statistical Abstract of the United States: 2002, 122nd ed. (Washington, DC, 2002).

at similar ages, with the most noticeable differences at the 60 to 64 age bracket (see Table 10.2). Specifically, among men born between 1906 and 1940, the oldest cohort (born 1906–10) had the highest labor force participation rates at virtually every age. When this oldest cohort was aged 60 to 64, three-quarters of them were in the workforce, compared with slightly more than one-half of the younger, 1921–40, cohorts when they were the same age. The decline in labor force participation for all male cohorts is most precipitous between the ages of 65 and 69 as well as 70 and 74, where participation rates are about half that of the prior five-year age category.

■ Elderly women have had more stable labor force participation over the years

Labor force participation among elderly women hovered between 7 and 11 percent in the latter half of the 20th century (see Chart 10.3).[21] Since 1985, the low point of elderly women's labor force participation (at 7.3 percent), rates have steadily increased, rising more than two percentage points to 9.8 percent in 2002. Younger women aged 55–64, on the other hand, have experienced dramatic increases in labor force participation rates throughout the last half of the 20th century (see Chart 10.3).

TABLE 10.2
Labor Force Participation Rates for Selected Cohorts, by Sex

	Year of Birth						
	1906-10	1911-15	1916-20	1921-25	1926-30	1931-35	1936-40
	%	%	%	%	%	%	%
Men aged:							
45-49 years	97.1	96.6	96.1	95.3	94.1	93.2	93.3
50-54	94.7	95.0	93.0	90.1	89.2	88.6	88.8
55-59	90.2	89.5	84.4	81.7	79.6	79.8	77.4
60-64	75.0	65.5	60.8	55.6	55.5	53.2	54.8
65-69	31.7	28.5	24.5	26.0	24.9	27.8	NA
70-74	17.9	14.9	15.4	15.5	16.5	NA	NA
75+	7.0	7.1	7.0	7.4	NA	NA	NA
Women aged:							
45-49 years	45.8	50.7	51.7	55.0	55.9	62.1	67.8
50-54	48.7	50.1	53.8	55.3	57.8	60.8	66.9
55-59	47.1	49.0	47.9	48.5	50.3	55.3	57.0
60-64	36.1	33.2	33.2	33.4	35.5	36.4	38.5
65-69	14.5	15.1	13.5	17.0	15.8	17.5	NA
70-74	7.5	7.6	8.2	8.4	9.0	NA	NA
75+	2.2	2.7	2.6	3.2	NA	NA	NA

Source: Murray Gendell. (October 2001). "Retirement Age Declines Again in the 1990s." *Monthly Labor Review Online.* 12–21. Available online at www.bls.gov/opub/mlr/archive.htm.

The 20th-century trend of increasing labor force participation among women is particularly evident when assessing longitudinal data, even among older women.[22] When elderly women in the oldest cohort (1906–10) were aged 45 to 49, they were substantially less likely to be in the workforce than were the youngest, 1936–40, cohort at the same age (46 percent versus 68 percent). Also like men, women increasingly withdraw from the workforce at older ages.

Despite higher in-going labor force participation rates, older and younger female cohorts very quickly converge to similar participation rates from age 60 onward. For men, these rates converge at age 65 onward.

■ "Retirement age" has also been declining

Social Security statistics reflect the decline in labor force participation rates of older people. The original Social Security legislation set retirement at age 65, with reduced benefits at age 62 made available to women in 1956 and to men in 1961. Since then, there has been a dramatic change in the age structure among those first receiving their Social Security retirement benefits.

In 1940, the average age at which men first started collecting their Social Security retirement benefit was 68.1 years (see Chart 10.4). Twenty-five years later in 1965, several years after early benefits had been extended to age 62, the average age had

CHART 10.4
Average Age of New Social Security Beneficiaries, by Sex: 1940–2002

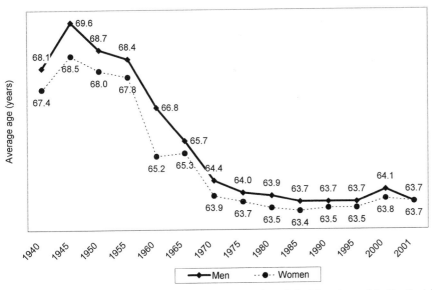

Source: Social Security Administration. (2002). "Annual Statistical Supplement to the Social Security Bulletin," Table 6.B5. Available online at www.ssa.gov/policy/docs/statcomps/supplement/2002.

dropped more than two years, to 65.7 years. Over the next 36 years, an additional two years were trimmed from the average age to 63.7 years in 2001. Women have experienced similar declines.

■ Elderly labor force participation has been increasing since 1985

For both elderly men and women, labor force participation trends reached their low point in 1985 and have been slowly, but steadily, increasing since then. A statistical analysis conducted by economist Joseph Quinn indicates that, for both men and women, the post-1985 trends are higher than what the prior trends would have predicted.[23]

Quinn also compared the average annual change in labor force participation rates for two time periods, 1970–85 and 1985–2002 (see Charts 10.5A and B). Over the earlier time period, labor force participation rates for men aged 55 to 70 declined, especially for men aged 62 to 64. On the other hand, over the more recent 1985–2002 period, labor force participation rates either declined slightly or increased. The increased participation was greatest for men aged 65 to 68.

The pattern for women is somewhat different (see Chart 10.5B). Over the 1970–85 period, annual labor force participation rates declined for women aged 59+, but

CHART 10.5A
Average Annual Change in Labor Force Participation Rate for Men, by Individual Age: 1970–1985 and 1985–2002

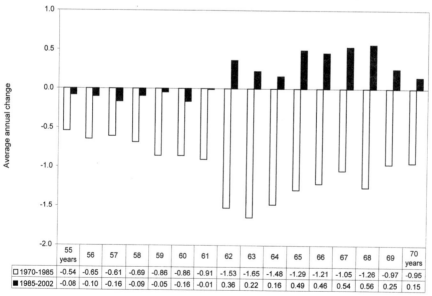

	55 years	56	57	58	59	60	61	62	63	64	65	66	67	68	69	70 years
□ 1970-1985	-0.54	-0.65	-0.61	-0.69	-0.86	-0.86	-0.91	-1.53	-1.65	-1.48	-1.29	-1.21	-1.05	-1.26	-0.97	-0.95
■ 1985-2002	-0.08	-0.10	-0.16	-0.09	-0.05	-0.16	-0.01	0.36	0.22	0.16	0.49	0.46	0.54	0.56	0.25	0.15

Source: Joseph F. Quinn. (May 1999). "Has the Early Retirement Trend Reversed?" Boston College Economics. Working Paper No. 424. Available online at http://fmwww.bc.edu/ec/research.php. Updated data provided to the authors.

CHART 10.5B
Average Annual Change in Labor Force Participation Rate for Women, by Individual Age: 1970–1985 and 1985–2002

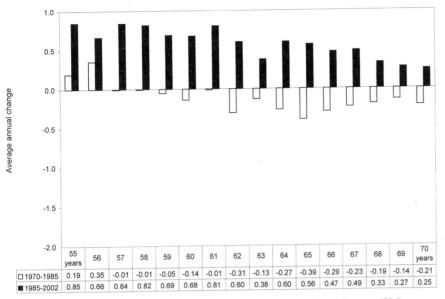

	55 years	56	57	58	59	60	61	62	63	64	65	66	67	68	69	70 years
☐ 1970-1985	0.19	0.35	-0.01	-0.01	-0.05	-0.14	-0.01	-0.31	-0.13	-0.27	-0.39	-0.29	-0.23	-0.19	-0.14	-0.21
■ 1985-2002	0.85	0.66	0.84	0.82	0.69	0.68	0.81	0.60	0.38	0.60	0.56	0.47	0.49	0.33	0.27	0.25

Source: Joseph F. Quinn. (May 1999). "Has the Early Retirement Trend Reversed?" Boston College Economics. Working Paper No. 424. Available online at http://fmwww.bc.edu/ec/research.php. Updated data provided to the authors.

to a much smaller degree than men. During the subsequent 1985–2002 period, labor force participation increased for all women aged 55+ and to a much greater degree than for men.

REASONS FOR CHANGING WORK AND RETIREMENT TRENDS

■ Many factors have affected work and retirement trends

Public policy, especially with regards to Social Security, has had a very large effect on the working behavior of older people, as have corporate policies, the economy, and health insurance availability.

■ Social Security has affected work and retirement behavior

Federal policy has been an important influence on labor force participation rates among older Americans.[24] Like their predecessors, today's retirees continue to receive Medicare benefits that exceed the value of their contributions and inclusive earnings. Also, up until the mid-1980s, retired Social Security beneficiaries received pensions that were larger than what they would have gotten had they invested those contributions in safe investments. More specifically, in earlier years, Social Security rules favored earlier retirement, including:

- the Social Security Act amendment in 1960, to allow disability payments to people under the age of 50,

- reduced Social Security retirement benefits offered to women at age 62 beginning in 1956 and to men in 1961

- Social Security payments that were over-adjusted for inflation in the 1970s.

More recently, though, Social Security rules have changed to encourage continued work:

- In 1978, the federal government raised mandatory retirement age from 65 to 70 and then outlawed it completely in 1986 for virtually all workers.

- Social Security payments were re-adjusted relative to inflation in the 1980s.

- The earnings test has been eliminated for beneficiaries at, or above, the normal retirement age.

- The normal retirement age is presently increasing to 67 years.

- Delayed retirement credits have increased to make Social Security more age-neutral.

Definition: A *defined benefit (DB) plan* provides a retired employee with a benefit based on earnings and length of employment. The employer bears the financial risk of maintaining sufficient funds to pay for future benefits. The plan sets a retirement age for full benefits and may also set an early retirement age for reduced benefits. DB plans provide a lifetime benefit usually based on the number of years worked and the salary in the last few years before retirement.

Definition: In a *defined contribution (DC) plan*, employer and/or employee contributions are put into the employee's individual account. These plans mostly consist of 401(k) or 403(b) plans. The employee's account consists of these contributions along with investment returns. The employer contributions are subject to a vesting schedule upon which the employee is fully vested. When an employee leaves the employer, the value of the account (less any unvested amounts) is transferable. Unlike a DB plan, DC retirement proceeds are not guaranteed and the financial risk rests with the employee/retiree.

▉ Private-sector benefit plans have affected labor force participation

Private-sector influences have also affected labor force participation in various ways. One such factor has been the lowered retirement age in many defined benefit (DB) plans. One analysis that studied the same plans in two periods, 1974 and 1983, found that slightly more than half of the plans in 1974 provided unreduced benefits at age

62 or younger.[25] By 1983, the figure increased to nearly 90 percent. In addition, 76 percent of DB plans in 1974 allowed early retirement at age 55 with reduced benefits, and this rose to 85 percent in 1983.

During the 1980s, corporate downsizing resulted in early retirement incentives that frequently included early pensions or lump-sum payments.[26] Many of these retirement programs subsidized early retirement, as they were not sufficiently adjusted to compensate for the additional benefits received prior to the standard age 65 retirement.[27]

On the other hand, defined contribution (DC) plans do not have such early retirement subsidies. In fact, if an employer matches part of a worker's contributions, that could actually encourage longer employment. Longer employment may also be encouraged by the unpredictability of DC plans. Increases in DC plan wealth are due to earnings on accumulated wealth and yearly contributions. Thus, much of the risk has been transferred to the worker, as the accumulated wealth is a function of a worker's investment choices and how well those investments pay off. Poorly performing investments, due to a sluggish or bearish stock market or to lower risk/lower performing investments, may motivate longer employment. Additionally, DC plans are voluntary; not all companies offer such plans and when they are offered, a worker may not participate at all, or may not participate at an early enough age to accrue enough assets for retirement.

One recent study indicates that people with DB pensions retire sooner than those with DC pensions or no pension at all. Specifically, for typical workers with DB pension coverage, their expected retirement age was 1.2 years earlier than those who had DC coverage or no pension coverage at all (63.9 years versus 65.1).[28] Retirement is moved up by seven-tenths of a year due to the characteristics of the DB plan, and it is moved up another half of a year due to the amount of an individual's DB plan wealth (in this case, calculated as an individual with an average level of wealth). More or less wealth would respectively move up, or delay, the expected retirement age.

Since the 1980s, DC plans have steadily become more popular such that they have now overtaken DB plans (see Table 10.3). Between 1975 and 1997, growth in DC plans outpaced that of DB plans on assets, benefits paid out, active participants, and contributions.[29]

TABLE 10.3
Percent of Full-Time Employees Covered by Pension Plans in Medium and Large Private Establishments: 1989, 1993, and 1997

	1985	1989	1993	1997
	%	%	%	%
Defined benefit	80	63	56	50
Defined contribution	41	48	49	57

Source: William J. Wiatrowski. (April 2001). "Changing Retirement Age: Ups and Downs." *Monthly Labor Review Online*. 3–12. Available online at www.bls.gov/opub/mlr/archive.htm.

◾ A strong economy offers more job opportunities for the elderly

The strong economy in the late 1980s and 1990s resulted in historically low unemployment rates and theoretically more employment opportunities for older workers. While economists Gary Burtless and Joseph Quinn state that the strong economy has likely had some effect on older worker's recent increase in labor force participation rates, they believe it has not had a large effect.[30] They cite a strong economy and low unemployment in the 1960s, when older men's participation rates continued to decline and older women's participation rates remained relatively unchanged.

Today's work environment is also less strenuous than in the past, as our economy has shifted away from manufacturing and more toward service-related activities.[31] Thus, it is easier for older people to find employment in less physically demanding occupations.

◾ Increasing wealth has aided retirement

Burtless and Quinn state that retirement has been more viable due to increasing wealth.[32] During the latter half of the 20th century, the nation as a whole prospered and some of that wealth was used to "purchase" more leisure. Retired workers additionally benefited from generous Medicare and Social Security benefits and a strong housing market that increased housing wealth.

◾ Health insurance availability influences retirement decisions

Medicare benefits are available at age 65. However, those retiring at an earlier age will be left with no health insurance coverage unless they have access through their own employer, that of another family member, Medicaid, or a privately purchased plan.[33] Research has shown that if workers have access to a retiree health plan, they tend to delay their retirement until they are eligible. Once eligible, such a plan encourages earlier retirement than if no such plan were offered. A 2003 AARP study finds that 75 percent of pre-retirees state that being eligible for retiree health benefits is a very important consideration in determining when they will retire.[34]

◾ Declining labor force participation + increased life expectancy = longer retirement

Since 1940, elderly labor force participation declined at the same time life expectancies increased. Burtless and Quinn state that male life expectancies increased 0.8 years per decade at a time that retirement age dropped 1.2 years per decade.[35] Thus, the net affect is about two more years per decade so that almost 12 years have been added to the amount of time men spend in retirement.

◾ FUTURE LABOR FORCE PARTICIPATION RATES

While recent elderly labor force participation rates have been on the increase, the direction of future rates has been debated. One school of thought, voiced by Quinn, believes that the aforementioned public policy and private-sector changes are making work in later life more attractive and thus contributing to the recent upturn in labor force participation rates.[36]

Dora Costa provides another school of thought—that these policy and private-sector changes are not strong enough to counter the underlying factors affecting the trend to early retirement.[37] Costa's research on retirement trends provides evidence that private pension plans and Social Security are not the primary factors in long-term trends, nor are improvements in health. Rather, it has been the increased income of the elderly that has been a major driving force behind increased retirement rates. Contributing to this are factors that make retirement more attractive, such as affordable retirement communities in areas of favorable climate, more travel and entertainment options for older Americans, and societal norms promoting retirement. Additionally, Costa argues that any permanent labor force participation increase would require an inherent change in motivation.

■ The non-working elderly have become a larger share of those who are economically dependent upon the labor force

Since 1987, Americans in the labor force have outnumbered those who do not work (see Table 10.4). Projections to 2010 indicate that this should hold. Specifically, in 1975 there were 126 non-working Americans being supported by 100 workers. This declined to 103 in 1985 and has continued downward to 94 in 2000. Most of the decline in this quarter century was due to a decline in births, with the ratios for those under 16 years dropping from 61 to 40. The rest was due to the higher labor force participation of non-elderly women.

Over the last quarter of the 20th century, the number of elderly Americans being supported by workers has remained relatively stable at about 21 per 100 workers. However, since the overall dependency ratio has declined, the elderly now represent a larger proportion of those who are economically dependent upon workers.

TABLE 10.4
Economic Dependency Ratio,* by Age: 1975–2000 and 2010 Projection

	Total Population	Under 16 Years	16-64 Years	65+ Years	Percent of Total that are 65+
1975	126.3	61.4	44.2	20.7	16
1980	108.9	50.7	37.4	20.8	19
1985	103.3	47.3	34.2	21.8	21
1990	98.3	45.8	30.5	22.1	22
1995	96.6	48.6	25.7	22.3	23
2000	93.9	44.1	28.3	21.6	23
2010	90.3	40.1	28.9	21.3	24

*Number of non-working Americans supported per 100 people in the labor force.
Source: Howard N. Fullerton, Jr., and Mitra Toossi. (November 2001). "Labor Force Projections to 2010: Steady Growth and Changing Composition." *Monthly Labor Review Online*. 21–38. Available online at www.bls/gov/opub/mlr/archive.htm

RETIREE ATTITUDES

Today's retirees are more likely to state that they wanted to retire

According to economists Gary Burtless and Joseph Quinn, poor health or layoffs dominated the reasons for retirement among survey respondents from the 1940s through the early 1970s, with a very small percentage of men saying they wanted to retire.[38] By the early 1980s, though, nearly half of all retiring elderly men stated they wanted to retire, more than 1 in 5 stated poor health, and about 15 percent indicated involuntary layoffs. It is postulated that some of this increase in an expressed desire to retire may be due to a change in societal norms, in which retirement is considered a more normal, and even desirable, aspect of older life.

According to the 1998 Health and Retirement Survey, reasons for retirement differ by age.[39] The oldest and youngest retirees (61 years and younger, and 75+, respectively) are the most likely to mention poor health or being forced to retire. The desire to spend time with family or to do other things is stated more often by younger retirees. Fewer than one in ten retirees state their dislike for work as a very important reason for retiring.

Half of retirees find their retirement years to be better than those just prior to retirement

A recent MetLife study, conducted by RAND[40] and based on the 2000 Health and Retirement Survey, finds that about half of retirees (48 percent) state their retirement years have been better than those just before retirement, one-third (34 percent) state they are about the same, and 18 percent state they are not as good.*

Virtually all retirees are satisfied with their retirement, with little difference by gender. Specifically, 59 percent of retirees state it as being "very satisfying" and 33 percent say it is moderately satisfying; less than one in ten, 8 percent, find it not at all satisfying.

Satisfaction in retirement years heavily related to health, income, and wealth

The MetLife study finds that health status, income and wealth are the most influential factors affecting retirement satisfaction.[41] Specifically, better health, along with higher incomes and wealth, correlate with higher "very satisfied" ratings. Retirees in excellent health are nearly three times more likely to be very satisfied than those in poor health (more than 8 in 10 versus 1 in 3). Those with the highest incomes (over $50,000) are almost twice as likely as those with the lowest incomes (under $15,000) to be very satisfied (74 percent versus 40 percent). Those with the highest net worth (over $400,000) are twice as likely as those with the lowest net worth (under $50,000) to be very satisfied (about 75 percent versus 38 percent).

---

*Half of the 2000 HRS sample was composed of people 65+.

▨ Separated or divorced retirees are the least satisfied

Separated or divorced retirees are the least satisfied with their retirement, with about 40 percent expressing "very satisfied" compared with about 60 percent of their married, widowed, or never married counterparts.[42]

▨ Retirees with defined benefit pensions are happier in retirement, especially those with lower incomes . . .

Retirees with income from DB plans (which guarantee lifetime income) are more satisfied with their retirement than those who do not have such income.[43] Specifically, about 7 in 10 of those who have some DB pension income are very satisfied with their retirement, compared with 54 percent of retirees who have no DB pension income. About half of the survey respondents had no DB pensions.

The positive effect of guaranteed income is most noticeable among those with lower incomes. Among retirees with the lowest incomes (under $15,000), 39 percent of those with no DB pension are very satisfied, versus 50 percent of those with at least some DB pension. Among those with the highest incomes (above $50,000), the differential is smaller, 70 percent versus about 77 percent.

▨ . . . and they maintain that happiness longer than those without a defined benefit pension

For retirees with DB pensions, retirement satisfaction remains stable over the duration of their retirement, while it declines for those without any lifelong guaranteed pension.[44] Satisfaction for the latter declines from 58 percent very satisfied shortly after retirement to 47 percent 10 years later. One possible explanation is that people without DB pensions become more concerned about outliving their savings than do those with lifelong income streams.

▨ Social Security dependency affects retirement satisfaction

Not surprisingly, retirement satisfaction declines as reliance on Social Security increases.[45] Among retirees who are the least dependent upon Social Security (no more than 25 percent of their potential total retirement spending is supported by Social Security), about two-thirds are very satisfied with their retirement, compared with fewer than half of those who are the most dependent upon Social Security (Social Security supports more than half of their potential total retirement spending). The researchers found that this was due to their low economic status rather than to the Social Security reliance itself.

▨ Financial involvement increases retirement satisfaction

Regardless of their income level, retirees who have engaged in some sort of financial planning activity are also more satisfied with their retirement.[46] Whether it is attending a retirement planning meeting, having long-term care insurance, or having a financial advisor, those retirees who met these conditions were more satisfied with their retirement than those who did not.

WORKING IN RETIREMENT

■ One in 20 working retirees had retired at age 65+ but decided to return to work

The 2003 AARP Working in Retirement Study interviewed 2,000 employed individuals aged 50 to 70 years.[47] Of that group, 15 percent had already retired from a job but either remained in the workforce or subsequently rejoined the workforce. Among these working retirees, only 5 percent had retired at age 65 or older. One in five (19 percent) retired between the ages of 60 and 64, 43 percent while in their fifties, and 32 percent before the age of 50. The average age of retirement was 52.7 years. Of those who retired under age 50, 32 percent had been in the military prior to retirement, compared with 4 percent of those in the 50+ group.

■ Nearly half of working retirees are working in a job very different from their pre-retirement career

Almost half (47 percent) of working retirees are currently working in jobs that are entirely different from their pre-retirement occupation.[48] Eighty percent of working retirees work for someone else, and they are most likely to be engaged in teaching (13 percent), office support (9 percent), management (6 percent), or driver/courier (5 percent). One in five (21 percent) are self-employed and most commonly involved in consulting (10 percent), real estate (10 percent), farming/ranching (6 percent), and private investigation (6 percent).

Working retirees most commonly state the need for money as the one major factor for working in retirement; 35 percent do so. The most important aspects of a job are: keeping you mentally active (74 percent state it as "very important"), making you feel useful (70 percent), being fun or enjoyable (68 percent), and interacting with other people (61 percent).

Half of working retirees (49 percent) plan to stop working before they reach age 70. More than one-quarter (28 percent) plan to stop working when in their 70s, while 12 percent plan to stop in their 80s, and 8 percent do not plan on stopping work or will work for as long as possible.

The Good Life

The elderly are quite similar to younger people in aspects they most consider as part of the "good life"; the life they'd like to have. At the top of the list are some of the things money can't buy, like good health, a happy marriage, and children as well as some big ticket items like a home and car (see Table 10.5).

TABLE 10.5
Aspects Considered as Part of the "Good Life" and Achievement of Those Aspects, by Age (Ranked by Aspect for 65+ Years): 2003

	Considered to be Part of the "Good Life"			Those that have Achieved the "Good Life*		
	18-64 Years	65+ Years	Ratio of 65+	18-64 Years	65+ Years	Ratio of 65+
	%	%	to 18-64	%	%	to 18-64
Owning a home	89	88	0.99	56	78	1.39
Good health	87	86	0.99	78	58	0.74
Happy marriage	81	81	1.00	57	56	0.98
Children	76	78	1.03	75	89	1.19
Car	79	74	0.94	84	86	1.02
Spiritual enrichment	63	70	1.11	75	84	1.12
Free time	68	53	0.78	46	70	1.52
A lot of money	60	48	0.80	5	8	1.60
Travel abroad	49	39	0.80	25	44	1.76
Second car	55	36	0.65	57	61	1.07
Vacation home	50	34	0.68	6	10	1.67
Really nice clothes	41	33	0.80	31	40	1.29
Computer	50	23	0.46	66	71	1.08
Home entertainment center	42	22	0.52	60	49	0.82
Swimming pool	40	19	0.48	10	9	0.90

*Among those for whom it was part of the "good life."
Source: NOP World, 2003.

The other end of the list is dominated by more tangible goods, such as a lot of money, computers, pools, vacation homes, and travel abroad. It is these more consumable items that the elderly are substantially less likely than younger people to identify with the good life. Free time is also substantially less associated with the elderly's impressions of the good life, perhaps because it is something they have in greater abundance. On the other hand, spiritual enrichment is the only "good life" aspect where the elderly hold an edge over younger people.

Thirty percent of the elderly feel they have already achieved the good life, substantially higher than the 4 percent of younger people who have reached this goal.[49] Among those who have not yet achieved the good life, there is optimism: two-thirds of the elderly (63 percent) feel their chances of achieving it are good, although they are less optimistic than younger people, of whom 80 percent feel good about achieving the good life.

The elderly have most likely achieved their "good life" goals of children, a car, spiritual enrichment, and homeownership; at least three-quarters of the elderly, for whom these aspects are considered part of the good life, have achieved them (see Table 10.6). Good health and a happy marriage have been a little harder

TABLE 10.6

Aspects Considered as Part of the "Good Life" and Achievement of Those Aspects, by Age (Ranked by Achievement for 65+ Years): 2003

	Considered to be Part of the "Good Life"			Those that have Achieved the "Good Life*		
	18-64 Years	65+ Years	Ratio of 65+ to 18-64	18-64 Years	65+ Years	Ratio of 65+to 18-64
	%	%		%	%	
Children	76	78	1.03	75	89	1.19
Car	79	74	0.94	84	86	1.02
Spiritual enrichment	63	70	1.11	75	84	1.12
Owning a home	89	88	0.99	56	78	1.39
Computer	50	23	0.46	66	71	1.08
Free time	68	53	0.78	46	70	1.52
Second car	55	36	0.65	57	61	1.07
Good health	87	86	0.99	78	58	0.74
Happy marriage	81	81	1.00	57	56	0.98
Travel abroad	49	39	0.80	25	44	1.76

Note: some aspects from Table 10.5 are not included due to extremely small sample sizes.
*Among those for whom it was part of the "good life."
Source: NOP World, 2003.

to achieve with 6 in 10 elderly who aspire to these aspects having achieved them. Six in ten elderly who desire to travel abroad have yet to achieve those goals.

NOTES

1. William J. Wiatrowski. (April 2001). "Changing Retirement Age: Ups and Downs," *Monthly Labor Review Online*, 3–12. Available online at www.bls.gov/opub/mlr/archive.htm.
2. Ibid.
3. Donald Bruce, Douglas Holtz-Eakin, and Joseph Quinn. (November 2000). "Self-Employment and Labor Market Transitions at Older Ages." Available online at http://fmwww.bc.edu/EC-P/WP490.pdf.
4. Joseph F. Quinn. (2002). "Changing Retirement Trends and Their Impact on Elderly Entitlement Programs." In *Policies for an Aging Society* (pp. 293–315). Edited by Stuart H. Altman and David I. Shactman. Baltimore, MD: Johns Hopkins University Press.
5. Patrick J. Purcell. (October 2000). "Older Workers: Employment and Retirement Trends." *Monthly Labor Review Online*, 19-30. Available online at www.bls.gov/opub/mlr/archive.htm.
6. Quinn.
7. Ibid.
8. Joseph Quinn, Kevin Cahill, Richard Burkhauser, and Robert Weather. (February 1998). "The Microeconomics of the Retirement Decision in the United States." Available online at http://econpapers.hhs.se/paper/oedoecdec/203.htm.

9. Bureau of Labor Statistics. "Employment Status of the Civilian Noninstitutional Population by Age, Sex, and Race," Available online at www.bls.gov/cps.
10. Howard N. Fullerton, Jr., and Mitra Toossi. (November 2001). "Labor Force Projections to 2010: Steady Growth and Changing Composition." *Monthly Labor Review Online*, 21–38. Available online at www.bls.gov/opub/mlr/archive.htm.
11. Ibid.
12. Wiatrowski.
13. Purcell.
14. Steven Haider and David Loughran. (September 2001). "Elderly Labor Supply: Work or Play?" Center for Retirement Research at Boston College, Working Paper No. 2001-04. Available online at www.bc.edu/centers/crr.
15. Ibid.
16. Ibid.
17. Ibid.
18. Ibid.
19. Gary Burtless and Joseph F. Quinn. (2001). "Retirement Trends and Policies to Encourage Work Among Older Americans," Boston College Economics Working Papers, Working Paper 436. In *Ensuring Health and Income Security for an Aging Workforce* (pp. 375–415). Edited by Peter Budetti, Richard Burkhauser, Janice Gregory and Allan Hunt. Kalamazoo: Upjohn Institute for Employment Research. Available online at http://fmwww.bc.edu/ec/research.php.
20. Murray Gendell. (October 2001). "Retirement Age Declines Again in the 1990s." Monthly Labor Review Online. 12–21. Available online at www.bls.gov/opub/mlr/archive.htm.
21. Ibid.
22. Ibid.
23. Joseph F. Quinn. (May 1999). "Has the Early Retirement Trend Reversed?," Boston College Economics, Working Paper No. 424,. Available online at http://fmwww.bc.edu/ec/research.php.
24. Burtless and Quinn.
25. Wiatrowski.
26. Fullerton and Toossi.
27. Alicia H. Munnell, Kevin E. Cahill, and Natalia A. Jivan. (September 2003). "How has the Shift to 401(k)s Affected the Retirement Age?" Center for Retirement Research at Boston College, Issue in Brief No. 3. Available online at www.bc.edu.crr.
28. Ibid.
29. Alicia H. Munnell, Annika Sunden, and Elizabeth Lidstone. (February 2002). "How Important are Private Pensions?," Center for Retirement Research at Boston College, Issue in Brief No. 8. Available online at www.bc.edu.crr.
30. Burtless and Quinn.
31. Quinn, "Changing Retirement Trends."
32. Burtless and Quinn.
33. Ibid.
34. S. Kathi Brown. (2003). "Staying Ahead of the Curve 2003: The AARP Working in Retirement Study." Washington, DC: AARP. Available online at http://research.aarp.org/econ/multiwork_2003.pdf.
35. Burtless and Quinn.
36. Ibid.
37. Gendell; and Dora Costa. (May 20–21, 1999). "Has the Trend Toward Early Retirement Reversed?" Paper presented at the First Annual Joint Conference for the Retirement Research Consortium. Available online at www.bc.edu.

38. Burtless and Quinn.
39. Haider and Loughran.
40. Metropolitan Life Insurance Company. (February 2002)."MetLife Retirement Crossroads Study: Paving the Way to a Secure Future." Available online at www.metlife.com.
41. Ibid.
42. Ibid.
43. Ibid.
44. Ibid.
45. Ibid.
46. Ibid.
47. Brown.
48. Ibid.
49. NOP World, 2003.

CHAPTER 11

Social Security and Supplemental Security Income

We have tried to frame a law which will give some measure of protection to the average citizen and his family against the loss of a job and against poverty-ridden old age.

—Franklin Delano Roosevelt, upon signing the Social Security Act in 1935

Since its inception, SSI has been viewed as the "program of last resort."

—Comment on the Web site of the Office of the Assistant Secretary for Planning and Evaluation, Department of Health and Human Services

This chapter covers the Social Security and Supplemental Security programs.

The original purpose of the Social Security program was to *partially replace* income lost due to retirement or disability. However, today Social Security is the sole source of financial support for many beneficiaries (see Chapter 7 for detailed information on the importance of Social Security income).

Supplemental Security Income (SSI) is a safety net program for people of all ages with low incomes. Low-income seniors are able to get SSI in addition to monthly Social Security benefits, if their Social Security benefit is low.

Highlights from the chapter include:

- Nine in 10 elderly receive Social Security benefits.

- About two-thirds of elderly (aged 65+) Social Security beneficiaries receive 50 percent or more of their income from Social Security.

- Most Social Security beneficiaries are retired workers.

- Most Social Security beneficiaries are over age 62.

- Men's average Social Security benefit is higher than women's.

- Social Security's demographics are challenging the system.

- In 2003, about 2 million elderly persons receive SSI payments.

- Three in 5 elderly SSI beneficiaries also receive Social Security.

Social Security celebrates its 70th birthday

President Franklin Roosevelt signed the Social Security Act into law on August 14, 1935. The program, popularly referred to as "Social Security," provides monthly benefits to retired and disabled workers as well as their survivors and dependents. The technical name for Social Security is Old-Age, Survivor's and Disability Insurance (OASDI).·

Workers pay into Social Security through taxes

Workers contribute to Social Security through payroll or self-employment taxes (FICA and SECA). The maximum taxable amount is updated annually based on increases in the average wage. In 2002, of the 153 million workers with Social Security taxable earnings, 6 percent had earnings that equaled or exceeded the maximum amount subject to taxes.

Social Security benefits are earned by individuals based on their tax contributions to the program during their working years. Others are entitled to benefits because of marriage or another relationship to a worker.

In 2003 the OASDI tax rate shared by employer and employee is 15.3 percent. Employer and employee each contribute 7.65 percent on wages; 6.2 percent for Social Security (OASDI), and 1.45 percent for Medicare.

Taxes collected for OASDI are put into trust funds that are created to receive income and disburse benefits. Separate funds support OASI (Old-Age and Survivor's Insurance) and DI (Disability Insurance).

The trustees of the funds invest the assets in securities issued or guaranteed by the federal government. According to the Social Security Administration (SSA), less than 1 percent of every Social Security tax dollar is spent on administrative costs.

Social Security beneficiaries can elect full, early, or delayed benefits

Retirees can collect full retirement benefits, reduced benefits beginning at age 62 or delayed benefits. Their decision will impact the date when payments begin and the amount of the benefit.

The age of full retirement benefits is gradually increasing to 67

Beneficiaries begin receiving "full" benefit payments once they reach the legally defined "full" retirement age. Historically, the "full" retirement age has been 65. However, beginning in 2000, the age at which full benefits could be collected started to gradually increase by increments of two months a year. This will continue until 2005, when the "full" retirement will be age 66. Then, in 2017, the age for full retirement gradually increases again in two months increments for each year until year 2022, at which point, "full" retirement will be defined as age 67.

▇ Beneficiaries can elect to receive reduced payments as early as age 62

Social Security benefits are decreased by five-ninths of a percent for each month before the full retirement age. Currently if benefits are started at age 62, the payment is 80 percent of what it would be at the full retirement age. As Social Security's full retirement age increases toward 67, the percentage of benefits received for selecting early retirement will gradually decrease from 80 percent to 70 percent.

The trade-off in electing early benefits is that payments are permanently reduced. However, the beneficiary receives checks for a longer period of time. According to SSA, as a general rule, early retirement gives beneficiaries about the same total Social Security benefits over their lifetimes.

Retirees who delay their Social Security benefits past age 65 receive increased payments (see Table 11.1). The increase stops at age 70, even if the beneficiary continues to delay taking benefits.

▇ Social Security is a pay-as-you-go system

Most of the payroll taxes collected from today's workers are used to pay Social Security benefits to *today's* recipients. They are not saved and invested for tomorrow's beneficiaries. In 2002, the OASDI Trust Funds collected $627 billion in revenues. Of that amount, 85 percent was derived from payroll taxes and 2 percent from income taxes on Social Security benefits. Interest earned on the government bonds held by the trust funds provided the remaining 13 percent of income. Assets increased in 2002 because income exceeded expenditures for benefit payments and administrative expenses.

▇ Social Security Trust Fund assets total over a trillion dollars

In December 2002, a total of 39.2 million people were receiving Old Age and Survivor's Insurance (OASI) benefits and 7.2 million were receiving DI benefits. Trust fund operations, in billions of dollars, are shown below (see Table 11.2).

TABLE 11.1
Increase in Social Security Payments for Delaying Retirement
Past Age 65

Year of Birth	Yearly Rate of Increase	Monthly Rate of Increase
1930	4.5%	3/8 of 1%
1931-1932	5.0%	5/12 of 1%
1933-1934	5.5%	11/24 of 1%
1935-1936	6.0%	1/2 of 1%
1937-1938	6.5%	13/24 of 1%
1939-1940	7.0%	7/12 of 1%
1941-1942	7.5%	5/8 of 1%
1943 or later	8.0%	2/3 of 1%

Source: Social Security Administration.

TABLE 11.2
Social Security Trust Fund Operations in Billions of Dollars

	Old Age and Survivor's Insurance	Disability Insurance
	Billions of Dollars	
Assets (end of 2001)	1,071.5	141.0
Income during 2002	539.7	87.4
Outgo during 2002	393.7	67.9
Net increase in assets	146.0	19.5
Assets (end of 2002)	1,217.5	160.5

Source: Social Security Administration.

According to the Social Security Board of Trustees, projected assets of the OASDI Trust Funds will be exhausted by 2042.[1]

SOCIAL SECURITY BENEFITS

Over 46 million people receive monthly checks from SSA

In 2002 more than 46 million people received monthly Social Security checks. SSA paid benefits totaling $454 billion.

The monthly Social Security benefit increases every year

Social Security benefits increase automatically each year based on the rise in the Bureau of Labor Statistics' Consumer Price Index for Urban Wage Earners and Clerical Workers (CPI-W). In July 2003, the average Social Security monthly benefit to a retired worker was $895, while the average benefit for his or her spouse was $452.

The amount of earnings needed for Social Security credits will increase in the future

Eligibility for Social Security benefits is based on employment and payment of taxes into the Social Security system. Social Security credits (also called quarters of coverage) are earned as workers pay taxes. Since 1978, credits have been based on annual earnings, with a maximum of four credits per year. In 2003, one credit is earned for each $890 in earnings, up to a maximum of four credits. In the future, the amount of earnings needed for a credit will increase as the average wage level increases. According to current SSA guidelines, a worker needs 40 credits to qualify for retirement benefits.

▒ Most beneficiaries are retired workers

In 2002 the majority (63 percent) of Social Security beneficiaries were retired work-ers and 12 percent were disabled workers. The remaining 25 percent were spouses, children, survivors, or dependents of retired or disabled workers.

▒ Most beneficiaries are over age 62

In 2002, 93 percent of all Social Security beneficiaries were aged 62 or older. Eighty-nine percent of disabled beneficiaries were under age 62.

▒ Elderly women who are Social Security beneficiaries outnumber elderly men

Of all adults receiving monthly Social Security benefits, 43 percent were men and 57 percent were women. Eighty-one percent of the men and 57 percent of the women received retired-worker benefits. About one-fifth of the women received survivor's benefits.

▒ The proportion of women among retired-worker beneficiaries has quadrupled since 1960

The percentage of women receiving benefits because of their own work histories climbed steadily from 12 percent in 1940 to 47 percent in 1980, leveling off at 48 percent in 1990 (see Chart 11.1). The proportion of women among disabled-worker

CHART 11.1
Women Beneficiaries as a Percentage of Retired
Workers and Disabled Workers: Selected Years

Source: Social Security Administration, *Fast Facts & Figures about Social Security*.

beneficiaries has more than doubled since disability benefits first became payable in 1957. The percentage rose steadily from 20 percent in 1957 to 35 percent in 1990 and 45 percent in 2002.

▣ Monthly benefits depend on the worker's wage history and time of retirement

A covered worker who had worked continuously at low wages (45 percent of the national average wage) and who claimed benefits at age 62 in January 2003 would receive a monthly benefit of $572. One who had earnings at or above the maximum amount subject to Social Security taxes and who claimed benefits at age 65 would receive $1,721. Someone who claimed benefits at age 70, which maximizes the effect of the delayed retirement credit, would receive $2,045 (see Table 11.3).

▣ Men's average benefit is higher than women's

Among retired and disabled workers who collected benefits based on their own work records in 2003, men receive a higher average monthly benefit than women. For those with benefits based on another person's work record (spouses and survivors), women had higher average benefits (see Table 11.4).

▣ The proportion of women who receive benefits based only on their husband's work record is decreasing

The proportion of women aged 62 or older who are receiving benefits as dependents on the basis of their husband's earnings record only has been declining—from 57 percent in 1960 to 34 percent in 2002 (see Chart 11.2). At the same time, the proportion of women with dual entitlement (that is, paid on the basis of both their own earnings record and that of their husbands) has been increasing—from 5 percent in 1960 to 28 percent in 2002.

TABLE 11.3
Hypothetical Social Security Monthly Benefits

	62 Years	65 Years	70 Years
Earnings Level	$	$	$
Low	572	701	833
Average	943	1,158	1,387
High	1,236	1,513	1,786
Maximum	1,404	1,721	2,045

Note: Low earnings are defined as 45% of the national average index, average earnings are equal to the index, high earnings are 160% of the index, and maximum earnings are equal to the OASDI contribution and benefits base.
Source: Social Security Administration, Office of the Chief Actuary.

TABLE 11.4
Hypothetical Social Security Benefits, Average Monthly Benefits

	Men	Women
	$	$
Total	983	740
Retired workers	1,008	774
Spouses	256	454
Disabled workers	936	709
Spouses	168	214
Survivors		
Nondisabled widow(er)s	663	863
Disabled widow(er)s	385	553
Mothers and fathers	547	646

Source: Social Security Administration.

CHART 11.2
Women Aged 62 or Older, by Basis of Entitlement:
Selected Years

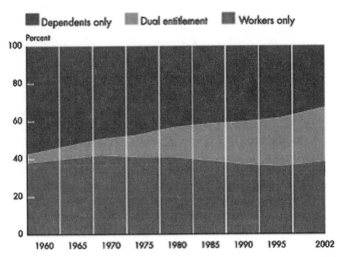

Source: Social Security Administration, *Fast Facts & Figures about Social Security*.

SOCIAL SECURITY FINANCING
▪ Social Security's demographics are challenging the system

The number of retired workers is projected to grow rapidly starting in 2008, when the members of the post–World War II baby boom begin to reach early retirement

CHART 11.3
Ratio of Covered Workers to Social Security Beneficiaries

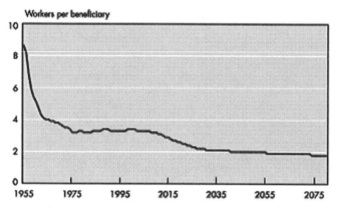

Source: The 2003 Annual Report of the Board of Trustees of the Federal Old-Age and Survivor's Insurance and Disability Insurance Trust Funds.

age, and will double in less than 30 years. People are also living longer, and the birth rate is low. As a result, the ratio of workers paying Social Security taxes to people collecting benefits will fall from 3.3 to 1 in 2003 to 2.1 to 1 by 2031 (see Chart 11.3). At that ratio there will not be enough workers to pay scheduled benefits at current tax rates.

■ Social Security is not sustainable over the long term at present benefit and tax rates

Within 15 years Social Security will begin paying more in benefits than it collects in taxes. By 2042 the trust funds will be exhausted. At that point, payroll taxes and other income will flow into the fund but will be sufficient to pay only 73 percent of program costs (see Chart 11.4).

■ Social Security's unfunded obligation is $3.5 trillion

Each year, Social Security's trustees provide an estimate of the financial status of the program for the next 75 years. In changing from the valuation period of one year's Trustees Report to the next, an additional year with a large imbalance between taxes and benefits is added to the projection. As a result, the estimated cost of meeting Social Security's financial shortfall tends to go up every year. In the year 2003 it was $3.5 trillion, up from $3.3 trillion in 2001 and $2.9 trillion in both 2000 and 1999 (all figures in 2002 dollars).

CHART 11.4
Cumulative Income Less Cost Based on Present Taxes
and Scheduled Benefits

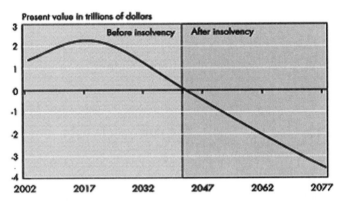

Source: The 2003 Annual Report of the Board of Trustees of the Federal
Old-Age and Survivor's Insurance and Disability Insurance Trust Funds.

SUPPLEMENTAL SECURITY INCOME (SSI)

▦ SSI is a safety net program for people with low incomes

The federal SSI program provides monthly income to people who are age 65 or older, are blind or disabled, or have limited income and financial resources. The Social Security Administration runs the program. In 2003, about 2 million elderly persons received SSI payments, 71 percent of whom were women.[2] Low-income seniors are able to get SSI in addition to monthly Social Security benefits, if their Social Security benefit is low.

▦ One in 5 SSI beneficiaries is elderly

In 2002, nineteen percent of SSI beneficiaries had benefits awarded on the basis of age, the rest on the basis of disability (see Chart 11.5) Twenty-nine percent of beneficiaries were aged 65 or older. (In the SSI program—unlike the OASDI program—a disabled beneficiary is still classified as "disabled" after reaching age 65.)

▦ Three in 5 elderly beneficiaries also receive Social Security

In 2002, fifty-eight percent of SSI beneficiaries aged 65 or older also received OASDI benefits.[3] Sixteen percent received other unearned income such as veterans' pensions or income from assets.

CHART 11.5
Distribution of SSI Beneficiaries, by Basis for Eligibility and Age

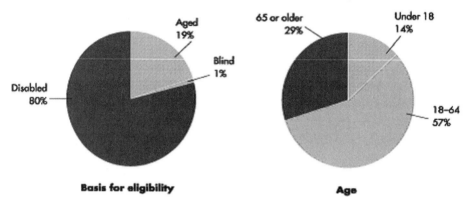

Source: Social Security Administration, *Fast Facts & Figures about Social Security*.

▓ Participation of the disabled are responsible for the growth in the SSI program

The elderly's share of SSI participation has decreased from 61 percent in January 1974 to 29 percent in December 2002 (see Chart 11.6). The overall long-term growth of the SSI program has occurred because of an increase in the number of disabled beneficiaries, most of whom are under age 65.

The amount of the SSI benefit depends on the state in which recipients live. The basic SSI check is the same nationwide. In 2003, the SSI payment for an eligible

CHART 11.6
Percentage of SSI Beneficiaries Aged 65 or Older: Selected Years

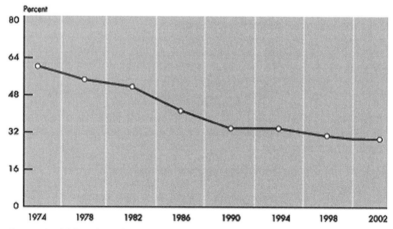

Source: Social Security Administration, *Fast Facts & Figures about Social Security*.

individual was $552 per month and $829 per month for an eligible couple. The following is a list of all states that supplement the basic SSI amount:

- California
- Hawaii
- Massachusetts
- Nevada
- New Jersey
- New York
- Pennsylvania
- Rhode Island
- Vermont
- Washington, DC

Like Social Security benefits, Supplemental Security Income benefits increase automatically each year based on the rise in the Bureau of Labor Statistics' Consumer Price Index for Urban Wage Earners and Clerical Workers (CPI-W).

The elderly who get SSI may also be able to get other low-income assistance, such as Medicaid and food stamps, from their states or counties.

NOTES

1. Social Security and Medicare Boards of Trustees. (2004) Status of the Social Security and Medicare Programs. Available online at http://www.ssa.gov.
2. SSA. (2003). *Fast Facts & Figures about Social Security*.
3. Ibid.

World Records and Fascinating Facts

ARTS AND ENTERTAINMENT

Greatest age span portrayed by an actor in a film: Dustin Hoffman aged from 17 to 121 in *Little Big Man.*

Longest screen career: Curt Bois, who made his debut at age eight in *Der Fidele Bauer* (Germany, 1908) and his final film in 1988 in *Wings of Desire* (Germany).

Oldest Oscar winner: Jessica Tandy won the Oscar for *Driving Miss Daisy* at age 80.

Oldest person to have a number 1 hit: At age 69 Louis Armstrong had the number one hit in the United Kingdom for "What a Wonderful World." Armstrong was almost 64 when he had his first U.S. number 1 hit, "Hello Dolly."

Oldest authors: Sisters Sarah and Elizabeth Delaney have this honor for publishing the *Delaney Sisters' Book of Everyday Wisdom* in 1994 when they were 105 and 103 years old.

Oldest chorus line performer: Irus Guarino has been dancing in the line of the Ziegfield Girls of Florida since 1986 when she was 77 years old.

LONGEST CONTRACT IN RADIO AND TV

Bob Hope completed the 60th year of his NBC contract on November 23, 1996. The TV veteran also holds Guinness World Records for Most Honored Entertainer, Most Oscar Ceremonies Presented, and Longest Hollywood Marriage.

Oldest film director: Manoel de Oliveira (Portugal), who began directing films in 1931, made his most recent film, *O Prinipio da Incerteza* (*The Principle of Uncertainty*, Portugal, 2002), at the age of 94. The film was presented at the Cannes film festival, France, on May 18, 2002.

SPORTS

Oldest person to ski to the North Pole: Canada's Jack MacKenzie joined a ski expedition to the geographic North Pole at the age of 77 years, 10 months, and 13 days. He reached the North Pole on April 28, 1999. The expedition was led by Richard Weber.

Oldest athlete: Baba Joginder Singh won a gold medal in 1998 at the Indian National Athletics Meet for Veterans held in Thane, Bombay. He was believed to be 105 years old. As a teenager he represented India in a 1910 world championship.

Oldest cresta run rider: Prince Constantin of Liechtenstein rode the Cresta run tobogganing course at the age of 85 on February 11, 1997.

Oldest tightrope walker: William Ivy Baldwin crossed South Boulder Canyon in Colorado on a 320-foot-high-wire with a 125-foot drop on his 82nd birthday on July 3, 1948.

Oldest hot air balloonist: Florence Lain of New Zealand flew in a balloon at age 102 in Cust, New Zealand on September 26, 1996.

Oldest boardsailer: Charles Ruiijter of the Netherlands took up boardsailing in 1978 at age 63.

Oldest man to climb Mount Everest: Japan's Yuichiro Miura (b. October 12, 1932) reached the summit of Mount Everest aged 70 years and 222 days on May 22 2003, becoming the oldest person ever to have done so. The previous holder was fellow Japanese climber Tomiyasu Ishikawa, who reached the summit aged 65 years and 181 days in May 2002.

Oldest person to complete an around-the-world flight: In 1994, Fred Lasby made a solo around-the-world flight at the age of 82 in his single engine Piper Comanche.

Oldest person to climb Mt. Kilimanjaro: William Masheu (Tanzania) was born in 1929 and was still climbing the mountain regularly in 1999.

Oldest pilots: Burnet Patten of Victoria, Australia, obtained his flying license in 1997 at the age of 80. Clarence Cornish of Indiana piloted aircraft until age 97. He died in 1995, eighteen days after his last flight.

Oldest wall-of-death rider: Oldest to regularly perform in public is 71-year-old Jerry deRoyce, riding a 1927 "Scout."

Oldest parachutist: Hildegarde Ferrara became the oldest-ever parachutist in 1996 when she made a tandem jump at age 99 in Hawaii.

Oldest high earning sportsman: In 1997, 68-year-old golfer Arnold Palmer earned $16.1 million from a salary, winnings, and endorsements. He still plays on the PGA tour.

Oldest U.S. Open golf champion: Hale Irwin won the U.S. Open at the age of 45 years 15 days. In 1997, he set the single season earnings record for the Senior PGA tour at over $2 million.

Oldest National golf champion: Pamela Fernando was 54 years and 282 days old when she won the Sri Lankan Women's Championship on July 17, 1981.

Oldest U.S. Open tennis champion: Margaret Du Pont (USA) won the mixed doubles title at the age of 42 years and 166 days in 1960.

Oldest ever U.S. Open singles champion: William Larned (USA) won the U.S. Open at age 38 years and 242 days in 1911.

Oldest Australian Open champion: Norman Brookes (Australia) was 46 years and 2 months when he won the 1924 Australian Open mixed doubles.

Oldest French Open champion: Elizabeth Ryan (USA) won the 1934 women's doubles at the age of 42 years and 88 days.

Oldest French Open singles champion: Andres Gimeno (Spain) won the championship at the age of 34 years and 301 days.

Oldest regular player in the NBA: Robert Parish retired at age 43 from the Chicago Bulls.

Oldest weight-lifting world record breaker: Norman Schemansky (USA) was 37 years and 333 days when he lifted 362 pounds in Detroit, Michigan in 1962.

Oldest Grand Prix driver: The oldest driver of the Grand Prix is Louis Alexandre Chiron (Monaco), who finished sixth in the Monaco Grand Prix on May 22, 1955 at the age of 55 years, 292 days.

Oldest Olympic champions: The oldest winner of an Olympic event was Patrick "Babe" McDonald (USA), who was 42 years and 26 days old when he won the 56 lb. weight throw in Belgium in 1920.

The oldest female Olympic champion was Lia Manoliu (Romania) who was 36 years and 176 days old when she won the gold medal for the discus in Mexico in 1968.

Oldest Olympic bobsled champion: Jay O'Brien (USA) was 47 years and 357 days old when he was a member of a four man team that won a gold medal at the Olympics in 1932.

Oldest professional drag racer: Eddie Hill (USA), who is now 63 years old, is still regularly racing at speeds in excess of 300 mph.

Oldest windsurfer: When he retired in 1986, Australia's Otto Comanos (b. November 16, 1913), took up windsurfing and now regularly windsurfs two to three times a week in and around the lakes of Sydney, New South Wales, Australia.

Oldest lifeguard: The oldest lifeguard in the world is Haywood Leroy Stewart (USA, b. May 22, 1916) of Wheat Ridge, Colorado, USA, who has been a lifeguard since 1938.

Oldest Wimbledon champion: The oldest Wimbledon tennis champion is Margaret Evelyn Du Pont (USA). She won the mixed doubles with Neale Fraser (Australia) in 1962 at the age of 44 years, 125 days.

Oldest Ryder Cup player: Raymond Floyd (USA) competed in the Ryder Cup in 1993 at the age of 51 years 20 days. Floyd was inducted into the World Golf Hall of Fame in 1989 and still plays on the Senior PGA tour.

Longest time as an Olympic competitor: Four Olympic competitors have participated in games over a period of 40 years: Ivan Joseph Martin Osiier (Denmark) in fencing (1908–32 and 1948); Magnus Andreas Thulstrup Clasen Konow (Norway) in yachting (1908–20, 1928, and 1936–48); Paul Elvstrom (Denmark) in yachting (1948–60, 1968–72, and 1984–88); and Durward Randolph Knowles (UK, then Bahamas) in yachting (1948–72 and 1988).

Oldest Tour de France winner: The oldest winner of the Tour de France was Firmin Lambot (Belgium), aged 36 years and 4 months in 1922.

RECORD HOLDERS

Oldest person in space: John Glenn in October 1998 at age 77.

Longest career: Shigechiyo Izumi lived to a greater age than any other man on record and worked for 98 years. He died at age 120 in 1986.

Oldest president: Joaquin Balaguer (1907–2002) was president of the Dominican Republic 1960–62, 1966–78, and 1986–96. He ultimately left office at the age of 89. He held the presidency for no fewer than 22 years.

Oldest mother: Arceli Keh of Highland, California gave birth to a daughter at age 63 years, 9 months. It was reported that Rosanna Dalla Corte (Italy, b. February 1931) gave birth to a baby boy on July 18, 1994, at the age of 63 years.

Oldest kidney donor and recipient: 78-year-old Victoria Whybrew, became the oldest kidney donor in 1995 when she donated one of her kidneys to her 77-year-old husband, who became the oldest kidney recipient.

Longest-serving U.S. senator: The longest serving senator in U.S. history is Republican Strom Thurmond (b. 1902), who served the state of South Carolina, USA, a total of 48 years in the Senate between 1954 and 2002, seeing the terms of 18 U.S. presidents.

Longest teaching career: Medarda de Jesus Leon de Uzcategui (Venezuela) taught in Caracas, Venezuela, for over 80 years from 1911.

Oldest couple to marry: On February 1, 2002 French couple Francois Frenandez (b. April 17, 1906) and Madeleine Francineau (b. July 15, 1907) exchanged vows at the rest home Le Foyer du Romarin, Clapiers, France, at the age of 96 and 94, respectively. The total aggregate years between them at the time of the wedding ceremony was a record 190. The oldest recorded bride is Minnie Munro (Australia), age 102, who married fellow Australian Dudley Reid, age 83, at Point Clare, New South Wales, Australia, on May 31, 1991.

Oldest drivers: There are three drivers who were issued with new driving licenses at age 104: Maude Tull (USA) of Inglewood, California—who took to driving at age 91 after her husband died—was issued a renewal to her license on February 5, 1976, when 104; Layne Hall (USA), whose date of birth is uncertain (b. 1884 or 1880), was issued with a New York State license on June 15, 1989, when he was either 104 or 109; and most recently, Fred Hale Sr. (USA, b. December 1, 1890) was issued with a driving license on February 29, 1995, at age 104. The license was valid until his 108th birthday in 1998.

Oldest doctorate: At the age of 90 years, 58 days, Elizabeth Eichelbaum (USA) became the oldest person to receive a doctorate (PhD). She received her doctorate in education on May 12, 2000 from the University of Tennessee, USA.

LONGEST LIVING

Oldest worker: At 102, property developer is named oldest U.S. worker. Russell Clark started working in real estate development after a 60-year career as a physician according to National Geographic News.

Oldest people: The greatest fully authenticated age to which a human being has ever lived is 122 years and 164 days by Jeanne Calment (France). She died in 1997.

Supercentenarians: As of September 2004 there were 59 documented supercentenarians in the world. Supercentenarians have lived to be 110 years or older.

Longest-lived parasite: A lifespan of 27 years has been recorded for a medicinal leech, Hirrudo medicinalis

Longest-lived chelonian: A Madagascar radiated tortoise (Astrochelys Radiata) was at least 188 years old when it died in 1965.

Longest-lived insects: The longest lived insects are the splendor beetles (family Buprestidae). One specimen appeared in 1983 after at least 51 years as a larvae.

Longest-lived rodent: The greatest age for a rodent is 27 years and 3 months for a Sumatran crested porcupine *(Hystrix brachyura)*.

Longest lived primate: The greatest age for a non-human primate is 59 years and 5 months for a chimpanzee who died at the Yerkes Primate Research Center in Atlanta in 1992.

OLDEST LIVING THING

Oldest living thing: "King Clone," a creosote plant, estimated to be 11,700 years old.

WHO LIVES LONGEST?

The longest living mammals: *Homo sapiens.*

The second longest-living mammal: the Asiatic elephant.

AVERAGE LIFE SPANS

Of an alligator: 55 years.

Of a cat: 15 years.

Of a dog: 8 to 15 years.

Of a dolphin: 65 years.

Of an elephant: 60 years.

Of a facelift: 6 to 10 years.

Of a hippopatamous: 40 years.

Of a horse: 30 years.

Of a housefly: 6 weeks.

Of a lion: 25 years.

Of a lobster: up to 50 years.

Of a macaw: 63 years.

Of a mayfly: 1 day.

Of a mouse: 2 to 3 years.

Of an ostrich: 50 years.

Of an owl: 24 years.

Of a pelican: 45 years.

Of a rattlesnake: 18 years.

Of a rabbit: 12 years.

Of a raven: 69 years.

Of a rhinoceros: 70 years.

Of a sheep: 10 to 15 years.

Of a squirrel: 11 years.

Of a trout: 5 to 10 years.

Of a turtle: 1 plus years.

SOME SENIOR ACHIEVEMENTS

When he was 100 years old, George Abbot opened a play on Broadway.

At 100, Grandma Moses illustrated *'Twas the Night before Christmas.*

At 99, Strom Thurmond retired from the Senate (in 2002). It was the end of his 8th term. He served 47 years and five months in the Senate. He also was the oldest person to serve in Congress, turning 100 on December 5, 2002, just a month before his retirement from the legislative body.

At 96, Martha Graham premiered her ballet, *Maple Leaf Rag.*

At 93, George Bernard Shaw wrote the play *Far Fetched Fables.*

At 93, Lillian Gish starred in the film, *The Whales of August.*

At 92, George Burns was performing on stage with 86-year-old Bob Hope.

At 90, Pablo Picasso was producing drawings and engravings.

At 90, Bertrand Russell intervened with heads of state during the Cuban missile crisis.

At 90, Duncan McLean won the 1975 World Veterans Olympics silver medal for the 2000-meter run.

At 90, Jenny Wood-Allen of Scotland completed the London Marathon in 11 hours, 34 minutes.

Between the ages of 66 and 91, Hulda Crooks, nicknamed "Grandma Whitney," made two dozen climbs up 14,495-foot Mount Whitney. Crooks Peak on Mount Whitney was named for her. She was the oldest woman to scale Mt. Whitney and 12,388-foot Mount Fuji in Japan.

At 89, Arthur Rubenstein gave one of his greatest recitals at Carnegie Hall.

At 89, "Granny D," whose real name was Diris Haddock, walked 3,200 miles across the United States in support of campaign reform.

At 87, Konrad Adenauer was chancellor of West Germany.

At 87, Jeanette Rankin, the first female member of Congress, led an anti–Viet Nam war protest on Capitol Hill.

At 81, Benjamin Franklin effected the compromise that led to the adoption of the U.S. Constitution.

At 81, Thomas Edison patented his last invention.

In his 80s, Titian was producing some of his finest works.

At 80, Norman Vincent Peale published his 34th book.

At 79, Marc Chagall produced two magnificent murals for the Metropolitan opera in New York.

At 75, Duke Ellington made his last recording.

At 79, actor Paul Newman is going strong as co-founder and director of Newman's Own, Inc., which has donated more than $150 million to charity.

At 78, Eleanor of Aquitaine led an army to crush a rebellion against her son, King John of England.

At 74, Claude Monet painted his famous Nympheas water lilies.

At 71, Cecil B. DeMille produced and directed the award-winning *Greatest Show on Earth.*

At 71, Michelangelo was appointed chief architect of St. Peter's Basilica in Rome.

At 70, Verdi finished *Falstaff.*

In his 70s, Frank Lloyd Wright designed many of his masterpieces, including the Solomon R. Guggenheim Museum in New York.

OLDEST AMERICAN PRESIDENTS

Inaugurated at age 69: Ronald Reagan.

Inaugurated at age 68: Martin Van Buren.

Inaugurated at age 65: James Buchanan.

Inaugurated at age 64: Zachary Taylor.

Inaugurated at age 62: Dwight David Eisenhower.

AGE OF CONGRESS AND THE SUPREME COURT

In 1999, the average age of the U.S. House of Representatives was 52.6, up from 51.6 in 1997. The average age of the U.S. Senate was 58.3, up from 57.5 in 1997.

In 2003, the average age of the Supreme Court was 69. The oldest member was Justice John Paul Stevens, age 83.

IN AN AVERAGE LIFETIME

The amount of time spent waiting for traffic lights to change: 5 months.

The amount of time on household chores: 4 years.

The amount of time spent eating: 6 years.

The amount of time spent standing in line: 6 years.

Resources in Aging Services, Gerontology, and Geriatrics

Alliance for Aging Research
2021 K Street, NW, Suite 305
Washington, DC 20006
Phone: 202-293-2856
1-800-639-2421 (toll-free)
Fax: 202-785-8574
E-mail: info@agingresearch.org
Web site: http://www.agingresearch.org
   The Alliance is a national, citizen advocacy organization offering free publications including *Investing in Older Women's Health*, *Meeting the Medical Needs of the Senior Boom*, *Delaying the Diseases of Aging*, and other aging-related subjects such as menopause, how to age with ease, and health care options under Medicare.

Alzheimer's Association
919 North Michigan Avenue, Suite 1100
Chicago, IL 60611
Phone: 1-800-272-3900 (toll-free)
312-335-8700
TTY: 312-335-8882
Fax: 312-335-1110
Email: info@alz.org
Web site: http://www.alz.org
   The Association is a nonprofit organization offering information and support services to people with Alzheimer's disease (AD) and their families. Contact the 24-hour, toll-free telephone line to link with local chapters and community resources. The Association funds research to find a cure for AD and provides information on caregiving. A free catalog of educational publications is available in English and Spanish.

Alzheimer's Disease Education and Referral (ADEAR) Center
PO Box 8250
Silver Spring, MD 20907-8250
Phone: 1-800-438-4380 (toll-free) (English, Spanish)
Fax: 301-495-3334
Email: adear@alzheimers.org
Web site: http://www.alzheimers.org

The ADEAR Center, funded by the National Institute on Aging, distributes information about Alzheimer's disease (AD) to health professionals, patients and their families, and the public. Contact the Center for information about the symptoms, diagnosis, and treatment of AD; recent research; and referrals to State and other national services. On its Web site, the Center offers searchable publications and databases, including the AD Clinical Trials Database of studies accepting volunteers.

American Association for Geriatric Psychiatry (AAGP)
7910 Woodmont Avenue, Suite 1050
Bethesda, MD 20814-3004
Phone: 301-654-7850
Fax: 301-654-4137
Email: main@aagponline.org
Web site: http://www.aagponline.org
The Association works to improve the mental health and well-being of older people. Contact AAGP for information on geriatric psychiatry and to receive referrals to specialists. Available publications include *Growing Older, Growing Wiser: Coping with Expectations, Challenges and Changes in Later Years*, and brochures on topics such as Alzheimer's disease, depression, and the role of the geriatric psychiatrist. Some consumer publications are free.

American Association of Health Plans (AAHP)/Health Insurance Association of America (HIAA) (AAHP-HIAA)
601 Pennsylvania Avenue, NW
South Building, Suite 500
Washington, DC 20004
Phone: 202-778-3200
Fax: 202-331-7487 fax
Email: webmaster@aahp.org
Web site: http://www.aahp.org/template.cfm
AAHP-HIAA is a trade association representing the interests of privately insurers. They have insurance information on health, long-term care, dental, disability, and supplemental coverage. HIAA also provides information and publications on health care issues, including continuation of group health benefits, major medical, and Medicare supplements.

American Association of Homes and Services for the Aging (AAHSA)
2519 Connecticut Avenue, NW
Washington, DC 20008-1520
Phone: 202-783-2242
Fax: 202-783-2255
Email: memberservices@aahsa.org
Web site: http://www.aahsa.org
AAHSA is a national, nonprofit organization providing older people with services and information on housing, health care, and community involvement. Visit the AAHSA Web site for information for seniors and caregivers.

American Association of Retired Persons (AARP)
601 E Street, NW
Washington, DC 20049
Phone: 202-434-2277
800-424-3410

Web site: www.aarp.org
http://research.aarp.org
Email: member@aarp.org

AARP is a nonprofit, nonpartisan membership organization for people 50 and over. The organization sells products to its members such as health and automobile insurance. Local chapters provide information and services on crime prevention, consumer protection, and income tax preparation. In addition, AARP advocates on legislative, consumer, and legal issues; assists members in serving their communities; and offers a wide range of services for its members. These include AARP's Web site at www.aarp.org, the AARP lifestyle magazines, the monthly AARP *Bulletin,* and a Spanish-language newspaper, *Segunda Juventud.* AARP is active in every state, the District of Columbia, Puerto Rico, and the U.S. Virgin Islands. AARP's AgeLine database, available on CD-ROM, contains extensive resources on issues of concern to older people.

American Bar Association
Commission on the Legal Problems of the Elderly
740 15th Street, NW
Washington, DC 20005-1019
Phone: 202-662-8690
Email: askaba@abanet.org
Web site: http://www.abanet.org/aging

The Commission examines and responds to law-related needs of older people. It makes referrals and maintains a listing of legal aid offices where older people can get free or low-cost legal assistance. The Commission's Web site lists available publications and videos.

American Federation for Aging Research (AFAR)
70 West 40th Street, 11th Floor
New York, NY 10018
Phone: 212-703-9977
Toll-free: (888) 582-2327
Fax: 212-997-0330
Email: info@afar.org
Web sites: http://www.afar.org
http://www.infoaging.org

AFAR is a nonprofit organization dedicated to supporting basic aging research. AFAR funds a wide variety of cutting-edge research on the aging process and age-related diseases. Visit the Web site for a list of free publications.

American Geriatrics Society (AGS)
350 Fifth Avenue
New York, NY 10118
Phone: 212-308-1414
Fax: 212-832-8646
Email: info@americangeriatrics.org
Web site: http://www.americangeriatrics.org

AGS is a nonprofit organization of physicians and health care professionals supporting the study of geriatrics. Contact AGS for information on geriatrics, long-term care, acute and chronic illnesses, rehabilitation, and nursing home care. Publications include the *AGS Complete Guide to Aging and Health* and the *AGS Medical Reference Guide.*

American Health Care Association (AHCA)
1201 L Street, NW
Washington, DC 20005
Phone: 202-842-4444
Fax: 202-842-3860
Web site: http://www.ahca.org
   AHCA is an organization representing the interests of for-profit nursing homes, assisted living centers, and subacute care facilities. Publications are available about nursing homes, guardianship, assisted living, financing, and long-term care services.

American Psychiatric Association (APA)
Council on Aging
1000 Wilson Boulevard, Suite 1825
Arlington, VA 22209-3901
Phone: 703-907-7300
Email: apa@psych.org
Web site: http://www.psych.org
   APA is an association of psychiatrists, physicians specializing in diagnosing and treating people with mental and emotional disorders. Its Council on Aging establishes standards for psychiatric care of older people. APA provides information on elder care issues, including medication use by older people, treatment of Alzheimer's disease, and nursing homes. APA provides referrals to local psychiatrists.

American Psychological Association (APA)
750 First Street, NE
Washington, DC 20002-4242
Phone: 202-336-6135
202/336-6040 fax
Web site: http://www.apa.org/pi/aging/
   APA is a professional society of psychologists that provides assistance and information on mental, emotional, and behavioral disorders. Contact the APA for a list of state chapters, information on the psychosocial aspects of aging, and referrals to APA-member psychologists. The APA's section on older people produces publications on topics such as dementia and dementia research. Publications include a quarterly subscription magazine, *Psychology and Aging*.

American Society on Aging (ASA)
833 Market Street, Suite 511
San Francisco, CA 94103
Phone: 1-800-537-9728 (toll-free)
415-974-9600
Fax: 415-974-0300
Email: info@asaging.org
Web site: http://www.asaging.org
   ASA is a nonprofit membership organization providing information about medical and social practice, research, and policy pertinent to the health of older people. The organization publishes *Generations*, a quarterly journal, and *Aging Today*, the Society's bimonthly news magazine. A catalog of books for sale and other educational materials is available on the Web site.

Assisted Living Federation of America (ALFA)
11200 Waples Mill Road, Suite 150
Fairfax, VA 22030
Phone 703-691-8100
Fax: 703-691-8106
E-mail: info@alfa.org
Web site: http://www.alfa.org
ALFA represents for-profit and nonprofit providers of assisted living, continuing care retirement communities, independent living, and other forms of housing and services. The Federation works to advance the assisted living industry and enhance the quality of life for consumers.

Association for Gerontology in Higher Education (AGHE)
1030 15th Street, NW, Suite 240
Washington, DC 20005-1503
Phone: 202-289-9806
Fax: 202-289-9824
Email: aghetemp@aghe.org
Web site: www.aghe.org
AGHE's members are organizations and institutions of higher education. Through conferences, publications, technical assistance, research studies, and consultation with policymakers, AGHE, an educational unit of the Gerontological Society of America, seeks to advance gerontology as a field of study at institutions of higher education.

Beverly Foundation
566 El Dorado Street #100
Pasadena, CA 91101
Phone: 626-792-2292
Fax: 626-792-6117
Email: info@beverlyfoundation.org
Web site: http://www.beverlyfoundation.org
The Foundation focuses on mobility and transportation for older people within the community, service delivery within home and institutional settings, and overall life enrichment. It engages in research and education projects and provides information for professionals and caregivers.

B'nai B'rith
Center for Senior Housing and Services
2020 K Street, NW, 7th Floor
Washington, DC 20006
Phone: 202-857-6600
Email: internet@bnaibrith.org
Web site: http://www.bnaibrith.org
B'nai B'rith is the world's oldest and largest Jewish service organization, providing community service, education, and advocacy. Its Center for Senior Housing and Services sponsors housing and travel for senior citizens. A list of publications is available.

Brookdale Center on Aging (BCOA) of Hunter College
The City University of New York
425 East 25th Street, 13th Floor North
New York, NY 10010-2590
Phone: 212-481-3780
Fax: 212-481-3791
Email: info@brookdale.org
Web site: http://www.brookdale.org
  BCOA sponsors a variety of programs, including the Institute on Law and Rights of Older Adults, that fight for grandparent rights. Other programs focus on elder care services, guardianship, caregiving, Medicare, intergenerational activities, and Alzheimer's disease. Contact BCOA about publications (some available in Spanish) including *Senior Rights Reporter*, *Benefits Checklist for Seniors*, *Help for Seniors*, and *Help for Grandparent Caregivers*, which are for sale.

The Center for Social Gerontology (TCSG)
2307 Shelby Avenue
Ann Arbor, MI 48103
Phone: 734-665-1126
Fax: 734-665-2071
Email: tcsg@tcsg.org
Web site: http://www.tcsg.org
  TCSG is a nonprofit research, training, and social policy organization. Particular attention is focused on law and aging, tobacco use and older people, guardianship service providers, and adult guardianship. Contact the Center for information on publications, videos, training, and technical assistance.

Center for the Study of Aging/International Association of Physical Activity, Aging and Sports (IAPAAS)
706 Madison Avenue
Albany, NY 12208-3604
Phone: 518-465-6927
Fax: 518-462-1339
Email: iapaas@aol.com
Web site: http://www.rit.edu/~pjr0120/csa/iapaas/
  The Center is a free-standing, nonprofit organization promoting research, education, and training in the field of aging. IAPAAS is the Center's membership division. It organizes programs on health, fitness, prevention, and aging. Contact the Center for a list of publications and information about the quarterly newsletter, *Lifelong Health and Fitness*.

Clearinghouse on Abuse and Neglect of the Elderly (CANE)
University of Delaware
Department of Consumer Studies
Alison Hall West, Room 211
Newark, DE 19716
Phone: 302-831-3525
Email: CANE-UD@udel.edu
Web site: http://www.elderabusecenter.org/clearing/index.html
  CANE, funded by the Administration on Aging, is a database of elder abuse materials and resources operated by the University of Delaware's National Center on Elder Abuse (NCEA).

CANE staff will conduct customized information searches and provide resources and referrals to elder abuse support groups. *NCEA Exchange*, CANE's newsletter, is available free.

Continuing Care Accreditation Commission (CCAC)
2519 Connecticut Avenue, NW
Washington, DC 20008-1520
Phone: 202-783-7286
Fax: 202-220-0022
Email: afinnega@ccaconline.org
Web site: http://www.ccaconline.org
    CCAC helps consumers identify quality retirement options. CCAC also accredits aging services that meet or exceed industry-generated standards of excellence in three areas: governance and administration; financial resources and disclosure; and resident life, health, and wellness.

Eldercare Initiative in Consumer Law (EICL)
National Consumer Law Center, Inc. (NCLC)
77 Summer Street, 10th Floor
Boston, MA 02110
Phone: 617-542-8010
Fax: 617-542-8028
Email: nclc@consumerlaw.org
Web site: http://www.consumerlaw.org
    The Initiative provides assistance on legal issues of older people. The EICL conducts regional and national legal workshops focusing on aging issues, including threats to loss of shelter and financial exploitation. Contact the Initiative for publications and references.

Elderhostel
11 Avenue de Lafayette
Boston, MA 02111-1746
Phone: 1-877-426-8056 (toll-free)
TTY: 1-877-426-2167 (toll-free)
Fax: 1-877-426-2166 (toll-free)
Email: registration@elderhostel.org
Web site: http://www.elderhostel.org
    Elderhostel is a nonprofit organization providing educational travel programs to people over age 55. Their catalog, published 10 times a year, lists thousands of national and international programs.

Elderweb
1305 Chadwick Drive
Normal, IL 61761
Phone: 309-451-3319
Email: info@elderweb.com
Web site: http://www.elderweb.com
    Elderweb is a research Web site for older people, professionals, and families seeking information on elder care and long-term care. Visit Elderweb for news and information on legal, financial, medical, and housing issues for older people and links to other Web sites.

Experience Works (formerly Green Thumb, Inc.)
2200 Clarendon Blvd, Suite 1000
Arlington, VA 22201
Phone: 703-522-7272
866-EXP-WRKS (866-397-9757)
Fax: 703-522-0141
Web site: http://www.experienceworks.org

Experience Works is a national, nonprofit organization helping older, low-income workers train for and find work, particularly in rural areas. One of the services of Experience Works is the Senior Community Service Employment Program, funded by the Department of Labor, it provides training, work experience, educational opportunities, and placement in community service jobs. The Geezer.com Web site has information to help seniors supplement their income, launch new businesses, and market their handcrafted goods.

Generations Online
108 Ralston House
3615 Chestnut Street
Philadelphia, PA 19104
Phone: 215-222-6400
Web site: http://www.generationsonline.com

Generations Online is a nonprofit Web site offering resources for older people unfamiliar with computers or the Internet. Generations Online provides self-training software for senior centers, libraries, retirement homes, and other locations for a one-time fee. The program is free for seniors. Its feature, Memories, links older people with schoolchildren for cultural, experiential, and personal exchanges on aging.

Generations Together (GT)
University of Pittsburgh
121 University Place, Suite 300
Pittsburgh, PA 15260-5907
Phone: 412-648-7150
Fax: 412-648-7446
Web site: http://www.gt.pitt.edu

GT promotes mutually beneficial interaction between young and old through community outreach, education, research, and dissemination of knowledge. GT develops, supports, and studies intergenerational programs and related issues. GT sponsors the annual International Intergenerational Training Institute, which furthers collaboration between generations in workshops and resource development. Contact GT for a catalog of publications.

Gerontological Society of America (GSA)
1030 15th Street, NW, Suite 250
Washington, DC 20005-1503
Phone: 202-842-1275
Fax: 202-842-1150
Email: geron@geron.org
Web site: http://www.geron.org

GSA is a nonprofit professional organization with more than 5000 members in the field of aging. GSA provides researchers, educators, practitioners, and policy makers with opportunities to understand, advance, integrate, and use basic and applied research on aging to improve the quality of life as one ages.

GSA publishes refereed journals (*Journals of Gerontology*—four journals of original research in the biological, medical, behavioral, and social sciences—and *The Gerontologist,* a multidisciplinary applied research journal); a monthly newsletter (*Gerontology News*); and special books and papers.

GSA members affiliate with one of the Society's four sections: Biological Sciences; Clinical Medicine; Behavioral and Social Sciences; or Social Research, Policy and Practice.

GSA organizes a four-day Annual Scientific Meeting that attracts about 3,000 professionals. The Society also conducts special projects such as the Minority Issues in Aging Project. GSA offers a public education program, the Expert Referral Service, a computerized database of researchers by area of expertise, and a program of press releases on current gerontological research.

Gray Panthers (GP)
733 15th Street, NW, Suite 437
Washington, DC 20005
Phone: 1-800-280-5362 (toll-free)
202-737-6637
Fax: 202-737-1160
Email: info@graypanthers.org
Web site: http://www.graypanthers.org

Gray Panthers is a national advocacy organization of activists concentrating on social and economic issues. Local chapters organize intergenerational groups to address issues including universal health care, Medicare, preserving Social Security, affordable housing, and discrimination.

John Douglas French Alzheimer's Foundation
11620 Wilshire Boulevard, Suite 270
Los Angeles, CA 90025
Web site: http://www.jdfaf.org

The Foundation funds scientific research into the causes and cure for Alzheimer's disease. They offer a free publication *Caring for a Person with Memory Loss and Confusion.*

Legal Counsel for the Elderly (LCE)
American Association of Retired Persons (AARP)
601 E Street, NW
Washington, DC 20049
Phone: 202-434-2120
TTY: 202-434-6562
Fax: 202-434-6464
Web site: http://www.aarp.org

LCE, part of AARP, works to expand the availability of legal services to older people and to enhance the quality of those services. The National Volunteer Lawyers Project matches legal cases affecting large numbers of older people with volunteer law firms. The Senior Lawyers Project tests ways retired lawyers can provide free legal services to older people in need. The National Elderlaw Studies Program provides individual home study courses as well as a paralegal certificate from the Department of Agriculture Graduate School. Publications are available.

Legal Services for the Elderly (LSE)
130 West 42nd Street, 17th Floor
New York, NY 10036
Phone: 212-391-0120
Fax: 212-719-1939
Email: hn4923@handsnet.org

LSE is an advisory center for lawyers specializing in legal problems of older people. While LSE does not provide direct services to clients, staff lawyers offer advice and write memoranda and briefs to lawyers who serve older clients on issues including Medicaid, Medicare, Social Security, disability, voluntary and involuntary commitment, age discrimination, pensions, rent-increase exemptions for older people, and nursing home care. A list of publications is available.

Lighthouse National Center for Vision and Aging (LNCVA)
111 East 59th Street
New York, NY 10022
Phone: 1-800-829-0500 (toll-free)
212-821-9200
TTY: 212-821-9713
Fax: 212-821-9705
Email: info@lighthouse.org
Web site: http://www.lighthouse.org

LNCVA provides advocacy, support, information, and resources on vision impairment and blindness. The Lighthouse makes referrals to specialists and resources on visual disability, vision rehabilitation, links to related services, as well as information on eye diseases such as macular degeneration, glaucoma, cataracts, and diabetic retinopathy. Publications and audiovisual materials are available on topics including vision, vision disorders, treatment options, and rehabilitation strategies.

Meals on Wheels Association of America (MOWAA)
1414 Prince Street, Suite 302
Alexandria, VA 22314
Phone: 703-548-5558
Email: mowaa@mowaa.org
Web site: http://www.mowaa.org

MOWAA is a national, nonprofit organization providing training and grants to programs that provide food to older people, and those who are frail, disabled, at-risk, or homebound.

Medicare Rights Center (MRC)
1460 Broadway, 11th Floor
New York, NY 10036
Phone: 212-869-3850
800-333-4114
Fax: 212-869-3532
Email: info@medicarerights.org
Web site: http://www.medicarerights.org

MRC is the largest independent source of Medicare information and assistance in the United States. Founded in 1989, MRC helps older adults and people with disabilities get high-quality, affordable health care. The organization provides telephone hotline services to individuals who need answers to Medicare questions or help securing coverage and getting the health care they need. Their education department works to teach people with Medicare and those who counsel them—health care providers, social service workers, family members, and others—about Medicare benefits and rights. MRC offers a wide range of useful, practical publications to help consumers understand Medicare. A list of publications is available on their Web site.

National Academy of Elder Law Attorneys, Inc. (NAELA)
1604 North Country Club Road
Tucson, AZ 85716
Phone: 520-881-4005
Fax: 520-325-7925
Web site: http://www.naela.org
NAELA is a nonprofit association assisting lawyers, bar associations, and others who work with older people and their families. NAELA provides information on lawyers specializing in issues pertinent to older people, resources to legal information, assistance, and education. A list of publications is available.

National Academy on an Aging Society
1030 15th Street, NW, Suite 250
Washington, DC 20005
Phone: 202-408-3375 |
Fax: 202-842-1150 (fax)
info@agingsociety.org
Web site: agingsociety/org.
The National Academy on an Aging Society is the policy institute of The Gerontological Society of America. As a non-partisan public policy institute, the Academy conducts research on issues related to population aging and provides information to the public, the press, policymakers, and the academic community. The Academy publishes reports and papers on Social Security, Medicare and Medicaid, the federal budget and related topics; the quarterly *Public Policy and Aging Report,* and Fact Sheets on health literacy, state demographics, Medicare and Medicaid, long-term care and related topics.

National Asian Pacific Center on Aging (NAPCA)
PO Box 21668
Seattle, WA 98101
Phone: 206-624-1221
Fax: 206-624-1023
Email: web@napca.org
Web site: http://www.napca.org
NAPCA is a nonprofit agency dedicated to serving aging Asian and Pacific Islanders. It offers employment programs, multilingual community forums and health care education. The Center works with elders, policy makers, program administrators, and community leaders. Publications include a newsletter and translated health care materials.

National Association for Hispanic Elderly (Asociación Nacional Por Personas Mayores)
234 East Colorado Boulevard, Suite 300
Pasadena, CA 91101
Phone: 626-564-1988
Fax: 626-564-2659
The Association is a national, private, nonprofit organization providing a variety of services for older Hispanic people. Resources include a national Hispanic research center, research and consultation for organizations seeking to reach older Spanish-speaking people, and

dissemination of written and audiovisual materials in English and Spanish. The Association administers Project AYUDA, a program providing employment counseling and placement services.

National Association for Home Care (NAHC)
228 7th Street, SE
Washington, DC 20003
Phone: 202-547-7424
Fax: 202-547-3540
Web site: http://www.nahc.org

NAHC promotes hospice and home care, sets standards of care, and conducts research on aging, health, and health care policy. Association publications include *How to Choose a Home Care Provider* and other free consumer guides on home care and hospice care.

National Association of Area Agencies on Aging (N4A)
1730 Rhone Island Ave, NW, Suite 1200
Washington, DC 20036
Phone: 1-800-677-1116 (toll-free) (Eldercare Locator)
202-872-0888
Fax: 202-872-0057
Web site: http://www.n4a.org

N4A is the umbrella organization for the 655 area agencies on aging (AAAs) and more than 230 Native American aging programs in the U.S. Through its presence in Washington, DC, N4A advocates on behalf of the local aging agencies to ensure that needed resources and support services are available to older Americans. The fundamental mission of the AAAs and Title VI programs is to provide services that make it possible for older individuals to remain in their home, thereby preserving their independence and dignity. These agencies coordinate and support a wide range of home- and community-based services, including information and referral, home-delivered and congregate meals, transportation, employment services, senior centers, adult day care and a long-term care ombudsman program.

National Association of Nutrition and Aging Service Programs (NANASP)
1612 K Street, NW Suite 400
Washington, DC 20006
Phone: 202-682-6899
Fax: 202-223-2099
Web site: http://www.nanasp.org

NANASP, a membership organization, supports a broad range of nutrition and related services for community-dwelling older people by training nutrition providers and advocating for older people. Publications include a *Legislative Action Manual* and *The Washington Bulletin*.

National Association of Professional Geriatric Care Managers (NAPGCM)
1604 North Country Club Road
Tucson, AZ 85716-3102
Phone: 520-881-8008
Fax: 520-325-7925
Email: info@caremanager.org
Web site: http://www.caremanager.org

NAPGCM is a nonprofit organization representing the interests of elder care practitioners and advocating for older peoples' independence, autonomy, and quality of health care. Geriatric care managers are professionals, such as social workers, counselors, nurses, or gerontologists who specialize in assisting older people and their families to attain the highest quality of life given their circumstances. NAPGCM has 1,500 members. Their Web site has a geriatric care locator, "Find a Geriatric Manager," which lists practitioners by local area. Publications are available through the Web site.

National Association of State Units on Aging (NASUA)
1225 I Street, NW, Suite 725
Washington, DC 20005
Phone: 202-898-2578
Fax: 202-898-2583
Email: info@nasua.org
Web site: http://www.nasua.org
NASUA is a national nonprofit membership organization comprised of the 57 state and territorial government agencies on aging. NASUA is the voice at the national level through which the state agencies on aging join together to promote social policy in the public and private sectors responsive to the challenges and opportunities of an aging America. The organization has four key organizational components: Public Policy, Advancement of State Community Service Programs, State Action on Elder Rights, and State Promotion of Productive Aging. NASUA makes available a number of publications free of charge. However, most of them were written in the 1990s.

National Bar Association (NBA)
1225 11th Street, NW
Washington, DC 20001
Phone: 202-842-3900
Fax: 202-289-6170
Web site: http://www.nationalbar.org
NBA uses its national membership, statewide minority bar programs, minority law students, minority bar group alliances, and private attorneys, to form links with community groups providing legal assistance to low-income, minority older people. Publications include *Saving the Home* and *Defending against Fraud and Scams*, a resource book on second mortgages.

National Caucus and Center on Black Aged, Inc. (NCBA)
1220 L Street, NW, Suite 800
Washington, DC 20005
Phone: 202-637-8400
Fax: 202-347-0895
Web site: http://www.ncba-aged.org
NCBA is a national, nonprofit organization providing health and social service information, advocacy, and assistance to African Americans and low-income older people. Contact NCBA for information on its local chapters and programs including senior employment and training, housing, health promotion, and advocacy. Publications include a support-service reference guide, job placement guides, and a *Profile of Black Elderly*.

National Center on Elder Abuse (NCEA)
1201 15th Street, NW, Suite 350
Washington, DC 20005-2800
Phone: 202-898-2586
Fax: 202-898-2583
Email: NCEA@nasua.org
Web site: http://www.elderabusecenter.org/
   NCEA is operated jointly by the National Association of State Units on Aging, the National Committee for the Prevention of Elder Abuse, and the University of Delaware to disseminate information about abuse and neglect of older people. NCEA operates the Clearinghouse on Abuse and Neglect of the Elderly and can provide referrals to agencies and specialists. Publications are available on prevention of abuse, neglect, and state regulations.

National Citizen's Coalition for Nursing Home Reform (NCCNHR)
1424 16th Street, NW, Suite 202
Washington, DC 20036-2211
Phone: 202-332-2275
Fax: 202-332-2949
Web site: http://www.nccnhr.org
   NCCNHR provides information on nursing home reform, promotes quality standards, and works to empower nursing home residents. The organization provides information and leadership on federal and state regulatory and legislative policy development and models and strategies to improve care and life for residents of nursing homes and other long term care facilities. Ongoing work addresses issues such as:

 • Inadequate staffing in nursing homes, particularly all levels of nursing staff

 • Poor working conditions, salaries and benefits for long-term care workers

 • Maintenance of residents' rights and empowerment of residents

 • Minimizing the use of physical and chemical restraints.

NCCNHR publishes materials for consumers and professionals on nursing homes and long-term care.

National Committee to Preserve Social Security and Medicare (NCPSSM)
10 G Street, NE, Suite 600
Washington, DC 20002
Phone: 1-800-966-1935 (toll-free)
202-216-0420
Web site: http://www.ncpssm.org
   NCPSSM, an advocacy and education membership organization, works to protect and enhance federal programs vital to seniors' health and economic well-being. Free informational brochures are available.

National Council on Aging, Inc. (NCOA)
409 3rd Street, SW, Suite 200
Washington, DC 20024
Phone: 202-479-1200
Fax: 202-479-0735

Email: info@ncoa.org
Web sites: http://www.ncoa.org; www.benefitscheckup.org

NCOA is a national network of organizations and individuals dedicated to improving the health and independence of older persons; increasing their continuing contributions to communities, society and future generations; and building caring communities. Its 3,800 members include senior centers, adult day service centers, area agencies on aging, faith congregations, senior housing facilities, employment services, and other consumer organizations. NCOA also includes a voluntary network of more than 14,000 leaders from academia, business and labor who support our mission and work. The organization develops decision support tools, such as BenefitsCheckUp® and the Long-Term Care Counselor, enabling consumers to make optimal decisions and maximize all available resources and opportunities.

The NCOA BenefitsCheckUp, www.benefitscheckup.org, is a comprehensive online service to screen for federal, state and some local private and public benefits for older adults (ages 55 and over). It contains over 1,150 different programs from all fifty states (including the District of Columbia). On average there are 50 to 70 programs available to individuals per state. Information includes detailed descriptions of the programs, local contacts for additional information (typically the addresses and phone numbers of where to apply for the programs), and materials to help successfully apply for each program.

NCOA also offers specialized publications for members and aging-field professionals and general-interest publications for seniors. Free downloads of research reports are also available.

National Family Caregivers Association (NFCA)
10400 Connecticut Avenue, #500
Kensington, MD 20895-3944
Phone: 1-800-896-3650 (toll-free)
Fax: 301-942-2302
Email: info@nfcacares.org
Web site: http://www.nfcacares.org

NFCA is a grassroots organization providing advocacy, support, and information for family members who care for chronically ill, older, or disabled relatives. There is no charge for family members to be on the mailing list and to receive the newsletter, *Take Care!*

National Gerontological Nursing Association (NGNA)
7794 Grow Drive
Pensacola, FL 32514
Phone: 1-800-723-0560 (toll-free)
850-473-1174
Fax: 850-484-8762
Email: ngna@puetzamc.com
Web site: http://www.ngna.org

NGNA, an organization of nurses specializing in care of older adults, informs the public on health issues affecting older people, supports education for nurses and other health care practitioners, and provides a forum to discuss topics such as nutrition in long-term care facilities and elder law for nurses. NGNA offers information on gerontological nursing and conducts nursing research related to older people.

National Hispanic Council on Aging (NHCoA)
2713 Ontario Road, NW
Washington, DC 20009
Phone: 202-265-1288
Fax: 202-745-2522
Email: nhcoa@worldnet.att.net
Web site: http://www.nhcoa.org
   NHCoA is a national organization providing advocacy, education, and information for older Hispanic people. The organization provides facts and resources on health, employment, housing, strengthening families, and building communities, as well as referrals to local Council chapters. Publications in English and Spanish are available.

National Indian Council on Aging (NICOA)
10501 Montgomery Boulevard, NE, Suite 210
Albuquerque, NM 87111-3846
Phone: 505-292-2001
Fax: 505-292-1922
Web site: http://www.nicoa.org
   NICOA provides services, advocacy, and information on aging issues for older American Indian and Alaska Native people. The organization has a clearinghouse for issues affecting older Indian people. Publications are available, including the newsletter *Elder Voices*.

National Interfaith Coalition on Aging (NICA)
National Council on Aging (NCOA)
409 3rd Street, SW, Suite 200
Washington, DC 20024
Phone: 1-800-424-9046 (toll-free)
202-479-1200
Fax: 202-479-0735
Web site: http://www.ncoa.org
   The Coalition, a constituent unit of NCOA, consists of individuals and organizations of various faiths concerned with issues of religion, spirituality, and aging. NICA provides networking opportunities and educational programs.

National Long-Term Care Ombudsman Resource Center (NLTCORC)
National Citizens' Coalition for Nursing Home Reform (NCCNHR)
1424 16th Street, NW, Suite 202
Washington, DC 20036
Phone: 202-332-2275
Fax: 202-332-2949
Email: ombudcenter@nccnhr.org
Web site: http://www.nccnhr.org
   NLTCORC is operated by the NCCNHR in collaboration with the National Association of State Units on Aging. The Center supports groups under federal mandate to identify and resolve residents' problems at long-term care facilities. Contact the Center for information and publications on nursing home reform and adult care.

National Long-Term Care Resource Center (NLTCRC)
Division of Health Services, Research and Policy
University of Minnesota School of Public Health
Mayo Mailcode 729
420 Delaware Street, SE
Minneapolis, MN 55455
Phone: 612-624-5171
Email: ihsr@umn.edu
Web site: http://www.hsr.umn.edu
   The Center assists State and Area Agencies on Aging and other community-based service agencies to monitor, develop, and refine community long-term care systems through legal reform. NLTCRC provides information on long-term health care, rehabilitation and acute care reform, ethics, and quality of life issues in nursing homes. A list of publications is available.

National Osteoporosis Foundation (NOF)
1232 22nd Street, NW
Washington, DC 20037-1292
Phone: 202-223-2226
Web site: http://www.nof.org
   NOF is a nonprofit, voluntary health organization dedicated to promoting lifelong bone health to reduce the widespread prevalence of osteoporosis and related fractures. NOF works to find a cure for osteoporosis through research, education, and advocacy. The Foundation provides general information on osteoporosis; its quarterly newsletter and booklets are available through membership.

National Policy and Resource Center on Nutrition and Aging
Department of Dietetics and Nutrition
Florida International University (FIU)
University Park, OE200
Miami, FL 33199
Phone: 305-348-1517
Fax: 305-348-1518
Email: nutreldr@fiu.edu
Web site: http://www.fiu.edu/~nutreldr
   The FIU Center, funded primarily by the Administration on Aging, works to reduce malnutrition and promotes good nutritional practices among older adults nationwide. The Center provides information dissemination, training and technical assistance, and policy analysis.

National Policy and Resource Center on Women and Aging (NPRCWA)
National Center on Women & Aging
The Heller School for Social Policy and Management, MS 035
Brandeis University
Waltham, MA 02454-9110
Phone: 1-800-929-1995 (toll-free)
781-736-3866
Fax: 781-736-3865

Email: NATWOMCTR@brandeis.edu
Web site: http://www.brandeis.edu/heller/national/
   NPRCWA focuses on older women's issues and provides policy analysis, research, and assistance to the network of Administration on Aging–funded State and Area Agencies on Aging. The Center provides information and publications on women's health, caregiving, income security, and housing as well as prevention of crime and violence toward older women.

National Rehabilitation Information Center (NARIC)
4200 Forbes Boulevard, Suite 202
Lanham, MD 20706
Phone: 1-800-346-2742 (toll-free)
301- 459-5900
TTY: 301- 459-5984
Email: naricinfo@heitechservices.com
Web site: http://www.naric.com
   NARIC, funded by the Department of Education, provides information on rehabilitation of people with physical or mental disabilities. Contact NARIC for database searches on all types of physical and mental disabilities, as well as referrals to local and national facilities and organizations. All of NARIC's database information is available online, free.

National Resource Center: Diversity and Long-Term Care (NRCDLTC)
Schneider Institute for Health Policy
Heller School for Social Policy and Management, Brandeis University
415 South Street, Waltham, MA 02454-9110
Phone: 781-736-3900
TTY/TDD: 781-736-3009
Web site: http://www.sihp.brandeis.edu
   NRCDLTC, a partnership between Brandeis University and San Diego State University, provides information on methods, resources, systems, and services for caring for older people. The Center provides referrals to health policy resources and information on issues of diversity in aging, including disabilities, race, ethnicity, gender, generations, and chronic diseases. A list of publications is available on request.

National Resource Center on Native American Aging (NRCNAA)
PO Box 9037
Grand Forks, ND 58202-9037
Phone: 1-800-896-7628 (toll-free)
701-777-3437
Fax: 701-777-6779
Web site: http://www.med.und.nodak.edu/depts/rural//nrcnaa/
   The Resource Center, funded by the Administration on Aging, provides support, advocacy, and information for older Native Americans, including American Indians, Alaska Natives, and Native Hawaiians. Contact the Center for legal information and references, geriatric leadership training, cultural awareness, and a variety of publications.

National Senior Citizens Education and Research Center (NSCERC)
8403 Colesville Road, Suite 1200
Silver Spring, MD 20910
Phone: 301-578-8900

Email: contact@ssa-i.org
Web site: http://www.seniorserviceamerica.org/
  NSCERC is a nonprofit organization providing employment opportunities, conducting research programs and workshops, and publishing its research findings.

National Senior Citizens Law Center (NSCLC)
1101 14th Street, NW, Suite 400
Washington, DC 20005
Phone: 202-289-6976
Fax: 202-289-7224
Web site: http://www.nsclc.org
  NSCLC offers assistance to Legal Aid Offices and private lawyers working on behalf of low-income older and disabled people. The Center does not accept individual clients but acts as a clearinghouse of information on legal problems such as age discrimination, Social Security, pension plans, Medicaid, Medicare, nursing homes, and protective services.

Native Elder Health Care Resource Center (NEHCRC)
University of Colorado Health Sciences Center
Campus Box A011-13
4455 East 12 Avenue
Denver, CO 80220
Phone: 303-315-9228
Fax: 303-315-9579
Email: dawn.wright@uchsc.edu
Web site: http://www.uchsc.edu/sm/nehcrc
  NEHCRC promotes the health of older Native people, including Alaska Natives and Native Hawaiians by increasing cultural competence among health care professionals. The Center focuses on four target areas: determining health status, improving medical standards, increasing access to care, and mobilizing community resources.

Older Women's League (OWL)
666 11th Street, NW, Suite 700
Washington, DC 20001
Phone: 1-800-TAKE-OWL (825-3695) (toll-free)
1-800-863-1539 (toll-free) (PowerLine)
202-783-6686
202-783-6689 (PowerLine)
Fax: 202-638-2356
Email: owlinfo@owl-national.org
Web site: http://www.owl-national.org
  OWL is a national organization advocating for the special concerns of older women. OWL helped develop the Campaign for Women's Health and the Women's Pension Policy Consortium. Contact OWL's 24-hour PowerLine for information about legal and political activity related to health care, access to housing, economic security, individual rights, and violence against women and older people. OWL newsletters are available.

Pension Rights Center (PRC)
1140 19th Street, NW, Suite 602
Washington, DC 20036

Phone: 202-296-3776
Fax: 202-833-2472
Email: pnsnrights@aol.com
Web site: http://www.pensionrights.org

PRC's Legal Outreach Program advocates for the pension rights of workers, retirees, and their families. The organizations provide referrals to pension attorneys or for publications on pension law, divorce, federal retirement plans, self-help guides on pension problems, or pension plan handbooks. Spanish language resources are also available.

Project Aliento
National Association for Hispanic Elderly (Asociación Nacional Pro Personas Mayores)
1452 West Temple Street, Suite 100
Los Angeles, CA 90026
Phone: 213-487-1922
Fax: 213-202-5905

Project Aliento works to make the Administration on Aging–funded network of State and Area Agencies on Aging accessible to older Hispanic people and their families. The organization provides information, publications, and videos about community care and in-home support issues, as well as links to the formal aging network. Publications are available in English and Spanish.

Senior Job Bank
PO Box 30064
Savannah, GA 31410
Email: Comment@SeniorJobBank.org
Web site: http://www.seniorjobbank.org

Senior Job Bank is an online resource that provides free job information and resources for members. The organization provides listings for occasional, part-time, flexible, temporary, or full-time jobs for older people.

SeniorNet (SN)
121 Second Street, 7th Floor
San Francisco, CA 94105
Phone: 415-495-4990
Fax: 415-495-3999
Web site: http://www.seniornet.org

SeniorNet is a nonprofit, educational organization that provides information and services to help older people become computer literate. Locally funded SN teaching sites offer introductory computer classes on various topics, providing older people with discounts on computer hardware, software, and publications. Members can access SN from any online computer and order publications on buying and using computers.

SPRY Foundation
10 G Street, NE, Suite 600
Washington, DC 20002
Phone: 202-216-0401
Fax: 202-216-0779
Email: info@spry.org
Web site: http://www.spry.org

SPRY—Setting Priorities for Retirement Years—is a nonprofit foundation that develops research and education programs to help older adults plan for a healthy and financially secure future. The Web site links consumers to national health resources.

United Seniors Health Council (USHC)
409 3rd Street, NW, Suite 200
Washington, DC 20024
Phone: 1-800-637-2604 (toll-free) (orders only)
202-479-6973
Fax: 202-479-6660
Email: info@unitedseniorshealth.org
Web site: www.unitedseniorshealth.org/
USHC is a nonprofit organization dedicated to helping older consumers, caregivers, and professionals. The Council produces publications on topics such as financial planning, managed care, and long-term care insurance. The Council pioneered a Health Insurance Counseling Program, which helps consumers understand their many insurance options. Its Eldergames program is a comprehensive series of materials designed to stimulate the imagination and memories of older people.

GOVERNMENT AGENCIES

Administration on Aging (AoA)
Department of Health and Human Services (DHHS)
330 Independence Avenue, SW
Washington, DC 20201
Public Inquiries: 202-619-0724
202-619-7501
Eldercare Locator: 1-800-677-1116 (toll-free)
Fax: 202-260-1012
E-mail: AoAInfo@aoa.gov
Web site: http://www.aoa.gov
AoA is the federal focal point and advocate agency for older persons and their concerns. The agency is one of the nation's largest providers of home- and community-based care for older persons and their caregivers. Created in 1965 with the passage of the Older Americans Act (OAA), AoA is part of a federal, state, tribal and local partnership called the National Network on Aging. The network, serving about 7 million older persons and their caregivers, consists of 56 State Units on Aging; 655 Area Agencies on Aging; 233 Tribal and Native organizations; two organizations that serve Native Hawaiians; 29,000 service providers; and thousands of volunteers. These organizations provide assistance and services to older individuals and their families in urban, suburban, and rural areas throughout the United States.

While all older Americans may receive services, the OAA targets those older individuals who are in greatest economic and social need: the poor, the isolated, and those elders disadvantaged by social or health disparities.

Access to services, especially for those who need them the most, has been a critical priority of AoA and the National Aging Services Network. In the 2001 fiscal year AoA provided over 15 million units of information and assistance and outreach to older Americans, and case management services were provided to over 433,000 older people.

Services funded by the OAA

There are six core services funded by the OAA including:

Supportive services, which enable communities to provide rides to medical appointments, and grocery and drug stores. Supportive services provide handyman, chore and personal care services so that older persons can stay in their homes. These services extend to community services such as adult day care and information and assistance as well.

Nutrition services, which include more than meals. Since its creation, the Older Americans Act Nutrition Program has provided nearly 6 billion meals for at-risk older persons. Each day in communities across America, senior citizens come together in senior centers or other group settings to share a meal, as well as comradery and friendship. Nutrition services also provide nutrition education, health screenings, and counseling at senior centers. Homebound seniors are able to remain in their homes largely because of the daily delivery of a hot meal, sometimes by a senior volunteer who is their only visitor. March 2002, marked the 30th anniversary of the OAA Nutrition Program, and AoA will be celebrating this successful community-based service throughout the year.

Preventive health services, which educate and enable older persons to make healthy lifestyle choices. Many chronic diseases can be prevented through healthy lifestyles, physical activity, appropriate diet and nutrition, smoking cessation, active and meaningful social engagement, and regular screenings. The ultimate goal of the OAA health promotion and disease prevention services is to increase the quality and years of healthy life.

The National Family Caregiver Support Program (NFCSP), which was funded for the first time in 2000, is a significant addition to the OAA. It was created to help the millions of people who provide the primary care for spouses, parents, older relatives and friends. The program includes information to caregivers about available services; assistance to caregivers in gaining access to services; individual counseling, organization of support groups and caregiver training to assist caregivers in making decisions and solving problems relating to their caregiving roles; and supplemental services to complement care provided by caregivers.

The program also recognizes the needs of grandparents caring for grandchildren and for caregivers of those 18 and under with mental retardation or developmental difficulties and the diverse needs of Native Americans.

Services that protect the rights of vulnerable older persons, which are designed to empower older persons and their family members to detect and prevent elder abuse and consumer fraud as well as to enhance the physical, mental, emotional and financial well-being of America's elderly. These services include, for example, pension counseling programs that help older Americans access their pensions and make informed insurance and health care choices; long-term care ombudsman programs that serve to investigate and resolve complaints made by or for residents of nursing, board and care, and similar adult homes. AoA supports the training of thousands of paid and volunteer long-term care ombudsmen, insurance counselors, and other professionals who assist with reporting waste, fraud, and abuse in nursing homes and other settings; and senior Medicare patrol projects, which operate in 47 states, plus the District of Columbia and Puerto Rico. AoA awards grants to state units on aging, area agencies on aging, and community organizations to train senior volunteers how to educate older Americans to take a more active role in monitoring and understanding their health care.

Services to Native Americans, which include nutrition and supportive services designed to meet the unique cultural and social traditions of tribal and native organizations and organizations serving Native Hawaiians. Native American elders are among the most disadvantaged groups in the country.

Eldercare Locator
Phone: 1-800-677-1116 (toll-free)
Fax: 202-296-8134
Funded by the Administration on Aging, the Eldercare Locator is a nationwide, directory assistance service helping older people and caregivers locate local support and resources for older Americans.

Information for Professionals
AoA also provides professionals and others interested in aging issues with statistical and related information including *A Profile of Older Americans*, brochure with the latest key statistics on older Americans; online links to statistical data on the aging; and statistics on minority aging.

AoA's Regional Offices
Region I: CT, MA, ME, NH, RI, VT
Regional Administrator
John F. Kennedy Bldg., Rm. 2075
Boston, MA 02203
Phone: 617-565-1158
Fax: 617-565-4511

Regions II & III: NY, NJ, PR, VI, DC, DE, MD, PA, VA, WV
Regional Administrator
26 Federal Plaza, Rm. 38-102
New York NY 10278
Phone: 212-264-2976
Fax: 212-264-0114

Region IV: AL, FL, GA, KY, MS, NC, SC, TN
Regional Administrator
Atlanta Federal Center
61 Forsyth Street, SW, Suite 5M69
Atlanta, GA 30303-8909
Phone: 404-562-7600
Fax: 404-562-7598

Region V: IL, IN, MI, MN, OH, WI
Regional Administrator
233 N. Michigan Ave., Suite 790
Chicago, IL 60601-5519
Phone: 312-353-3141
Fax: 312-886-8533

Region VI: AR, LA, OK, NM, TX
Regional Administrator
1301 Young Street, Rm. 736
Dallas, TX 75201
Phone: 214-767-2971
Fax: 214-767-2951

Region VII: IA, KS, MO, NE
Regional Administrator
601 East 12th Street, Rm. 1731
Kansas City, MO 64106
Phone: 816-426-3511
Fax: 816-426-3516

Region VIII: CO, MT, ND, SD, UT, WY
Regional Administrator
1961 Stout Street, Rm. 1022
Federal Office Bldg.
Denver, CO 80294-3538
Phone: 303-844-2951
Fax: 303-844-2943

Region IX: AS, AZ, CA, CNMI, GU, HI, NV
Regional Administrator
50 United Nations Plaza, Rm. 455
San Francisco, CA 94102
Phone: 415-437-8780
Fax: 415-437-8782

Region X: AK, ID, OR, WA
Regional Administrator
Blanchard Plaza, MS-RX-33
2201 Sixth Ave., Rm. 1202
Seattle, WA 98121-1828
Phone: 206-615-2298
Fax: 206-615-2305

State Agencies on Aging
Alabama
Alabama Department of Senior Services (Off Site)
770 Washington Avenue
RSA Plaza, Suite 470
Montgomery, AL 36130
Phone: 334-242-5743
Fax: 334-242-5594

Alaska
Division of Senior Services
Department of Administration
PO Box 110209
Juneau, AK 99811-0209
Phone: 907-465-4879
Fax: 907-465-4716

Arizona
Aging and Adult Administration Department of Economic Security
1789 West Jefferson Street, #950A
Phoenix, AZ 85007
Phone: 602-542-4446
Fax: 602-542-6575

Arkansas
Division Aging and Adult Services
Arkansas Dept of Human Services
PO Box 1437, Slot S-530
1417 Donaghey Plaza South
Little Rock, AR 72203-1437
Phone: 501-682-2441
Fax: 501-682-8155

California
California Department of Aging
1600 K Street
Sacramento, CA 95814
Phone: 916-322-5290
Fax: 916-324-1903

Colorado
Division of Aging and Adult Services
Department of Human Services
1575 Sherman Street, Ground Floor
Denver, CO 80203-1714
Phone: 303-866-2636
Fax: 303-866-2696

Connecticut
Director of Elderly Services
Division of Elderly, Community and Social Work Services
Department of Social Services
25 Sigourney Street, 10th floor
Hartford, CT 06106-5033
Phone: 860-424-5277
Fax: 860-424-5301 or if down (860)-424-4966

Delaware
Division of Services for Aging & Adults with Physical Disabilities
Department of Health & Social Services
1901 North DuPont Highway
New Castle, DE 19720
Phone: 302-577-4791
Fax: 302-577-4793

District of Columbia
District of Columbia Office on Aging
One Judiciary Square, 9th Floor
441 Fourth Street, NW
Washington, DC 20001
Phone: 202-724-5622
Fax: 202-724-4979

Florida
Department of Elder Affairs
Building B, Suite 152
4040 Esplanade Way

Tallahassee, FL 32399-7000
Phone: 850-414-2000
Fax: 850-414-2004
E-mail: information@elderaffairs.org

Georgia
Division of Aging Services
Department of Human Resources
2 Peachtree Street, NE, 9th Floor
Atlanta, GA 30303-3142
Phone: 404-657-5258
Fax: 404-657-5285
E-mail: dhrconstituentservices@dhr.state.ga.us

Guam
Division of Senior Citizens
Department of Public Health & Social Services
PO Box 2816
Agana, Guam 96910
Phone: 011-671-475-0263
Fax: 671-477-2930

Hawaii
Executive Office on Aging
#1 Capitol District
250 South Hotel Street, Ste 109
Honolulu, HI 96813-2831
Phone: 808-586-0100
Fax: 808-586-0185

Idaho
Idaho Commission on Aging
PO Box 83720
Boise, ID 83720-0007
Phone: 208-334-3833
Fax: 208-334-3033

Illinois
Department on Aging
421 East Capitol Avenue
Springfield, IL 62701
Phone: 217-785-2870
Fax: 217-785-4477

Indiana
Bureau of Aging/In Home Services
402 W. Washington Street
PO Box 7083
Indianapolis, IN 46207-7083
Phone: 317-232-7020
Fax: 317-232-7867

Iowa
Iowa Department of Elder Affairs
Clemens Building, 3rd Floor
200 Tenth Street
Des Moines, IA 50309-3609
Phone: 515-242-3333
Fax: 515-242-3300

Kansas
Department on Aging
New England Building
503 South Kansas
Topeka, KS 66603-3404
Phone: 785-296-5222
Fax: 785-296-0256

Kentucky
Office of Aging Services
Cabinet for Families and Children
Commonwealth of Kentucky
275 East Main Street
Frankfort, KY 40621
Phone: 502-564-6930
Fax: 502-564-4595

Louisiana
Governor's Office of Elderly Affairs
PO Box 80374
Baton Rouge, LA 70898-0374
Phone: 225-342-7100
Fax: 225-342-7133

Maine
Bureau of Elder and Adult Services
Department of Human Services
35 Anthony Avenue
State House, Station #11
Augusta, ME 04333
Phone: 207-624-5335
Fax: 624-5361

Mariana Islands
CNMI Office on Aging, DC&CA
PO Box 2178
Saipan, MP 96950
Phone: 011-671-734-4361
Fax: 011-670-233-1327

Maryland
Maryland Department of Aging
State Office Building, Room 1007

301 West Preston Street
Baltimore, MD 21201-2374
Phone: 410-767-1100
Fax: 410-333-7943

Massachusetts
Executive Office of Elder Affairs
1 Ashburton Place, 5th floor
Boston, MA 02108
Phone: 617-222-7451
Fax: 617-727-6944

Michigan
Office of Services to the Aging
PO Box 30676
7109 West Saginaw 48917
Lansing, MI 48909-8176
Phone: 517-373-8230
Fax: 517-373-4092

Minnesota
Minnesota Board on Aging
444 Lafayette Road
Street Paul, MN 55155-3843
Phone: 6510296-2770
TTY: 800-627-3529
Fax: 651-297-7855

Mississippi
Division of Aging and Adult Services
750 N. State Street
Jackson, MS 39202
Phone: 601-359-4925
Fax: 601-359-9664

Missouri
Director of Division of Senior Services
Department of Health & Senior Services
PO Box 570
615 Howerton Court
Jefferson City, MO 65102-0570
Phone: 573-751-3082
Fax: 573-751-8687

Montana
Senior and Long Term Care Division
Department of Public Health & Human Services
PO Box 4210
111 Sanders, Room 211
Helena, MT 59620
Phone: 406-444-4077
Fax: 406-444-7743

Nebraska
Division of Aging Services
Dept of Health & Human Services
PO Box 95044
301 Centennial Mall–South
Lincoln, NE 68509
Phone: 402-471-2307
Fax: 402-471-4619

Nevada
Division for Aging Services
Department of Human Resources
3416 Goni Road, Building D-132
Carson City, NV 89706
Phone: 775-687-4210
Fax: 775-687-4264

New Hampshire
Division of Elderly and Adult Services
State Office Park South
129 Pleasant Street, Brown Bldg. #1
Concord, NH 03301
Phone: 603-271-4680
Fax: 603-271-4643

New Jersey
Division of Aging & Community Services
Division of Senior Affairs
Department of Health & Senior Services
PO Box 807
Trenton, NJ 08625-0807
Phone: 609-943-3345
Fax: 609-943-3343

New Mexico
State Agency on Aging
La Villa Rivera Building
228 East Palace Avenue, Ground Floor
Santa Fe, NM 87501
Phone: 505-827-7640
Fax: 505-827-7649

New York
Office for the Aging
Two Empire State Plaza
Albany, NY 12223-1251
Phone: 518-474-7012
Fax: 518-474-1398

North Carolina
Department of Health and Human Services
Division of Aging

2101 Mail Service Center
Raleigh, NC 27699-2101
Phone: 919-733-3983
Fax: 919-733-0443

North Dakota
Department of Human Services
Aging Services Division
600 South 2nd Street, Suite 1C
Bismarck, ND 58504
Phone 701-328-891
800-451-8693
TDD: 701-328-8968
Fax: 701-328-8989

North Mariana Islands
Office on Aging
PO Box 2178
Saipan, MP 96950
011-671-734-4361
Fax: 011-670-233-1327

Ohio
Ohio Department of Aging
50 West Broad Street, 9th Floor
Columbus, OH 43215-5928
Phone: 614-466-5500
Fax: 614-466-5741

Oklahoma
Aging Services Division
Department of Human Services
PO Box 25352
312 NNE 28th Street
Oklahoma City, OK 73125
Phone: 405-521-2281 or 521-2327
Fax: 405-521-2086

Oregon
Senior & Disabled Services Division
500 Summer Street, NE, E02
Salem, OR 97301-1073
Phone: 503-945-5811
Fax: 503-373-7823

Pennsylvania
Department of Aging
Forum Place
555 Walnut Street, 5th Floor
Harrisburg, PA 17101-1919
Phone: 717-783-1550
Fax: 717-772-3382

Puerto Rico
Commonwealth of Puerto Rico
Governor's Office of Elderly Affairs
Call Box 50063
Old San Juan Station, PR 00902
Phone: 787-721-5710, 721-4560, 721-6121
Fax: 787-721-6510

Rhode Island
Department of Elderly Affairs
Benjamin Rush Bldg., #55, 2nd Floor
35 Howard Ave.
Cranston, RI 02920
Phone: 401-462-0500
Fax: 401-462-0503

Samoa (American)
Territorial Administration on Aging
American Samoa Government
Pago Pago, American Samoa 96799
Phone: 011-684-633-1251-1252
Fax: 684-633-2533

South Carolina
Department of Health & Human Services
PO Box 8206
1801 Main Street
Columbia, SC 29202-8206
Phone: 803-898-2513
Fax: 803-898-4515

South Dakota
Office of Adult Services and Aging
700 Governors Drive
Pierre, SD 57501-2291
Phone: 605-773-3656
Fax: 605-773-6834

Tennessee
Commission on Aging and Disability
Andrew Jackson Building 9th floor
500 Deaderick Street
Nashville, Tennessee 37243-0860
Phone: 615-741-2056
Fax: 615-741-3309

Texas
Texas Department on Aging
4900 North Lamar, 4th Floor
Austin, TX 78751-2316
Phone: 512-424-6840
Fax: 512-424-6890

Utah
Division of Aging & Adult Services
Box 45500
120 North 200 West
Salt Lake City, UT 84145-0500
Phone: 801-538-3910
Fax: 801-538-4395

Vermont
Vermont Department of Aging and Disabilities
Waterbury Complex
103 South Main Street
Waterbury, VT 05671-2301
Phone: 802-241-2400
Fax: 802-241-2325

Virgin Islands
Senior Citizen Affairs
Department of Human Services
#19 Estate Diamond Fredericksted
Street Croix, VI 00840
Phone: 340-692-5950
Fax: 340-692-2062

Virginia
Virginia Department for the Aging
1600 Forest Avenue, Suite 102
Richmond, VA 23229
Phone: 804-662-9333
Fax: 804-662-9354

Washington
Aging and Adult Services Administration
Department of Social & Health Services
PO Box 45050
Olympia, WA 98504-5050
Phone: 360-725-2310
In-state only: 800-422-3263
Fax: 360-438-8633
E-mail: askdshs@dshs.wa.gov

West Virginia
West Virginia Bureau of Senior Services
Holly Grove, Building 10
1900 Kanawha Boulevard East
Charleston, WV 25305
Phone: 304-558-3317
Fax: 304-558-5699
E-mail: info@boss.state.wv.us

Wisconsin
Bureau of Aging and Long Term Care Resources
Department of Health and Family Services

1 West Wilson Street
Room 450
Madison, WI 53707-7850
Phone: 608-266-2536
Fax: 608-267-3203

Wyoming
Division on Aging
Department of Health
6101 Yellow Stone Road, #259B
Cheyenne, WY 82002
Phone: 307-777-7986 or 800-442-2766
Fax: 307-777-5340

Agency for Healthcare Research & Quality (AHRQ)
540 Gaither Road
Rockville, MD 20850
Phone: 301-427-1364
Email: info@ahrq.gov
Web site: http://www.ahrq.gov
   AHRQ provides an information clearinghouse that distributes *Evidence-Based Summaries and Reports, Clinical Practice Guidelines,* and other medical statistics and information. Call to order copies of guidelines on topics such as cardiac rehabilitation, treatment of pressure sores, or other publications on elder and long-term health care, health insurance, and minority health data. Visit the Web site to download *Clinical Practice Guidelines* on topics such as urinary incontinence, screening for Alzheimer's disease, and post-stroke rehabilitation.

Centers for Medicare and Medicaid Services (CMS)
7500 Security Boulevard
Baltimore, MD 21244
Phone: 1-800-MEDICARE (633-4227) (toll-free) (Medicare hotline)
410-786-3000
Web sites: http://www.cms.gov
http://www.medicare.gov (Medicare information)
   CMS is responsible for Medicare, Medicaid, the State Children's Health Insurance Program (SCHIP), the Health Insurance Portability and Accountability Act, and Clinical Laboratory Improvement Amendments. CMS provides information for a variety of professional audiences, including health policy researchers and the medical community. The Medicare 800 number (1-800-633-4227) provides services to beneficiaries 24 hours a day, seven days a week.
   The CMS Web site medicare.gov provides useful information for elderly consumers and professionals including:

- *Home Health Compare* gives detailed information about Medicare-certified home health agencies. The database includes quality measures, which give information about how well home health agencies provide care for their patients. The measures provide information about patients' physical and mental health, and whether their ability to perform basic daily activities is maintained or improved.

- *The Medicare Handbook* is a summary of Medicare benefits, rights and obligations.

- *The Medicare Personal Plan Provider* helps compares health plan options in local areas.

- *Nursing Home Compare* compares nursing homes in local areas.

- *The Participating Physician Directory* provides information on physicians by specialty and geographic area, along with detailed physician profiles, maps and driving directions.

- *Your Medicare Coverage* provides information about health care benefits in the Original Medicare plan including some of the services and supplies the Original Medicare Plan covers; the conditions that must be met for services or supplies to be covered; how often services or supplies are covered (limits); how much beneficiaries must pay; and some of the services and supplies the Original Medicare Plan does not currently cover.

- *The Supplier Directory* provides names, addresses, and contact information for Medicare-approved suppliers. Suppliers provide health care equipment, items, or services under Medicare. They provide items such as: Durable Medical Equipment (wheelchairs, walkers, oxygen), Prosthetics (artificial limb replacements or dentures) or Orthotics (mechanical devices used to assist in mobility or supplement the joints and limbs). In addition, Pharmacy/Drug Stores and Optometry/Opticians may be suppliers.

The CMS Web site also provides researchers and other health care professionals with a broad range of quantitative information on CMS programs, from estimates of future Medicare and Medicaid spending to enrollment, spending, and claims data. CMS also provides updates on regulatory information. Examples of their publications include:

- *The Medicare Current Beneficiary Survey* (MCBS), the only comprehensive source of health characteristics of the entire spectrum of Medicare beneficiaries. The MCBS Profiles series uses MCBS data to offer interesting insights into health care delivery.

- *The CMS Data Compendium* contains historic, current, and projected data on Medicare enrollment and Medicaid recipients, expenditures, and utilization.

- *CMS in Graphic Detail* includes chartbooks on CMS programs, spending, and activities.

- *Health Care Financing Review* is the CMS peer-reviewed research journal.

- *Statistical Supplement* to the *Health Care Financing Review* contains over 100 tables of unique and detailed information on CMS programs.

- *Reports on CMS Research Projects* are available on a broad range of health care issues.

- *Updates on Laws And Regulations* provide information on recent laws and regulations that effect agency programs.

Corporation for National Service (CNS)
1201 New York Avenue, NW
Washington, DC 20525
Phone: 202-606-5000
TTY: 202-565-2799
Email: webmaster@cns.gov
Web site: http://www.nationalservice.org

   CNS oversees volunteer community enhancement programs including: the National Senior Services Corps (a network of federally supported programs helping older people get involved in community service); the Foster Grandparent Program (encouraging older people to work with children with special needs); and the Senior Companion Program (volunteers assisting older people with special needs in hospitals, social service agencies, or home health care agencies). Contact CNS for pamphlets, brochures, fact sheets, and program handbooks.

Department of Justice (DOJ)
950 Pennsylvania Avenue, NW
Washington, DC 20530-0001
Email: ASKDOJ@usdoj.gov
Web site: http://www.usdoj.gov/
DOJ has a Nursing Home Initiative that prosecutes institutions whose wrongdoing results in harm or death for residents. DOJ also prosecutes health care and consumer fraud and enforces civil rights addressing discrimination against older people. Publications and statistics on victimization of older people are available.

Department of Labor (DOL)
Frances Perkins Building
200 Constitution Avenue, NW
Washington, DC 20210
Phone: 1-866-4-USA-DOL
TTY: 1-877-889-5627
Web site: http://www.dol.gov
DOL is charged with protecting workers' rights. Contact DOL for information and assistance on pensions, employment, wages, discrimination, and occupational safety. The agency's Senior Community Service Employment Program helps low-income older people through part-time employment and job training. The DOL Web site includes links to information for employers, employees, and job seekers.

Department of Transportation (DOT)
National Highway Traffic Safety Administration (NHTSA)
Information
400 Seventh Street, SW
Washington, DC 20590
Phone: 1-888-327-4236 (toll-free)
Email: webmaster@nhtsa.dot.gov
Web site: http://www.nhtsa.dot.gov/
The NHTSA is responsible for reducing deaths, injuries, and economic losses resulting from car accidents. It sets standards, investigates safety defects, and conducts research on driver behavior. Contact NHTSA for information on older drivers.

Department of Veterans Affairs (VA)
Office of Public Affairs
810 Vermont Avenue, NW
Washington, DC 20420
Phone: 1-800-827-1000 (toll-free)
TTY: 1-800-829-4833 (toll-free)
Web site: http://www.va.gov
The VA provides benefits for eligible veterans, many of whom are elderly, and their families in outpatient clinics, medical centers, and nursing homes across the US. Contact the VA for information and publications on service locations and benefits, including comprehensive medical and dental care, other insurance benefits, vocational rehabilitation compensation, and pension.

Employee Benefits Security Administration (EBSA) (formerly Pension and Welfare Benefits Administration (PWBA))
Department of Labor
200 Constitution Avenue, NW
Washington, DC 20210
Phone: 1-866-444-3272
TTY: 1-877-889-5627
Web site: http://www.dol.gov/ebsa/
   PWBA protects the integrity of private pension, health, and other employee benefits plans. The Administration assists workers in obtaining inappropriately denied benefits. Contact PWBA for assistance with technical questions and publications on topics such as pension and health care benefits, 401(k) and cash balance plans, planning for retirement, simplified employee pensions, and retiree health benefits. Most publications are also found on the Web site.

Equal Employment Opportunity Commission (EEOC)
1801 L Street, NW
Washington, DC 20507
Phone: 1-800-669-3362 (toll-free) (publications)
202-663-4900 (headquarters)
TTY: 1-800-800-3302 (toll-free) (publications)
202-663-4494 (headquarters)
Web site: http://www.eeoc.gov
   The EEOC promotes equal opportunity in employment. It enforces the Age Discrimination in Employment Act (ADEA), conducts investigations, makes determinations, and effects reconciliations in age discrimination actions. Contact EEOC regarding age discrimination issues.

Federal Consumer Information Center (FCIC)
PO Box 100
Pueblo, CO 81009
Phone: 1-888-878-3256 (toll-free)
1-800-688-9889 (toll-free) (National Contact Center)
TTY: 1-800-326-2996 (toll-free)
1-800-326-2996 (toll-free) (National Contact Center)
Fax: 719-948-9724
Web site: http://www.pueblo.gsa.gov/
   FCIC distributes a wide range of consumer-oriented publications from many federal agencies. *The Consumer Information Catalog* lists more than 200 publications on topics ranging from health and housing to food and nutrition; from money management to employment. The National Contact Center answers questions and provides referral information on federal programs, benefits, and services.

Federal Trade Commission (FTC)
600 Pennsylvania Avenue, NW
Washington, DC 20580
Phone: 1-877-FTC-HELP (382-4357) (toll-free)
202-326-2222 (General Information Locator)
Email: UCE@FTC.GOV
Web site: http://www.ftc.gov

FTC regulates trade and protects consumers from unfair and deceptive business practices. Its consumer protection programs include truth in advertising, consumer fraud and nursing home business practices. Publications include "Staff Summary of Federal Trade Commission Activities Affecting Older Americans: September 2001–August 2003."

Food and Drug Administration (FDA)
HFE88
5600 Fishers Lane
Rockville, MD 20857
Phone: 1-888-INFO-FDA (463-6332) (toll-free)
1-888-723-3366 (toll-free) (Food Information Line)
1-800-822-7967 (toll-free) (Vaccine Adverse Event Reporting System)
1-800-838-7715 (toll-free) (Mammography Information Service)
Web site: http://www.fda.gov
   FDA regulates the safety and effectiveness of food products, additives, drugs, medical devices, and cosmetics. FDA has information for older people on topics including cancer, health fraud, nutrition, buying medicines online, and food safety.

Food and Nutrition Information Center (FNIC)
Department of Agriculture
Agricultural Research Service/National Agriculture Library
10301 Baltimore Avenue, Room 105
Beltsville, MD 20705-2351
Phone: 301-504-5719
TTY: 301-504-6856
Fax: 301-504-6409
Email: fnic@nal.usda.gov
Web site: http://www.nalusda.gov/fnic
   FNIC provides information, publications, and audiovisual materials on nutrition. Resource guides on nutrition and older people, heart disease, diabetes, vegetarianism, food safety, and food labeling are available.

National Arthritis and Musculoskeletal and Skin Diseases Information Clearinghouse
National Institute of Arthritis and Musculoskeletal and Skin Diseases (NIAMS)
National Institutes of Health
1 AMS Circle
Bethesda, MD 20892-3675
Phone: 1-877-22-NIAMS (226-4267) (toll-free)
301-495-4484
TTY: 301-565-2966
Fax: 301-881-2731
Email: NIAMSInfo@mail.nih.gov
Web site: http://www.nih.gov/niams
   NIAMS Information Clearinghouse is funded by NIAMS, part of the National Institutes of Health. The Clearinghouse provides information and resources on all forms of arthritis, musculoskeletal diseases such as fibromyalgia, as well as skin diseases. Publications are available on the causes, treatments, and prevention of arthritis, lupus, musculoskeletal disorders, and diseases of bones, joints, and skin.

National Diabetes Information Clearinghouse (NDIC)
National Institute of Diabetes and Digestive and Kidney Diseases (NIDDK)
National Institutes of Health (NIH)
1 Information Way
Bethesda, MD 20892-3560
Phone: 1-800-860-8747 (toll-free)
301-654-3327
Fax: 301-907-8906
Email: ndic@info.niddk.nih.gov
Web site: http://www.niddk.nih.gov
   NDIC provides referrals to diabetes specialists and organizations, and searches from its database of patient and professional education materials. Publications are available on topics such as alternative therapies, controlling diabetes, complications of diabetes, and diabetes in Asian, Hispanic, and other ethnic groups. Spanish-language publications are available.

National Digestive Diseases Information Clearinghouse (NDDIC)
National Institute of Diabetes and Digestive and Kidney Diseases (NIDDK)
National Institutes of Health (NIH)
2 Information Way
Bethesda, MD 20892-3570
Phone: 1-800-891-5389 (toll-free)
301-654-3810
Fax: 301-907-8906
Email: nddic@info.niddk.nih.gov
Web site: http://www.niddk.nih.gov
   NDDIC provides referrals to digestive diseases organizations and support groups, as well as searches from its database of patient and professional education materials. Fact sheets are available on gastroesophageal reflux disease, hemorrhoids, constipation, ulcers, and irritable bowel syndrome.

National Eye Health Education Program (NEHEP)
National Eye Institute (NEI)
National Institutes of Health (NIH)
2020 Vision Place
Bethesda, MD 20892-3655
Phone: 301-496-5248
Fax: 301-402-1065
Email: 2020@nei.nih.gov
Web site: http://www.nei.nih.gov
   NEHEP is a partnership of professional, civic, and voluntary organizations and federal agencies. NEHEP provides referrals to vision professionals and other health resources. The Program offers free materials to educate the public about how to protect eye health and prevent vision loss, and distributes information on such topics as preventing diabetic eye disease, glaucoma, and low vision.

National Health Information Center (NHIC)
Office of Disease Prevention and Health Promotion (ODPHP)
Department of Health and Human Services
PO Box 1133

Washington, DC 20013-1133
Phone: 1-800-336-4797 (toll-free)
301-565-4167
Fax: 301-984-4256
Email: info@health.org
Web site: http://www.health.gov/NHIC
    NHIC, a service of the federal government, links consumers and health professionals with resources and information. The Center provides health information, contacts for federally supported health information centers, lists of national health observances, and toll-free numbers sponsored by the federal government.

National Heart, Lung, and Blood Institute (NHLBI) Information Center
National Institutes of Health (NIH)
PO Box 30105
Bethesda, MD 20824-0105
Phone: 301-592-8573
TTY: 240-629 3255
Fax: 301-592-8563
Email: NHLBIinfo@rover.nhlbi.nih.gov
Web site: http://www.nhlbi.nih.gov
    The Information Center provides referrals to resource organizations and information on elevated cholesterol, high blood pressure, heart disease, exercise, risk of and recovery from stroke, chronic cough, asthma, cystic fibrosis, and sleep disorders. Publications include two newsletters, *HeartMemo* and *AsthmaMemo*.

National Institute of Dental and Craniofacial Research (NIDCR)
National Institutes of Health (NIH)
NIDCR Public Information & Liaison Branch
45 Center Drive, MSC 6400
Bethesda, MD 20892-6400
Phone: 301-496-4261
Web site: http://www.nidcr.nih.gov/
NIDCR conducts and supports research on the causes, treatment, and prevention of diseases of the teeth, gums, and facial bones. The organization provides publications, audiovisual materials, and fact sheets.

National Institute of Environmental Health Sciences (NIEHS)
National Institutes of Health (NIH)
PO Box 12233
Research Triangle Park, NC 27709
Phone: 919-541-3345
TTY: 919/541-0731
Web site: http://www.niehs.nih.gov/home.htm
    NIEHS conducts and supports research on potential environmental contributors to human illnesses and dysfunction, including asthma, Alzheimer's, bronchitis, cancer, lead poisoning, Parkinson's and other chronic diseases. NIEHS also studies variable human susceptibilities to these environmental factors. The National Toxicology Program, headquartered at NIEHS, tests natural and man-made chemicals for safety.

National Institute of General Medical Sciences (NIGMS)
National Institutes of Health (NIH)
Office of Communications and Public Liaison
45 Center Drive MSC 6200
Bethesda, MD 20892-6200
Phone: 301-496-7301
Email: pub_info@nigms.nih.gov
Web site: http://www.nigms.nih.gov

NIGMS conducts and supports research in medical fields such as genetics, cellular and molecular biology, and pharmacology. Publications include *Medicines for You* (also available in Spanish), and *Inside the Cell*.

National Institute of Mental Health (NIMH)
National Institutes of Health (NIH)
6001 Executive Boulevard, Room 8184, MSC 9663
Bethesda, MD 20892-9663
Phone: 301-443-4513 or 1-866-615-NIMH (6464), toll-free
TTY: 301-443-8431; Fax: 301-443-4279
Fax: 4U: 301-443-5158
Email: nimhinfo@nih.gov
Web site: http://www.nimh.nih.gov

NIMH conducts and supports mental health research including mental disorders of aging. Contact NIMH for information on mental health and aging, Alzheimer's disease, anxiety disorders, depression, and suicide.

National Institute of Neurological Disorders and Stroke (NINDS)
National Institutes of Health (NIH)
NIH Neurological Institute
PO Box 5801
Bethesda, MD 20824
Phone: 1-800-352-9424 (toll-free) (information service)
301-496-5751
TTY: 301- 468-5981
Web site: http://www.ninds.nih.gov

NINDS conducts and supports research on stroke and neurological disorders. NINDS provides information on its research targets, including stroke, head and spinal injuries, tumors of the central nervous system, epilepsy, multiple sclerosis, Huntington's disease, Parkinson's disease, and Alzheimer's disease. A directory of voluntary health agencies is available.

National Institute of Nursing Research (NINR)
Office of Science Policy and Public Liaison
National Institutes of Health (NIH)
31 Center Drive
Building 31, Room 5B10
Bethesda, MD 20892-2178
Phone: 301-496-0207
Email: info@ninr.nih.gov
Web site: http://www.nih.gov/ninr

NINR conducts and supports basic and clinical research to establish a scientific basis for the care of individuals across the life span. Studies addressed by nurse researchers include the management of chronic diseases, health disparities, improving palliative end-of-life care, and telehealth technology.

National Institute on Aging (NIA)
National Institutes of Health (NIH)
Building 31, Room 5C27
31 Center Drive, MSC 2292
Office of Communications and Public Liaison
Bethesda, MD 20892-2292
Phone: 1-800-222-2225 (toll-free) (NIA Information Center, NIAIC)
1-800-438-4380 (toll-free) (Alzheimer's Disease Education and Referral Center-ADEAR)
301-496-1752
Fax: 301-589-3014 (NIAIC)
301-495-3334 (ADEAR)
Email: adear@alzheimers.org (ADEAR)
Web sites: http://www.nih.gov/nia
http://www.alzheimers.org

The National Institute on Aging (NIA) leads a broad scientific effort to understand the nature of aging and to extend the healthy, active years of life. In 1974, Congress granted authority to form the National Institute on Aging to provide leadership in aging research, training, health information dissemination, and other programs relevant to aging and older people. Subsequent amendments to this legislation designated the NIA as the primary federal agency on Alzheimer's disease research.

The NIA's mission is to improve the health and well-being of older Americans through research, and specifically to:

- Support and conduct high quality research on:

  - aging processes

  - age-related diseases

  - special problems and needs of the aged

- Train and develop highly skilled research scientists from all population groups

- Develop and maintain state-of-the-art resources to accelerate research progress

- Disseminate information and communicate with the public and interested groups on health and research advances and on new directions for research.

NIA sponsors research on aging through extramural and intramural programs. The extramural program funds research and training at universities, hospitals, medical centers, and other public and private organizations nationwide. The intramural program conducts basic and clinical research in Baltimore, MD, and on the NIH campus in Bethesda, MD.

NIA develops and disseminates publications on topics such as the biology of aging, exercise, doctor-patient communication, and menopause. The Institute produces the Age Pages— a series of fact sheets for consumers on a wide range of subjects including nutrition, medications, forgetfulness, sleep, driving, and long-term care. Information, publications, referrals, resource lists, and database searches on Alzheimer's disease are available through the Institute-funded ADEAR Center.

NIA has established more than ten Centers on the Demography of Aging to provide innovative and policy-relevant research on health, social factors, economics, and other issues that affect the U.S. older population. Specialized data collection and services are provided by these centers located in California, Colorado, North Carolina, Illinois, Michigan, Pennsylvania, and Wisconsin.

Also see NIHSeniorHealth listed below.

National Institute on Alcohol Abuse and Alcoholism (NIAAA)
National Institutes of Health (NIH)
5635 Fishers Lane, MSC 9304
Bethesda, Maryland 20892-9304
Phone: 301-443-3860
Fax: 301-443-6077
Email: niaaaweb-r@exchange.nih.gov
Web site: http://www.niaaa.nih.gov
  NIAAA conducts and supports research on alcoholism and alcohol abuse. Contact the NIAAA for information on genetic and behavioral aspects of alcoholism, physiologic effects of alcohol abuse, and diagnosis, treatment, and prevention of alcohol-related problems.

National Institute on Deafness and Other Communication Disorders (NIDCD)
National Institutes of Health (NIH)
Office of Communication and Public Liaison
31 Center Drive, MSC 2320
Bethesda, MD 20892-2320
Phone: 1-800-241-1044 (toll-free) (NIDCD Information Clearinghouse)
301-496-7243
TTY: 1-800-241-1055 (toll-free) (NIDCD Information Clearinghouse)
301-402-0252
Fax: 301-402-0018
Email: nidcd@nidcd.nih.gov
Web site: http://www.nidcd.nih.gov
  NIDCD conducts and supports research on normal mechanisms as well as diseases and disorders of hearing, balance, smell, taste, voice, speech, and language. NIDCD develops and disseminates health information to the public based on scientific discovery.

National Institute on Drug Abuse (NIDA)
National Institutes of Health (NIH)
Public Information and Liaison Branch
6001 Executive Boulevard, Room 5213
Bethesda, MD 20892-9561
Phone: 1-800-729-6686 (toll-free) (National Clearinghouse for Alcohol and Drug Information–NCADI)
301-443-1124
Email: Information@lists.nida.nih.gov
Web site: http://www.nida.nih.gov
  NIDA conducts and supports research on the physiology of specific drug addictions, effects of abused substances, and current and potential treatments. Contact NIDA for scientific information, and patient and public education materials on drug abuse, its causes, consequences, prevention, and treatment. Spanish language resources are available.

National Institutes of Health (NIH)
2 AMS Circle
Bethesda, MD20892-3676
Phone: 1-800-624-BONE (2663) (toll-free)
202-223-0344
TTY: 202-466-4315
Fax: 202-293-2356
Email: osteoinfo@osteo.ord
Web site: http://www.osteo.org
   The Resource Center provides patients, health professionals, and the public with resources and information on osteoporosis, Paget's disease of the bone, osteogenesis imperfecta, and other metabolic bone diseases. The Center is supported by the National Institute of Arthritis and Musculoskeletal and Skin Diseases and six other Institutes and Offices.

National Kidney and Urological Diseases Information Clearinghouse (NKUDIC)
National Institute of Diabetes and Digestive and Kidney Diseases (NIDDK)
National Institutes of Health (NIH)
Office of Communications and Public Liaison
NIDDK, NIH, Building 31, Room 9A04
Center Drive, MSC 2560
Bethesda, MD 20892-2560
Phone: 1-800-891-5390 (toll-free)
301-654-4415
Fax: 301-907-8906
Email: nkudic@info.niddk.nih.gov
Web site: http://www.niddk.nih.gov
   NKUDIC provides referrals to specialists, resource organizations, and support groups. Publications and information on subjects such as kidney stones, prostate gland problems, urinary incontinence, and urinary tract infections are available.

National Library of Medicine (NLM)
National Institutes of Health (NIH)
8600 Rockville Pike
Bethesda, MD 20894
Phone: 1-888-FIND-NLM (346-3656) (toll-free)
301-594-5983
Fax: 301-402-1384
Email: custserv@nlm.nih.gov
Web sites: http://www.nlm.nih.gov (MEDLINE)
http://www.nlm.nih.gov/medlineplus (MEDLINEplus)
http://www.clinicaltrials.gov (Clinical Trials database)
   NLM is the world's largest medical library. The collection can be consulted in the reading room or requested on interlibrary loan. NLM offers nationwide access to information through a National Network of Libraries of Medicine. The database, MEDLINE, is available via the World Wide Web. MEDLINEplus links the public to many sources of consumer health information and researchers and professionals to materials of interest to them.

National Library Service for the Blind and Physically Handicapped (NLSBPH)
Library of Congress
Reference Section
1291 Taylor Street, NW
Washington, DC 20542
Phone: 1-800-424-8567 (toll-free)
202-707-5100
Fax: 202-707-0712
Email: nls@loc.gov
Web site: http://www.lcweb.loc.gov/nls/

NLSBPH, funded by the Library of Congress, is a network of regional and local libraries that provide free library services to blind and physically disabled people. Contact NLSBPH about programs such as postage-free delivery and return-mailing of audio-books and books and magazines in Braille. Specially designed Talking Books and cassette players also are lent to the public free. NLSBPH provides information on blindness and physical disabilities.

NIHSeniorHealth.gov

www.NIHSeniorHealth.gov is a Web site for older adults. NIHSeniorHealth makes aging-related health information easily accessible for family members and friends seeking reliable, easy-to-understand online health information. This site was developed by the National Institute on Aging (NIA) and the National Library of Medicine (NLM). NIHSeniorHealth features authoritative and up-to-date health information from Institutes and Centers at NIH. In addition, the American Geriatrics Society provides expert and independent review of some of the material found on this Web site. Each health topic includes general background information, open-captioned videos, quizzes and frequently asked questions (FAQs). New topics are added to the site on a regular basis.

A research-based approach guided the development of NIHSeniorHealth. The design of the site grew out of NIA's research on the types of cognitive changes that are a part of the normal aging process. Changes in memory, text comprehension, information processing speed and vision can interfere with older adults' use of computers. Research indicates older adults can effectively use computers if information is provided in a senior-friendly manner. NIH extensively tested NIHSeniorHealth with adults age 60 to 88 to ensure that it is easy for them to see, understand, and navigate.

The Web site's features include large print, short, easy-to-read segments of information and simple navigation. A "talking" function reads the text aloud and special buttons to enlarge the text or turn on high contrast make text more readable.

Social Security Administration (SSA)
Office of Public Inquiries
6401 Security Boulevard
Baltimore, MD 21235
Phone: 1-800-772-1213 (toll-free)
TTY: 1-800-325-0778
Web site: http://www.ssa.gov

SSA is the agency responsible for Social Security retirement programs, survivor benefits, disability insurance, and Supplemental Security Income. SSA provides information and assistance with Social Security benefits. A directory is available listing the SSA offices in each state. Social Security has a toll-free number that operates from 7 A.M. to 7 P.M., Monday to Friday: 1-800-772-1213. If you have a touch-tone phone, recorded information and services are available 24 hours a day, including weekends and holidays. People who are deaf or hard of hearing may call our toll-free TTY number, 1-800-325-0778, between 7 A.M. and 7 P.M. on Monday through Friday. Please have your Social Security number handy when you call us. Social Security's Office of Policy is responsible for analysis and research on policy initiatives for the Social Security Old-Age, Survivors, and Disability Insurance (OASDI) programs and the Supplemental Security Income program. The Office of Policy is the agency's source for statistics on the impact and operations of the OASDI and SSI programs and on the earnings of the working and beneficiary populations. Statistics available from SSA include:

- Information useful in evaluating current programs and proposed legislative and program changes and in running the programs;

- Data on beneficiaries in individual states, localities, or congressional districts;

- Information about beneficiaries and expenditures of the Social Security program and other major social insurance and welfare programs;

- Specialized tables related to current issues.

Substance Abuse and Mental Health Services Administration (SAMSHA)
Department of Health and Human Services
Rm 12-105 Parklawn Building
5600 Fishers Lane
Rockville, MD 20857
Phone: 1-800-729-6686 (toll-free) (National Clearinghouse for Alcohol and Drug Information-NCADI)
TTY: 1-800-487-4889 (toll-free)
Fax: 301-468-7394
Email: info@samhsa.gov
Web site: http://www.samhsa.gov
    SAMHSA is responsible for improving the quality and availability of prevention, treatment, and rehabilitation services in order to reduce the illness, death, disability, and cost resulting from substance abuse and mental illness. Spanish language resources are available from NCADI.

U.S. Census Bureau
Special Populations Branch
FB3 Room 2384
Washington, DC 20233
Phone: 301-457-2378
Fax: 301-457-6634
Web site: http://www.census.gov
    The Census Bureau collects and provides data about the people and economy of the U.S. Contact the Census Bureau for age-related data and statistics about the older populations in the United States.

Glossary

A comprehensive list of terms used in *Aging: Demographics, Health, and Health Services* and *Aging: Lifestyles, Work, and Money* as well as others commonly used in the fields of gerontology and geriatrics.

A

Activities of Daily Living (ADLs)
Basic personal activities which include bathing, eating, dressing, mobility, transferring from bed to chair, and using the toilet. ADLs are used to measure how dependent a person may be on requiring assistance in performing any or all of these activities.

Acute Care
Care that is generally provided for a short period of time to treat a certain illness or condition. This type of care can include short-term hospital stays, doctor's visits, surgery, and X-rays.

Acute Illness
Illness that is usually short-term and that often comes on quickly.

Administration on Aging
Federal agency within the Department of Health and Human Services (DHHS) responsible for administering all programs authorized by the Older Americans Act; they also performs an advocacy role for the elderly.

Adult Day Care
A daytime community-based program for functionally impaired adults that provides a variety of health, social, and related support services in a protective setting.

Adult Protective Services
Services provided to older people and people with disabilities who are in danger of being mistreated or neglected, are unable to protect themselves, and have no one to assist them.

Adverse Drug Events
An unintended injury caused by drugs.

Age Discrimination in Employment Act (ADEA)
A 1967 federal law that prohibits employers with 20 or more employees from discriminating on the basis of age in hiring, job retention, compensation, and benefits. ADEA also sets requirements for the duration of employer-provided disability benefits.

Aged Unit
A definition used by the Social Security Administration that includes either a married couple living together (at least one of whom is aged 55+) or a person aged 55+ who does not live with a spouse (either married or unmarried). This definition includes the aged population, whether or not they live with other relatives.

Aggregate Income
Sum total of all income received.

Aging
The lifelong process of growing older.

Aging Network
The system of federal, state, and local agencies, organizations and institutions that are responsible for serving and/or representing the needs of older persons. The network may be involved in service systems development, advocacy, planning, research, coordination, policy development, training and education, administration and direct service provision. The core organizations in the network include the Administration on Aging (AoA), State Units on Aging (SUAs), Area Agencies on Aging (AAAs), and local service provider agencies.

Alzheimer's Disease
A progressive, irreversible disease characterized by degeneration of the brain cells and serve loss of memory, causing the individual to become dysfunctional and dependent upon others for basic living needs.

Alzheimer's Facilities
Facilities designed for individuals with Alzheimer's disease and related disorders. They are staffed with professional care providers experienced in handling behavior associated with memory impairments.

Ambulatory Care
All types of health services which are provided on an outpatient basis, in contrast to services provided in the home or to persons who are inpatients. While many inpatients may be ambulatory, the term ambulatory care usually implies that the patient must travel to a location to receive services which do not require an overnight stay.

Americans with Disabilities Act (ADA)
Legislation that gives civil rights protection to individuals with disabilities. It guarantees equal opportunity for individuals with disabilities in employment, public accommodations, transportation, state and local government services, and telecommunications.

Annuity
A contract between an individual and an insurance company, which provides lifetime income to the person in return for either a lump-sum or periodic payment to the insurance company.

Area Agency on Aging (AAA)
A local (city or county) agency, funded under the federal Older Americans Act, that plans and coordinates various social and health service programs for persons 60 years of age or more. The network of AAA offices consists of more than 600 approved agencies.

Asset
Anything that has a monetary value.

Assisted Living
Residences that provide a "home with services" and that emphasize residents' privacy and choice. Residents typically have private locking rooms (only shared by choice) and bathrooms.

Personal care services are available on a 24-hour-a-day basis. (Licensed as **residential care facilities** or as **rest homes.**)

Assistive Devices
Tools that enable individuals with disabilities to perform essential job functions, for example, telephone headsets, adapted computer keyboards, enhanced computer monitors.

B

Beneficiaries
A person who receives benefits, profits and/or advantages. This term is commonly used to describe recipients of Social Security, Medicare, and related benefits.

Bequeathable Wealth
The sum of real estate, business and farm, IRA, stock, bond, cash, certificate of deposit, auto, trust, and housing equity wealth less non-mortgage debt.

Board and Care Facilities
(Also called **adult care home** or **group home.**) Residence which offers housing and personal care services for 3 to 16 residents. Services (such as meals, supervision, and transportation) are usually provided by the owner or manager. May be a single family home.

Body Mass Index
Body mass index (BMI) correlates to fatness, and applies to both men and women. To determine BMI, weight in kilograms is divided by height in meters, squared. A BMI of 25 to 29.9 is considered overweight and 30 or above is considered obese.

C

Caregiver
Person who provides support and assistance with various activities to a family member, friend, or neighbor. May provide emotional or financial support, as well as hands-on help with different tasks. Caregiving may also be done from a long distance.

Care/Case Management
Offers a single point of entry to the aging services network. Care/case management assess clients' needs, create service plans, and coordinate and monitor services; they may operate privately or may be employed by social service agencies or public programs. Typically case managers are nurses or social workers.

Cash Contribution Expenditures
Cash contributed to persons or organizations outside the consumer unit, including alimony and child support payments; care of students away from home; and contributions to religious, educational, charitable, or political organizations.

Cash Value Life Insurance
Life insurance that includes an investment vehicle.

Center for Medicare and Medicaid Services (CMS)
Federal agency responsible for Medicare, Medicaid, State Children's Health Insurance Program (SCHIP), the Health Insurance Portability and Accountability Act, and Clinical Laboratory Improvement Amendments.

Chronic Care
Care and treatment given to individuals whose health problems are of a long-term and continuing nature. Rehabilitation facilities, nursing homes, and mental hospitals may be considered chronic care facilities.

Chronic Illness (Condition)
Long-term or permanent illness (e.g., diabetes, arthritis) which often results in some type of disability and which may require a person to seek help with various activities.

Co-Insurance
(Also called **co-payment**.) The specified portion (dollar amount or percentage) that Medicare, health insurance, or a service program may require a person to pay toward his or her medical bills or services.

Co-Payment
(Also called **co-insurance**.) The specified portion (dollar amount or percentage) that Medicare, health insurance, or a service program may require a person to pay toward his or her medical bills or services.

Cognitive Impairment
Deterioration or loss of intellectual capacity which requires continual supervision to protect the insured or others, as measured by clinical evidence and standardized tests that reliably measure impairment in the area of (1) short or long-term memory, (2) orientation as to person, place and time, or (3) deductive or abstract reasoning. Such loss in intellectual capacity can result from Alzheimer's disease or similar forms of senility or Irreversible Dementia.

Cohort
A set of people born during a specific time period; also a set of people born during a historical era that creates different inter-cohort characteristics such as size, composition, experiences, and values.

Community-Based Care
Health and social services available to individuals and families in their local community.

Conditioning Excercisers
Conditioning exercisers are defined as those who reported exercising at least six times per month, with an intensity corresponding to at least vigorous walking for a mean duration of 30 minutes. Occasional exercisers are those who were neither sedentary nor conditioning exercisers. Sedentary people are those who reported no leisure physical activity.

Congregate Housing
Also known as retirement housing, congregate housing generally includes individual apartments in which residents may receive some services, such as a daily meal with other tenants. (Other services may be included as well.) Buildings usually have some common areas such as a dining room and lounge as well as additional safety measures such as emergency call buttons. May be rent-subsidized (known as Section 8 housing).

Consumer Unit
A measurement used by the Bureau of Labor Statistic's Consumer Expenditure Survey (CEX). A consumer unit comprises either: (1) all members of a particular household who are related by blood, marriage, adoption, or other legal arrangements; (2) a person living alone or sharing a household with others or living as a roomer in a private home or lodging house or in permanent living quarters in a hotel or motel, but who is financially independent; or (3) two or more persons living together who use their income to make joint expenditure decisions.

Continuing Care Retirement Community (CCRC)
Communities that offer multiple levels of care (independent living, assisted living, skilled nursing care) housed in different areas of the same community or campus and which give residents the opportunity to remain in the same community if their needs change. Provide residential services (meals, housekeeping, laundry), social and recreational services, health care services, personal care, and nursing care. Require payment of a monthly fee and possibly a large lump-sum entrance fee.

Continuum of Care
The entire spectrum of specialized health, rehabilitative, and residential services available to the frail and chronically ill. The services focus on the social, residential, rehabilitative and supportive needs of individuals as well as needs that are essentially medical in nature.

Cost of Living Adjustment (COLA)
Increase to a monthly long-term disability benefit, usually after the first year of payments. May be a flat percentage (e.g., 3 percent) or tied to changes in inflation. In some states, workers' compensation income replacement benefits also include annual COLAs.

Custodial Care
Care that does not require specialized training or services.

D

Debit Card
A card that allows customers to access their funds immediately through electronic means. Often a replacement for checks.

Deinstitutionalization
Policy which calls for the provision of supportive care and treatment for medically and socially dependent individuals in the community rather than in an institutional setting.

Defined Benefit (DB) Plan
A plan that provides a retired employee with a benefit based on earnings and length of employment. DB plans provide a lifetime benefit usually based on the number of years worked and the salary in the last few years before retirement.

Defined Contribution (DC) Plan
Employer and/or employee contributions are put into an employee's individual account. These plans mostly consist of 401(k) or 403(b) plans.

Dementia
Term which describes a group of diseases (including Alzheimer's Disease) which are characterized by memory loss and other declines in mental functioning.

Diagnosis-Related Group (DRG)
A classification system which uses diagnosis information to establish hospital payments under Medicare. This system groups patient needs into 467 categories, based upon the coding system of the International Classification of Disease, Ninth Revision-Clinical Modification (ICD-9-CM).

Disability
The limitation of normal physical, mental, social activity of an individual. There are varying types (functional, occupational, learning), degrees (partial, total), and durations (temporary, permanent) of disability. Moderate to severe disability means that an individual requires help

with one or more ADL tasks. Benefits are often available only for specific disabilities, such as total and permanent (the requirement for Social Security and Medicare).

Discharge
A formal termination of inpatient care.

Durable Medical Equipment (DME)
(Also called **home medical equipment**.) Equipment such as hospital beds, wheelchairs, and prosthetics used at home. May be covered by Medicaid and in part by Medicare or private insurance.

Durable Power of Attorney
A legal document giving a person the authority to handle financial or personal matters for another person that remains in effect even if the individual becomes incompetent and unable to handle his or her own affairs.

Durable Power of Attorney for Health Care
A legal document giving one person the authority to make medical decisions for another.

E

Elder Cottage Housing Opportunity (ECHO) units
Small, freestanding, removable housing units that are located on the same lot as a single-family house.

Emergency Medical Services (EMS)
Services utilized in responding to the perceived individual need for immediate treatment for medical, physiological, or psychological illness or injury.

Employee Retirement Income Security Act (ERISA)
A federal act, passed in 1974, that established new standards and reporting/disclosure requirements for employer-funded pension and health benefit programs.

Escort Services
(Also called **transportation services**.) Provides transportation for older adults to services and appointments. May use bus, taxi, volunteer drivers, or van services that can accommodate wheelchairs and persons with other special needs.

Estate Recovery
States are required by law to recover funds from certain deceased Medicaid recipients' estates up to the amount spent by the state for all Medicaid services (e.g., nursing facility, home and community-based services, hospital, and prescription costs).

F

Family Caregiver
An adult family member, or another individual, who is an informal provider of in-home and community care to an older individual.

Family Caregiver Support Services
Services provided under the National Family Caregiver Support Program authorized by Title III, Part E, of the Older Americans Act. Services include information about available services, assistance to caregivers in gaining access to the services, individual counseling, organization of support groups, caregiver training, respite care and supplemental services to complement the care provided by caregivers.

Fee-for-Service
The way traditional Medicare and health insurance work. Medical providers bill for whatever service they provide. Medicare and/or traditional insurance pay their share, and the patient pays the balance through co-payments and deductibles.

Foreign-Born
A resident who was not a U.S. citizen at birth.

For-Profit
Organization or company in which profits are distributed to shareholders or private owners.

Foster Grandparent Program
A volunteer program that matches low-income senior volunteers and special needs children in various settings. The FGP receives funding from a combination of federal and state grants.

Functionally Disabled
A person with a physical or mental impairment that limits the individual's capacity for independent living.

G

Generation
Though popularly used as a synonym for cohort, the term is technically applied to families. Children form one generation, their parents form another, their grandparents form a third generation, and so on.

Geriatrician
Physician who is certified in the care of older people.

Geriatrics
Medical specialty focusing on treatment of health problems of the elderly.

Gerontology
Study of the biological, psychological and social processes of aging.

Group Home
(Also called **adult care home** or **board and care home**.) Residence which offers housing and personal care services for three to 16 residents. Services (such as meals, supervision, and transportation) are usually provided by the owner or manager. May be single family home.

H

Handicapped
As defined by Section 504 of the Rehabilitation Act of 1973, any person who has a physical or mental impairment that substantially limits one or more major life activity, has a record of such impairment, or is regarded as having such an impairment.

Health Insurance
Financial protection against the medical care costs arising from disease or accidental bodily injury. Such insurance usually covers all or part of the medical costs of treating the disease or injury. Insurance may be obtained on either an individual or a group basis.

Health Insurance Portability and Accountability Act (HIPAA)
Federal health insurance legislation passed in 1996, which sets standards for access, portability, and renewability that apply to group coverage—both fully insured and self-funded—as

well as to individual coverage. HIPAA allows, under specified conditions, for long-term care insurance policies to be qualified for certain tax benefits.

Health Maintenance Organization (HMO)
Managed care organizations that offer a range of health services to its members for a set rate, but which requires its members to use health care professionals who are part of its network of providers. (See also **Medicare HMOs.**)

High Serum Cholesterol
An elevated blood level of cholesterol that constitutes an increased risk of developing coronary heart disease.

Home and Community-Based Services
Services provided to individuals who, without them, would require institutionalization. Also see Home and Community-Based Waivers.

Home and Community-Based Waivers
Section 2176 of the Omnibus Reconciliation Act permits states to offer, under a waiver, a wide array of home and community-based services that an individual may need to avoid institutionalization. Regulations to implement the act list the following services as community and home-based services which may be offered under the waiver program: case management, homemaker, home health aide, personal care, adult day health care, habilitation, respite care and other services.

Home Equity Conversion Mortgages (HECM)
Also known as "reverse mortgages," Home Equity Conversion Mortgage loans enable homeowners aged 62 and older to convert the equity in their homes into monthly income streams or lines of credit.

Home Health Agency (HHA)
A public or private organization that provides home health services supervised by a licensed health professional in the patient's home either directly or through arrangements with other organizations.

Home Health Aide
A person who, under the supervision of a home health or social service agency, assists elderly, ill or disabled person with household chores, bathing, personal care, and other daily living needs. Social service agency personnel are sometimes called **personal care aides**.

Home Health Care
Includes a wide range of health-related services such as assistance with medications, wound care, intravenous (IV) therapy, and help with basic needs such as bathing, dressing, mobility, etc., which are delivered at a person's home.

HOME Investment Partnership Program
A federally funded program for housing. The program is intended to foster partnerships among Federal, State, and local governments, and the private sector.

Home Medical Equipment
(Also called **durable medical equipment.**) Equipment such as hospital beds, wheelchairs, and prosthetics used at home. May be covered by Medicaid and in part by Medicare or private insurance.

Homebound
One of the requirements to qualify for Medicare home health care. Means that someone is generally unable to leave the house, and if they do leave home, it is only for a short time (e.g., for a medical appointment) and requires much effort.

Homemaker Services
In-home help with meal preparation, shopping, light housekeeping, money management, personal hygiene and grooming, and laundry.

Household head
The person providing information on surveys about household characteristics.

Hospice
A program that provides palliative and supportive care for terminally ill patients and their families, either directly or on a consulting basis with the patient's physician or another community agency. The whole family is considered the unit of care, and care extends through their period of mourning.

Hospice Care
Services for the terminally ill provided in the home, a hospital, or a long-term care facility. Includes home health services, volunteer support, grief counseling, and pain management.

Hospital
An institution whose primary function is to provide inpatient diagnostic and therapeutic services for a variety of medical conditions, both surgical and nonsurgical.

Housing Choice Vouchers
A federal rental assistance program, which was formerly the Section 8 certificate and voucher program. It is designed to help with rent affordability for very-low-income and extremely low income persons in existing private rental housing.

I

Impairment
Any loss or abnormality of psychological, physiological, or anatomical function.

Incontinence
Losing urine beyond ones control.

Independent Living Facility
Rental units in which services are not included as part of the rent, although services may be available on site and may be purchased by residents for an additional fee.

Indigent Care
Health services provided to the poor or those unable to pay. Since many indigent patients are not eligible for federal or state programs, the costs which are covered by Medicaid are generally recorded separately from indigent care costs.

Informal Caregivers
Family members, feinds, and other helpers who provide long-term care and are not paid for their services.

Inmigration
The number of migrants who moved into an area during a given period.

Inpatient
A person who has been admitted at least overnight to a hospital or other health facility (which is therefore responsible for his or her room and board) for the purpose of receiving diagnostic treatment or other health services.

Institutional Health Services
Health services delivered on an inpatient basis in hospitals, nursing homes, or other inpatient institutions. The term may also refer to services delivered on an outpatient basis by departments or other organizational units of, or sponsored by, such institutions.

Instrumental Activities of Daily Living (IADLs)
Household/independent living tasks which include using the telephone, taking medications, money management, housework, meal preparation, laundry, and grocery shopping.

Intermediate Care
Occasional nursing and rehabilitative care ordered by a doctor and performed or supervised by skilled medical personnel.

Intermediate Care Facility (ICF)
A nursing home, recognized under the Medicaid program, which provides health-related care and services to individuals who do not require acute or skilled nursing care, but who, because of their mental or physical condition, require care and services above the level of room and board available only through facility placement. Specific requirements for ICFs vary by state. Institutions for care of the mentally retarded or people with related conditions (ICF/MR) are also included. The distinction between "health-related care and services" and "room and board" is important since ICFs are subject to different regulations and coverage requirements than institutions which do not provide health-related care and services.

L

Labor Force Participation Rates
The percentage of a given population that is either working or is actively seeking work.

Level of Care (LOC)
Amount of assistance required by consumers, which may determine their eligibility for programs and services. Levels include: protective, intermediate, and skilled.

Life Cycle
The entire course of a person's life—from infancy to old age.

Life Expectancy
The number of years that an average person of a given age can be expected to live.

Living Will
A legal document that states what health care should be given once a person can no longer make decisions for himself or herself.

Longevity
The condition or quality of being long-lived.

Longitudinal Data
Data derived from the same group of people over a period of time.

Long-Term Care (LTC)
Range of medical and/or social services designed to help people who have disabilities or chronic care needs. Services may be short- or long-term and may be provided in a person's home, in the community, or in residential facilities (e.g., nursing homes or assisted living facilities).

Long-Term Care Insurance
Insurance policies that pay for long-term care services (such as nursing home and home care) that Medicare and Medigap policies do not cover. Policies vary in terms of what they will cover, and may be expensive. Coverage may be denied based on health status or age.

Long-Term Care Ombudsman
An individual designated by a state or a substate unit responsible for investigating and resolving complaints made by or for older people in long-term care facilities. Also responsible for monitoring federal and state policies that relate to long-term care facilities, for providing information to the public about the problems of older people in facilities, and for training volunteers to help in the ombudsman program. The long-term care ombudsman program is authorized by Title III of the Older Americans Act.

Low-Income Housing Tax Credit Program (LIHTC)
Created by Congress in 1986, the program provides a tax credit to those who invest in affordable housing.

M

Managed Asset
Includes annuities, trust, and managed investment accounts.

Managed Care
Method of organizing and financing health care services that emphasizes cost-effectiveness and coordination of care. Managed care organizations (including HMOs, PPOs, and PSOs) receive a fixed amount of money per client/member per month (called a capitation), no matter how much care a member needs during that month.

Means Test
The determination of eligibility for a program or service based upon an individual's or family's income.

Medicaid (Title XIX)
Federal and state-funded program of medical assistance to low-income individuals of all ages. There are income eligibility requirements for Medicaid.

Medical Necessity
Services or supplies which are appropriate and consistent with the diagnosis in accord with accepted standards of community practice and are not considered experimental. They also can not be omitted without adversely affecting the individual's condition or the quality of medical care.

Medically Indigent
People who cannot afford needed health care because of insufficient income and/or lack of adequate health insurance.

Medicare (Title XVIII)
Federal health insurance program for persons age 65 and over (and certain disabled persons under age 65). Consists of three parts: Part A (hospital insurance) and Part B (optional medi-

cal insurance which covers physicians' services and outpatient care in part and which requires beneficiaries to pay a monthly premium). Part C, Medicare+Choice, provides beneficiaries with managed care options for their health care. In addition, a new Medicare Part D drug benefit will begin January 1, 2006.

Medicare-Approved
Entity or provider approved for reimbursement for services by Medicare.

Medicare + Choice
Part C of Medicare introduced in the Balanced Budget Act of 1997. It provides beneficiaries with managed care options for their health care. These options are private plans and are not available in all geographic areas.

Medicare HMOs
Under Medicare HMOs (health maintenance organizations), members pay their regular monthly premiums to Medicare, and Medicare pays the HMO a fixed sum of money each month to provide Medicare benefits (e.g., hospitalization, doctor's visits, and more). Medicare HMOs may provide extra benefits over and above regular Medicare benefits (such as prescription drug coverage, eyeglasses, and more). Members do not pay Medicare deductibles and co-payments; however, the HMO may require them to pay an additional monthly premium and co-payments for some services. If members use providers outside the HMO's network, they pay the entire bill themselves unless the plan has a point of service option.

Medicare Supplemental Insurance
(Also called **Medigap**.) Insurance supplement to Medicare that is designed to fill in the "gaps" left by Medicare (such as co-payments). May pay for some limited long-term care expenses, depending on the benefits package purchased.

Medigap
(Also called **Medicare supplemental insurance**.) Insurance supplement to Medicare that is designed to fill in the "gaps" left by Medicare (such as co-payments). May pay for some limited long-term care expenses, depending on the benefits package purchased.

Mental Health
The capacity in an individual to function effectively in society. Mental health is a concept influenced by biological, environmental, emotional, and cultural factors and is highly variable in definition, depending on time and place. It is often defined in practice as the absence of any identifiable or significant mental disorder and sometimes improperly used as a antonym for mental illness.

Mental Health Services
Variety of services provided to people of all ages, including counseling, psychotherapy, psychiatric services, crisis intervention, and support groups. Issues addressed include depression, grief, anxiety, stress, as well as severe mental illnesses.

Mental Illness/Impairment
A deficiency in the ability to think, perceive, reason, or remember, resulting in loss of the ability to take care of one's daily living needs.

Metropolitan Area
A core area containing a substantial population nucleus, together with adjacent communities having a high degree of economic and social integration with that core.

Migration
Moves that cross jurisdictional boundaries such as counties. Migration can be differentiated as movement within the United States (*domestic*, or *internal*, migration) and movement into and out of the United States (*international* migration).

Money Income
The total income received by an aged unit before any deductions for taxes, union dues, or Medicare premiums. This income is from any source that is regularly received and includes wages and salaries, self-employment income (including losses), Social Security, Supplemental Security Income, public assistance, interest, dividends, rent, royalties, estates or trusts, veterans' payments, unemployment compensation, workers' compensation, private and government retirement and disability pensions, alimony, and child support. Capital gains and losses and lump-sum or one-time payments such as life insurance are excluded. Nonmoney transfers such as food stamps, health benefits, subsidized housing, payments in kind, and fringe benefits are not included.

Morbidity
The extent of illness, injury, or disability in a defined population. It is usually expressed in general or specific rates of incidence or prevalence.

Mortality
A term used to describe the relation of deaths to the population in which they occur.

Movers
Movers can be classified by type of move and are categorized as whether they moved within the same county, to a different county within the same state, to a different county from a different state region, or were movers from abroad.

Multigenerational families
Households with more than two generations living together.

N

National Institute on Aging
One of the National Institutes of Health, a federal agency supporting research in medicine and health issues. The NIA conducts research on aging in its Baltimore laboratories and funds projects focusing on general aging process as well as specific diseases.

Net Migration
The difference between inmigration and outmigration during a given time. A positive net, or *net inmigration*, indicates that more migrants entered an area than left during that time. A negative or *net outmigration* means that more migrants left an area than entered it.

Net Worth
The difference between gross assets and liabilities.

Nonprofit/Not-For-Profit
An organization that reinvests all profits back into that organization.

Nurse
An individual trained to care for the sick, aged, or injured. Can be defined as a professional qualified by education and authorized by law to practice nursing.

Nursing Home
Facility licensed by the state to offer residents personal care as well as skilled nursing care on a 24-hour-a-day basis. Provides nursing care, personal care, room and board, supervision,

medication, therapies and rehabilitation. Rooms are often shared, and communal dining is common.

Nursing Home Care
Full-time care delivered in a facility designed for recovery from a hospital, treatment, or assistance with common daily activities.

O

Occupational Therapy (OT)
Designed to help patients improve their independence with activities of daily living through rehabilitation, exercises, and the use of assistive devices. May be covered in part by Medicare.

Old-Age Survivors and Disability Insurance (OASDI)
Federal program under the Social Security Act providing benefits to eligible individuals who are fully insured, have reached entitlement age, and have applied for retirement insurance benefits, or to those persons who are the eligible survivors of the deceased, insured worker.

Older Americans Act (OAA)
Federal legislation that specifically addresses the needs of older adults in the United States. Provides some funding for aging services (such as home-delivered meals, congregate meals, senior center, employment programs). Creates the structure of federal, state, and local agencies that oversee aging services programs.

Ombudsman
A representative of a public agency or a private nonprofit organization who investigates and resolves complaints made by or on behalf of older individuals who are residents of long-term care facilities.

Omnibus Budget Reconciliation Act (OBRA) of 1993
Federal legislation that limits the amount of compensation that can be paid to employees covered by long-term disability plans funded through voluntary employees' beneficiary association trusts. Any such plan with participants earning more than $150,000 could lose its tax-exempt status.

Outmigration
The number of migrants who moved out of an area during a given period.

Outpatient
A patient who is receiving ambulatory care at a hospital or other facility without being admitted to the facility. Usually, it does not mean people receiving services from a physician's office or other program which also does not provide inpatient care.

P

Palliative Care
Pain and symptom management, physical care, counseling, and related services to patients who are terminally ill. Palliative care does not attempt to cure disease or health problems.

Paraprofessional Caregivers
Home health aides, certified nursing assistants (CNAs), personal attendants, and related non-professional workers employed in nursing homes, assisted living facilities, adult care homes, group homes, and individual clients' residences.

Pension
A regular payment given to a person in retirement by a former employer.

People Living in the Community
People who do not live in institutions such as nursing homes.

Personal Care
(Also called **custodial care**.) Assistance with activities of daily living as well as with self-administration of medications and preparing special diets.

Physical Therapy (PT)
Designed to restore/improve movement and strength in people whose mobility has been impaired by injury and disease. May include exercise, massage, water therapy, and assistive devices. May be covered in part by Medicare.

Point of Service
A health insurance benefits program in which subscribers can select between different delivery systems (i.e., HMO, PPO and fee-for-service) when in need of medical services, rather than making the selection between delivery systems at time of open enrollment at place of employment.

Post-Acute Care (PAC)
(Also called **subacute care** or **transitional care**.) Type of short-term care provided by many long-term care facilities and hospitals, which may include rehabilitation services, specialized care for certain conditions (such as stroke and diabetes) and/or post-surgical care and other services associated with the transition between the hospital and home. Residents on these units often have been hospitalized recently and typically have more complicated medical needs. The goal of subacute care is to discharge residents to their homes or to a lower level of care.

Preferred Provider Arrangement (PPA)
Selective contracting with a limited number of health care providers, often at reduced or pre-negotiated rates of payment.

Preferred Provider Organization (PPO)
Managed care organization that operates in a similar manner to an HMO or Medicare HMO except that this type of plan has a larger provider network and does not require members to receive approval from their primary care physician before seeing a specialist. It is also possible to use doctors outside the network, although there may be a higher co-payment.

Premium
The periodic payment (e.g., monthly, quarterly) required to keep an insurance policy in force.

Preventive Medicine
Care which has the aim of preventing disease or its consequences. It includes health care programs aimed at warding off illnesses (e.g., immunizations), early detection of disease (e.g., Pap smears), and inhibiting further deterioration of the body (e.g., exercise or prophylactic surgery).

Primary Care
Basic or general health care focused on the point at which a patient ideally first seeks assistance from the medical care system.

Probability
The likelihood that an event will occur.

Prospective Payment
Any method of paying hospitals or other health programs in which amounts or rates of payment are established in advance for a defined period (usually a year).

Provider
Individual or organization that provides health care or long-term care services (e.g., doctors, hospital, physical therapists, home health aides, and more).

Provider Sponsored Organization (PSO)
Managed care organization that is similar to an HMO or Medicare HMO except that the organization is owned by the providers in that plan and these providers share the financial risk assumed by the organization.

Public Health
The science dealing with the protection and improvement of community health by organized community effort.

Q

Qualified Medicare Beneficiary and Specified Low Income Medicare Beneficiary (QMB AND SLMB)
Programs for low income elderly and disabled. QMB pays all Medicare Part A and Part B premiums, deductibles and co-insurance. SLMB pays only Part B monthly premiums.

Quality of Care
A measure of the degree to which delivered health services meet established professional standards and judgments of value to the consumer.

R

Rehabilitation
The combined and coordinated use of medical, social, educational, and vocational measures for training or retaining individuals disabled by disease or injury to the highest possible level of functional ability. Several different types of rehabilitation are distinguished: vocational, social, psychological, medical, and educational.

Rehabilitation Services
Services designed to improve/restore a person's functioning; includes physical therapy, occupational therapy, and/or speech therapy. May be provided at home or in long-term care facilities. May be covered in part by Medicare.

Reimbursement
The process by which health care providers receive payment for their services. Because of the nature of the health care environment, providers are often reimbursed by third parties who insure and represent patients, such as Medicare or Medicaid.

Residential Care
The provision of room, board and personal care. Residential care falls between the nursing care delivered in skilled and intermediate care facilities and the assistance provided through social services. It can be broadly defined as the provision of 24-hour supervision of individuals who, because of old age or impairments, necessarily need assistance with the activities of daily living.

Residential Mobility
Moves within a jurisdiction.

Respite Care
Service in which trained professionals or volunteers come into the home to provide short-term care (from a few hours to a few days) for an older person to allow caregivers some time away from their caregiving role.

Retirement

Period or life stage following termination of and withdrawal from a regular job. It is difficult to define because some older persons retire from one job and change careers or take on other full or part-time work.

Retirement Account

Any of a number of programs that permit employees, *or, in some cases, people who are not in the labor force,* to invest money for their retirement.

Retirement Communities

Also known as congregate housing, retirement communities generally offer individual apartments in which residents may receive some services, such as a daily meal with other tenants. (Other services may be included as well.) Buildings usually have some common areas such as a dining room and lounge as well as additional safety measures such as emergency call buttons. May be rent-subsidized.

Reverse Mortgages

Also known as Home Equity Conversion Mortgages (HECMs,) reverse mortgages enable homeowners aged 62 and older to convert the equity in their homes into monthly income.

Retired Senior Volunteer Program (RSVP)

A program that coordinates volunteer opportunities for adults over the age of 60. The program receives a combination of federal and state funds.

S

Section 202 Housing

The Housing Act of 1959 (P.L. 86-372) established the Section 202 program, which provides low-income elderly with housing options that allow them to live independently but in an environment that provides support activities such as cleaning, cooking, and transportation. The federal program provides capital advances to private nonprofit organizations to pay for the costs of developing such housing.

Section 221(d)(3) and 221(d)(4)

A Federal program that insures mortgage loans to facilitate the construction or rehabilitation of multifamily rental or cooperative housing for moderate-income families, elderly, and the handicapped.

Section 236 Housing

A federal program that provides housing to low-income families, elderly, disabled and individuals under age 62.

The Section 504 Home Repair Loan and Grant Program

A rural program offered to elderly persons and very low-income families who own homes that need repairs.

Section 515 Rural Rental Housing Program

A multifamily direct-loan program administered by the Rural Housing Service (RHS) of the U.S. Department of Agriculture.

Senescence

The process of growing old, which occurs continuously at every biological level (chemical, cellular, tissue, organ systems, and organism).

Senility
The generalized characterization of progressive decline in mental functioning as a condition of the aging process. Within geriatric medicine, this term has limited meaning and is often substituted for the diagnosis of senile dementia and/or senile psychosis.

Senior Center
Provides a variety of on-site programs for older adults including recreation, socialization, congregate meals, and some health services. Usually a good source of information about area programs and services.

Severity of Illness
A risk prediction system to correlate the "seriousness" of a disease in a particular patient with the statistically "expected" outcome (e.g., mortality, morbidity, efficiency of care).

Shared Housing
A housing arrangement where two or more unrelated people choose to share a house, apartment, or other living arrangement. Each person usually has their own bedroom, but shares the common areas of the home.

Skilled Care
"Higher level" of care (such as injections, catheterizations, and dressing changes) provided by trained medical professionals, including nurses, doctors, and physical therapist.

Skilled Nursing Care
Daily nursing and rehabilitative care that can be performed only by or under the supervision of, skilled medical personnel.

Skilled Nursing Facility (SNF)
Facility that is certified by Medicare to provide 24-hour nursing care and rehabilitation services in addition to other medical services. (See also **nursing home**.)

Social Health Maintenance Organization (SHMO)
A managed system of health and long-term care services geared toward an elderly client population. Under this model, a single provider entity assumes responsibility for a full range of acute inpatient, ambulatory, rehabilitative, extended home health and personal care services under a fixed budget which is determined prospectively. Elderly people who reside in the target service area are voluntarily enrolled. Once enrolled, individuals are obligated to receive all SHMO covered services through SHMO providers, similar to the operation of a medical model health maintenance organization (HMO).

Social Security Disability Insurance (SSDI)
A system of federally provided payments to eligible workers (and, in some cases, their families) when they are unable to continue working because of a disability. Benefits begin with the sixth full month of disability and continue until the individual is capable of substantial gainful activity.

Social Services Block Grant (SSBG) Services
(Formerly known as **Title XX services.**) Grants given to states under the Social Security Act which fund limited amounts of social services for people of all ages (including some in-home services, abuse prevention services, and more).

Special Care Units
Long-term care facility units with services specifically for persons with Alzheimer's disease, dementia, head injuries, or other disorders.

Speech Therapy
Designed to help restore speech through exercises. May be covered by Medicare.

Spend-Down
Medicaid financial eligibility requirments are strict, and may require beneficiaries to spend down/use up assets or income until they reach the eligibility level.

Spousal Impoverishment
Federal regulations preserve some income and assets for the spouse of a nursing home resident whose stay is covered by Medicaid.

State Unit on Aging
Authorized by the Older Americans Act. Each state has an office at the state level which administers the plan for service to the aged and coordinates programs for the aged with other state offices.

Subacute Care
(Also called **post-acute care** or **transitional care.**) Type of short-term care provided by many long-term care facilities and hospitals which may include rehabilitation services, specialized care for certain conditions (such as stroke and diabetes) and/or post-surgical care and other services associated with the transition between the hospital and home. Residents on these units often have been hospitalized recently and typically have more complicated medical needs. The goal of subacute care is to discharge residents to their homes or to a lower level of care.

Supplemental Security Income (SSI)
A program of support for low-income aged, blind and disabled persons, established by Title XVI of the Social Security Act. SSI replaced state welfare programs for the aged, blind and disabled in 1972, with a federally administered program, paying a monthly basic benefit nationwide of $284.30 for an individual and $426.40 for a couple in 1983. States may supplement this basic benefit amount.

Support Groups
Groups of people who share a common bond (e.g., caregivers) who come together on a regular basis to share problems and experiences. May be sponsored by social service agencies, senior centers, religious organizations, as well as organizations such as the Alzheimer's Association.

Survey
An investigation in which information is systematically collected.

T

Tax-Deferred Retirement Accounts
Accounts that allow employees, *or, in some cases, people who are not in the labor force,* to invest money for their retirements with the benefit of deferring taxes until the time when the funds are withdrawn.

Title III Services
Services provided to individuals age 60 and older which are funded under Title III of the Older Americans Act. Include: congregate and home-delivered meals, supportive services (e.g., transportation, information and referral, legal assistance, and more), in-home services (e.g., homemaker services, personal care, chore services, and more), and health promotion/disease prevention services (e.g., health screenings, exercise programs, and more).

Title XIX (Medicaid)
Federal and state-funded program of medical assistance to low-income individuals of all ages. There are income eligibility requirements for Medicaid.

Title XVIII (Medicare)
Federal health insurance program for persons age 65 and over (and certain disabled persons under age 65). Consists of 2 parts: Part A (hospital insurance) and Part B (optional medical insurance which covers physicians' services and outpatient care in part and which requires beneficiaries to pay a monthly premium).

Title XX Services
(Now known as **Social Services Block Grant services.**) Grants given to states under the Social Security Act which fund limited amounts of social services for people of all ages (including some in-home services, abuse prevention services, and more).

Transaction Accounts
Financial accounts such as checking, savings, money market deposit, and money market mutual funds.

Transitional Care
(Also called **subacute care** or **post-acute care.**) Type of short-term care provided by many long-term care facilities and hospitals which may include rehabilitation services, specialized care for certain conditions (such as stroke and diabetes) and/or post-surgical care and other services associated with the transition between the hospital and home. Residents on these units often have been hospitalized recently and typically have more complicated medical needs. The goal of subacute care is to discharge residents to their homes or to a lower level of care.

Transportation Services
(Also called **escort services.**) Provides transportation for older adults to services and appointments. May use bus, taxi, volunteer drivers, or van services that can accommodate wheelchairs and persons with other special needs.

Treatment Plan
(Also called **care plan** or **service plan.**) Written document which outlines the types and frequency of the long-term care services that a consumer receives. It may include treatment goals for him or her for a specified time period.

U

Uncompensated Care
Service provided by physicians and hospitals for which no payment is received from the patient or from third party payers.

Underinsured
People with public or private insurance policies that do not cover all necessary medical services, resulting in out-of-pocket expenses that exceed their ability to pay.

Undue Hardship
With respect to the provision of accommodation for an individual with a disability under the Americans with Disabilities Act—significant difficulty or expense, considered in light of the employer's financial resources, facilities, workforce, and business operations.

Unrelated Individual
A term used by the U.S. Census Bureau to describe a householder living alone or with nonrelatives only.

V

Veterans Affairs (VA) Department
Administers benefits for former Armed Services members and their dependents. Coverage and benefits include disability and death, pensions, medical treatment and hospitalization, nursing home and domiciliary care, and burial.

Visiting Nurse Association (VNA)
A voluntary health agency which provides nursing and other services in the home. Basic services include health supervision, education and counseling; beside care; and the carrying out of physicians' orders. Personnel include nurses and home health aides who are trained for specific tasks of personal bedside care. These agencies had their origin in the visiting or district nursing provided to sick poor in their homes by voluntary agencies.

Vital Statistics
Statistics relating to births (natality), deaths (mortality), marriages, health, and disease (morbidity).

Voucher Rehab Loan Program
A federal program that provides 3 percent interest-rate loans for landlords to fix up their rental units. In return for receiving a 3 percent loan, landlords must rent to families with Housing Choice Vouchers.

W

Waivers (Medicaid)
Medicaid Waivers were made possible by the Omnibus Budget Reconciliation Act (OBRA) of 1981. OBRA '81 allows states to request federal approval to waive certain requirements of the Social Security Act related to coverage of services under the Medicaid program. Medicaid waivers allow the use of Medicaid funds for services that are not traditionally covered by the Medicaid program. States are required to make a variety of assurances to obtain a Medicaid waiver.

Selected Bibliography and Useful Web Sites

SELECTED BIBLIOGRAPHY

AARP. (May 2003). "These Four Walls . . . Americans 45+ Talk about Home and Community."

Aizcorbe, Ana M., Arthur B. Kennickell, and Kevin B. Moore. (January 2003). "Recent Changes in U.S. Family Finances: Evidence from the 1998 and 2001 Survey of Consumer Finances." *Federal Reserve Bulletin.*

Bayer, Ada-Helen, and Leon Harper. (May 2000). "Fixing to Stay: A National Survey on Housing and Home Modification Issues." AARP.

Brown, S. Kathi. (September 2003). "Staying Ahead of the Curve 2003: The AARP Working in Retirement Study." AARP.

Bruce, Donald, Douglas Holtz-Eakin, and Joseph Quinn. (November 2000). "Self-Employment and Labor Market Transitions at Older Ages."

Burtless, Gary, and Joseph F. Quinn. "Retirement Trends and Policies to Encourage Work among Older Americans." Boston College Economics Working Papers No. 436, January 2000. In *Ensuring Health and Income Security for an Aging Workforce*, edited by Peter Budetti, Richard Burkhauser, Janice Gregory and Allan Hunt. Kalamazoo, MI: Upjohn Institute for Employment Research.

Costa, Dora. (May 1999). "Has the Trend toward Early Retirement Reversed?" Paper presented at the First Annual Joint Conference for the Retirement Research Consortium, [Au: City?].

Federal Bureau of Investigation, Uniform Crime Reports. (2002). "Crime in the United States—2002."

Haider, Steven, and David Loughran. (September 2001). "Elderly Labor Supply: Work or Play?" Center for Retirement Research at Boston College, Working Paper No. 2001–04.

Hetzel, Lisa, and Annetta Smith. (October 2001). "The 65 Years and Over Population: 2000." U.S. Census Bureau.

Heumann, Leonard, Karen Winter-Nelson, and James Anderson. (January 2001). "The 1999 National Survey of Section 202 Housing for the Elderly." *AARP Public Policy Report.*

The Independent Sector. (November 2001). "Giving and Volunteering in the United States."

Insurance Institute for Highway Safety. (2002). "Fatality Facts: Older People 2002."

Kochera, Andrew. (May 2001). "A Summary of Federal Rental Housing Programs." AARP Public Policy Institute.

Kutner, Gail, and Jeffrey Love. (November 2003). "Multicultural Study 2003: Time and Money: An In-Depth Look at 45+ Volunteers and Donors." AARP.

Metropolitan Life Insurance Company. (February 2002). "MetLife Retirement Crossroads Study: Paving the Way to a Secure Future."

National Center for Assisted Living. (March 2001). "Assisted Living: Independence, Choice and Dignity."

National Center on Institutions and Alternatives. (1997). "Elderly Study."

National Council of State Housing Agencies, "State HFA Factbook: 2000 Annual Survey Results." 2000.

Proctor, Bernadette, and Joseph Dalaker. (2003). "Poverty in the United States: 2002." U.S. Census Bureau, Current Population Reports, P60-222, Washington, DC: U.S. Government Printing Office.

Purcell, Patrick J. (October 2000). "Older Workers: Employment and Retirement Trends." *Monthly Labor Review Online*, 19–30.

Quinn, Joseph F. (May 1999). "Has the Early Retirement Trend Reversed?" Boston College Economics Working Papers No. 424.

Quinn, Joseph, Kevin Cahill, Richard Burkhauser, and Robert Weather. (February 1998). "The Microeconomics of the Retirement Decision in the United States."

Ritter, Anita Stowell, Audrey Straight, and Ed Evans. (April 2002). "Understanding Senior Transportation: Report and Analysis of a Survey of Consumers 50+ – Report," AARP Public Policy Institute.

Social Security Administration. (March 2003). "The 2003 Annual Report of the Board of Trustees of the Federal Old-Age and Survivors Insurance and Disability Insurance Trust Funds."

Social Security Administration. (2000). *Income of the Population 55 or Older, 2000*.

———. (2000). *Income of the Aged Chartbook*.

Teaster, Pamela B. (2000). "A Response to the Abuse of Vulnerable Adults: The 2000 Survey of State Adult Protective Services." National Center on Elderly Abuse.

U.S. Census Bureau. (March 2002). "Foreign-Born Population of the United States Current Population Survey: Detailed Tables (PPL-162)."

———. (March 2002). "Educational Attainment in the United States: Detailed Tables (PPL-169)."

———. Census 2000 Summary File 3 (SF 3)—Sample Data, "P17, Age by Language Spoken at Home by Ability to Speak English for the Populations 5 Years and Older."

———. Census 2000 Summary File 3 (SF 3)—Sample Data, "Pct25, Sex by Age by Educational Attainment for the Population 18 Years and Over."

———. (October 2003). "Marital Status: 2000."

———. 2001 and 2002 American Housing Survey.

———. (2002). "Housing Vacancies and Homeownership Annual Statistics: 2002."

———. (February 2002). "Voting and Registration in the Election of November 2000."

U.S. Department of Health and Human Services, Administration on Aging. (2002). "Profile of Older Americans: 2002."

U.S. Department of Justice, Bureau of Justice Statistics. (January 2000). "Crimes against Persons Age 65 or Older, 1992–97."

———. (2001). "Criminal Victimization in the United States, 2001." Available online at www.ojp.usdoj.gov/bjs/pub/pdf/cvus01.pdf.

———. (July 2003). "Prisoners in 2002." Available online at www.ojp.usdoj.gov/bjs.

———. (May 1991). "Survey of State Prison Inmates."

U.S. Department of Labor, Bureau of Labor Statistics. (December 2002). "2001 Consumer Expenditure Survey."

———. (December 2003). "Volunteering in the United States, 2003." Available online at www.bls.gov/news.release/pdf/volun.pdf.

U.S. Department of Transportation, National Highway Traffic Safety Administration. *Fatality Analysis Reporting System* (FARS).

———. (2002). National Center for Statistics and Analysis. "Traffic Safety Facts 2002, Older Population."

Wiatrowski, William J. (April 2001). "Changing Retirement Age: Ups and Downs," *Monthly Labor Review Online*, 3–12.

WEB SITES

AARP (formerly known as the American Association of Retired Persons), www.aarp.org and http://research.aarp.org.

Benefits CheckUp, www.benefitscheckup.org.

Center for Retirement Research at Boston College, www.bc.edu/centers/crr.

Commission on Affordable Housing and Health Facility Needs for Seniors in the 21st Century, www.seniorscommission.gov.

Federal Bureau of Investigation, Uniform Crime Reports, www.fbi.gov/ucr.

Federal Reserve Board, Survey of Consumer Finances, www.federalreserve.gov/pubs/oss/oss2/2001/scf2001home.html.

The Gallup Organization, www.gallup.com.

General Accounting Office, www.gao.gov.

The Independent Sector, www.independentsector.org.

Insurance Institute for Highway Safety, www.highwaysafety.org.

Joint Center for Housing Studies of Harvard University, www.jchs.harvard.edu.

Mediamark, www.mediamark.com (Mediamark Research offers comprehensive demographic, lifestyle, product, and media usage data from a single sample).

Medline, http://www.nlm.nih.gov/medlineplus.

Monthly Labor Review Online, www.bls.gov/opub/mlr/archive.htm.

The National Center on Elderly Abuse, www.elderabusecenter.org.

National Center for Assisted Living, www.ncal.org.

National Council of State Housing Agencies, www.ncsha.org.

NIHSeniorHealth.gov, www.NIHSeniorHealth.gov (a website for older adults sponsored by the National Institutes of Health).

NOP World, www.nopworld.com (NOP World, formerly known as Roper Starch Worldwide, conducts an ongoing survey of American's attitudes and behavior called Roper Reports).

U.S. Census Bureau, www.census.gov.

U.S. Department of Health and Human Services, Administration on Aging, www.aoa.gov.

U.S. Department of Justice, Bureau of Justice Statistics, www.ojp.usdoj.gov/bjs.

U.S. Department of Labor, Bureau of Labor Statistics, Consumer Expenditure Survey, www.bls.gov/cex/home.htm.

U.S. Department of Labor, Bureau of Labor Statistics, Current Population Survey, www.bls.census.gov/cps/cpsmain.htm.

U.S. Department of Transportation, National Highway Traffic Safety Administration, www.nhtsa.dot.gov.

ACRONYMS AND ABBREVIATIONS

APS	Adult Protective Services
BAC	Blood Alcohol Concentration
CCRC	Continuing Care Retirement Community
CEX	Consumer Expenditure Survey
CNA	Certified Nursing Assistant
CPI	Consumer Price Index

DI	Disability Insurance
ECHO	Elder Cottage Housing Opportunity
FARS	Fatality Analysis Reporting System
FICA	Federal Insurance Contributions Act
HA	Housing Agency
HDS	Health and Disability Status
HECM	Home Equity Conversion Mortgage
HUD	Housing and Urban Development
LIHTC	Low-Income Housing Tax Credit Program
LTC	Long-Term Care
NAHA	National Affordable Housing Act
NCAL	National Center for Assisted Living
NCEA	National Center on Elder Abuse
NCIA	National Center on Institutions and Alternatives
NCVS	National Crime Victimization Survey
OASI	Old-Age and Survivor's Insurance
RHS	Rural Housing Service
RN	Registered Nurse
SECA	Self-Employment Contributions Act
SSA	Social Security Administration
SSI	Supplemental Security Income
SRO	Single Room Occupancy

Index

Note: Page numbers in *italic* type indicate the presence of a table, chart, or figure.

Abuse and neglect, 94–96
Aged units, 113
Aiken, Lewis R., 15
Alcohol, traffic fatalities and, 36, *36*
Allen, Woody, 113
Alzheimer's facilities, 52
Animal companionship, 70–71, *71*
Apparel and related services, 175–76, *176*
Assault, 83
Assets: equity, 139–40, *140, 141*; financial, 134–42; as income source, 115–16, 117, *120*, 120–21; nonfinancial, 142–44, *143, 144*; types of, 135, *135*
Assisted living, 50–53
ATM machines, 138

Banking practices, *138*, 138, 148
Bateson, Mary Catherine, 7
Baumgarten, Jane O'Dell, 48
Benefit plans, 190–91, 195. *See also* Pensions
Bergen, Edgar, 180
Blacks. *See* Race
Board and care facilities, 52–53
Bonds, 141, *142*
Bowman, John, 82
Bridge jobs, 180
Brown, Rita Mae, 97
Burtless, Gary, 192, 194
Business equity, 144
Butler, Samuel, 113

Card playing, 74
Car ownership, 33–34, 142, 164, *166*

Cash contributions, *172*, 172–73, *173*
Cash value life insurance, 137, *138*
Catholics, 79
Certificates of deposit (CDs), 137–38, *139*
Cities, 20, *21*
Citizenship, 97–98, *98*
Climate, migration and, 29
Clothing and related services, 175–76, *176*
Club or organizational membership, *58*, 58
Colorado, 106
Communication: information sources, 65–66, *66, 67*; interpersonal, 65, *66*
Community life: club or organizational membership, *58*, 58; political activity, 56–57; volunteering, 59–63
Computers, 64–65
Consumer units, 152
Continuing care retirement communities (CCRCs), 52
Contributions, *172*, 172–73, *173*
Costa, Dora, 193
Counties: population by, *18*, 18–19, *19*; relocation within, 23
Credit cards: debt from, 145, 150; use of, *150*
Crime, 82–94; elderly criminals, 92–94; fraud, 83; murder, 88, 92; nonlethal violent, 83, 91; personal, 83–86; personal theft, 88–89, *89*, 91, *92*; property, 83, 87, *88*, 88–89, *90*, 91; reporting of, 86, *87*; victims of, 83, *84, 85*, 86; victim survey results, 88–92; violent, *85*
Crossword puzzles, 74
Cultural entertainment, 73, *74*

Customer spending, 152–78; aggregate annual expenditures by age, *154*; apparel and related services, 175–76, *176*; average annual expenditures by age, *155*; average annual expenditures by income, *156*; average annual expenditures by region, *156*; cash contributions, *172*, 172–73, *173*; entertainment, *174*, 174–75; food, 168–71, *170*, *171*; health care, 166–68, *167*, *168*, *169*; housing, 156–63, *159*, *160*, *163*; overview of, 154–56; pension and Social Security expenditures, 176–78, *177*; share of, per household, 155–56, *157*; shopping preferences, *175*, 175; transportation, 164–66; utilities, 163

Deaths: pedestrian deaths, 36–37, *37*; traffic injuries and deaths, 34–37
Debit cards, 150
Debt, 145–46, *146*, *147*
Defined benefit plans, 190–91, 195
Defined contribution plans, 190–91
Demographics: geographic location, 15–21; mobility, 22–31; projections for, 3
Department of Housing and Urban Development (HUD), 46
Dining out, 68–70, *70*
Divorce, 10, 126, 195
Driver's licenses, 33
Driving, 33–34; amount of, 33, *33*, 38–39; attitudes about, 34, *34*, 39; health and disability status and, *38*; vehicle ownership, 33–34
Drugs, prescription, 167

Earnings. *See* Income: from employment
Educational attainment, 100, 102–9; by age and sex, *102*, *103*; attainment levels, *105*; income and, 103; by labor force status and sex, *104*; by metropolitan status, 105, *106*; by origin, 103, 105, *105*; by period of entry, *105*; by region, *107*; by sex, *102*, *103*, *105*, *107–8*
Elder abuse, 94–96
Elder care housing opportunity (ECHO) units, 52
Elderly, typical American, 1–3
Emerson, Ralph Waldo, 82
Employment, 180–98; bridge jobs, 180; causes of recent trends in, 189–92;

economic dependency ratio, *193*; educational attainment by, *104*; full- and part-time status by age and sex, *183*; future labor force participation rates, 192–93; as income source, 121, *121*, *122*; labor force participation rates by age and sex, *182*, *185*; labor force participation rates by sex and race, *183*; labor force participation rates for cohorts by sex, *186*; labor force participation rates for men by age, *188*; labor force participation rates for women by age, *189*; labor force statistics, 181–89; in retirement, 196
Entertainment: cultural, 73, *74*; games, 74, *75*; going out, 68–70; hobbies, 74–75, *76*; social entertainment, 68; sources of, *67*; spending on, *174*, 174–75; television as, 67–68
Equity assets, 139–40, *140*, *141*
Estate planning, 147
Exercise, 72
Expenditures, 154

Family, defined for financial purposes, 133
Fast-food restaurants, 69
Federal housing programs, 46–50
Finances, 133–50; assets, 134–44; attitudes about, 146–50, *147*, *148*, *149*; debt, 145–46, *146*, *147*; median net worth, *134*; savings, 145
Financial advice, 149, *149*
Financial planning, 145, 195–96
Financial support to children, 148
Florida: concentrations of elderly in, 20; migration to, 28
Food expenditures, 168–71, *170*, *171*. *See also* Dining out
Forbes, Malcolm S., 180
Foreign born citizens, 97–98, 129–30
Four-generation households, 13
Franklin, Benjamin, 133
Fraud, 83

Gambling, 63–64, *64*
Games, 74, *75*
Gardening, 74–75
Geographic location, 15–21; concentrations of elderly, *20*, 20–21, *21*; population by county, *18*, 18–19, *19*; population by

region, 17; population by state, 15–17, *16–17*, 20–21. *See also* Mobility
Good life, 196–98, *197*, *198*
Grandparent households, *12*, 12
Greeting cards, 71

Haider, Steven, 184
Happiness, 196–98, *197*, *198*
Harrington, Michael, 55
Hawes, Catherine, 95
Heads of households, 41
Health and disability status (HDS): board and care facilities, 52–53; mobility and transportation, 37, *38*; Section 202 housing and, 47–48, *48*
Health care, 166–68, *167*, *168*, *169*
Health insurance, 167, 192
Hobbies, 74–75, *76*
Home equity conversion mortgages, 50
Home improvement, 44–45, *45*
HOME Investment Partnership Program, 50
Homeownership, *41*, 41–43, 142–43, 160–61, *161*, *162*. *See also* Mortgages
Home safety, 41
Home values, 42, *43*, *162*
Hood, Thomas, 32
Household head, 41, 83
Households: as consumer units, 152–53; elderly heads of, 41; grandparent, 12; head of, 41, 83; living arrangements, 10–11; location of, 15–21; marital status, 8–10; mobility of, 22–31; multigenerational, 13; size by age of reference person, *153*; size of, *11*, 11–12
Housekeeping services, 44
Housing, 41–53; assisted living, 50–53; costs for lower income persons, *47*; federal programs, 46–50; heads of households, 41; home improvement, 44–45, *45*; home safety, 41; home values, 42, *43*, *162*; Housing Choice Vouchers, 48–49; planning for future, 45; problems with, 44; Section 202, 47–49; secured communities, 46; spending on, 156–63, *159*, *160*, *163*; subsidized, 46; utilities, 163. *See also* Home-ownership; Mortgages
Housing Choice Vouchers, 48–49
Howard, Jane, 7
Hubbard, Kin, 113

HUD. *See* Department of Housing and Urban Development
Huttman, Elizabeth D., 32

Immigrants: citizenship status of, *98*; and multigenerational families, 13; origins of, 98, *99*; percentage of elderly, 98; period of entry, *98*; poverty among, 129–30
Immigration, 22, 97
Income, 115–27, *123*; aggregate, *117*, *118*, *119*; average annual expenditures by, *156*; definition of, 114; distribution of, *124*; educational attainment and, 103, *104*; from employment, 121, *121*, *122*; food expenditures by, 170, *171*; home-owners versus renters, 43; housing issues for lower, 46–47; levels of, 123–27; median, by age and marital status, *125*; median, by age, marital status and race, *126*; of nonmarried persons, *127*; property crime rates by, 91; sources of, *115*, 115–22, *116*, *119*
Information sources, 65–66, *66*, *67*
Institutions, abuse and neglect in, 95–96
Insurance: health, 167, 192; life, 137, *138*, 178, *178*; long-term care, 51; personal, *178*, 178
Internal migration, 23–31
Internal Revenue Service, 141

James, William, 152

Labor. *See* Employment
Labor force participation rates, 180
Language, 98–100, *100*, *101–2*
Lappe, Anna, 152
Life insurance, 137, *138*, 178, *178*
Living arrangements, *10*, 10–11
Long-term care insurance, 51
Loughran, David, 184
Low-Income Housing Tax Credit, 49

Marital status, *8*, 8–10, *9*
Medical bills, concern about paying, 148
Membership in clubs or organizations, 58, *58*
Men: club or organizational membership of, 58; as crime victims, *85*, 85; educational attainment of, 100, *102*, 102–3, *103*, *104*, *105*, *107–8*; and elder abuse,

Men (*continued*)
94; hobbies of, 74–75, *76*; in labor force, 182, *188*; living arrangements of, 10–11; marital status of, 8, *9*; spectator sports favored by, *72*; sports favored by, 71–73; volunteering of, 59
Middle Atlantic, outmigration from, 28
Migration, *25–27*; by county, 30; definition of, 22; internal, 23–31; return, 30; by state, 30
Mobility, 22–31; by age, 22–23, *24*; internal migration, 23; residential, 22; by sex, 23, *24*
Money management, 145
Mortgages, 41–42, *42*, *43*, 50, 145–46, 160–61, *161*, *162*
Motorcycles, 34
Movers, 22
Multigenerational families, 13
Murder, 88, 92
Mutual funds. *See* Equity assets

National Affordable Housing Act, 50
Native citizens, 97–98
Net migration, 22
Net worth, 134
Nevada, migration to, 28
Never married, 10
Newspapers, 65–66, *67*
New York, outmigration from, 28
Nonlethal violence, 83, 91

Older Americans Act/Supplemental Security Income, 12
Online financial transactions, 138, 148
Outmigration, 22

Paar, Jack, 97
Pacific, outmigration from, 28
Pedalcycles, 35
Pedestrian deaths, 36–37, *37*
Pensions, 115, 117, 176–78, *177*, *191*. *See also* Benefit plans
Personal crime, 83–86
Personal insurance, 178, *178*
Pet ownership, 70–71, *71*
Philadelphia, 20
Political activity, *56*, 56–57
Poverty, 127–32; by citizenship status and sex, *130*; definition of, 114, 127; oldest-old below 125 percent level, *131*; oldest-

old by sex, race, and ethnicity, *131*; rates by age, *128*, 128–32; by sex and race, *129*; by sex and race below 125 percent level, *130*; states with highest rates of, 131–32
Poverty threshold, 114, 127
Prescription drugs, 167
Prisoners, elderly, *92*, 92–94
Property crime, 83, 87, *88*, 88–89, *90*, 91
Protestants, 79
Public assistance, 116, *122*, 122
Public policy, effect on work and retirement behavior of, 189–90
Public transportation, 40

Quinn, Joseph, 188, 192, 194

Race: crime victimization rates by, *86*, 86; income by, 124; nonlethal violence by, 91; poverty by, 129, 131; property crime rates by, 89; Social Security income by, 119–20, *120*
Reading, 74–75
Real estate holdings, 143–44
Reference persons, 153
Religion, 79–80; attendance, *80*; importance of, *79*; membership, *80*; preferences by age, *80*
Repplier, Agnes, 55
Residential mobility, 22
Retirement, 180–98; attitudes of retirees, 194–96; causes of recent trends in, 189–92; early, 191; incidence of, 185–86; length of, 192; measurement of, 180; onset of, 187–88; satisfaction with, 194–96; Social Security full benefits for, 202; working in, 196
Retirement accounts, 136–37, *137*
Retirement benefits, 116
Retirement communities, 52
Return migration, 30
Reverse mortgages, 50
Ride sharing, 39
Roosevelt, Franklin Delano, 201

Savings, 145
Savings bonds, 141, *142*
Seat belt use, 36
Section 202 housing, 47–49
Section 221d, 49
Section 236 housing, 49

Section 504 Home Repair Loan and Grant Program, 50
Section 515 Rural Rental Housing Program, 49–50
Secured communities, 46
Self-neglect, 94
Senior vans, 40
Separation, 10, 195
Shared housing, 52
Shopping preferences, *175*, 175
Simple assault, 83
Skinner, B. F., 97
Social and leisure activities, 63–79; communication, 65, *66*; entertainment, 67–70, 73–75; exercise, 72; gambling, 63–64; participation by age and sex, *69*; pet ownership, 70–71, *71*; religious participation, 79–80; sports, 71–73; technology and, 64–65; travel, 75–79
Social discourse, 65, *66*
Social Security, 201–11; benefits from, 204–7, *206*, *207*; contributions by elderly to, 176–78, *177*; financing of, 207–9, *208*, *209*; as income source, 117–19, *118*, 120; increase in payments for delaying retirement, *203*; overview of, 202–3; by race and marital status, *120*; retirement satisfaction and, 195; Supplemental Security Income (SSI), 209–11; trust fund operations, *204*; widows living alone and, 12; work and retirement behavior affected by, 189–90
South: customer spending in, 155; migration to, 23; population growth, 17
South Atlantic, migration to, 24
Spending. *See* Customer spending
Sports: exercise and, 72–73; particular sports by age and sex, *73*; spectator, 71, *72*
Stock brokerage industry, 141
Stocks. *See* Equity assets
Subsidized housing, 46
Supplemental Security Income (SSI), 209–11, *210*

Tax-deferred retirement accounts, 136
Taxis, 40
Technology: attitudes about, *64*, 64–65; electronic products or services, *65*
Television: as entertainment, 67–68; as information source, 65–66; types of show viewed, *68*

Theft, 88–89, *89*, 91, *92*
Thoreau, Henry David, 55
Traffic injuries and deaths, 34–37; fatality rates, 35, *35*; motorcycles, 34; pedalcycles, 35; pedestrian deaths, 36–37, *37*
Transaction accounts, 135–36, *136*
Transportation, 33–41; driving, 33–34, 38–39; health and disability status and, 37, *38*; needs and preferences, 37–40; public, 40; senior vans, 40; spending on, 164–66, *165*, *166*; taxis, 40; traffic injuries and deaths, 34–37; walking, 40
Travel, 75–79; destinations, 76–77; domestic, *78*, 79; extent of, 75–76; foreign, 77–78, *78*; interest in, 77; opinions about, *78*; vacation activities, *77*
Turley, Jonathan, 92
Typical American elderly, 1–3

Utilities, 163

Vacations. *See* Travel
Vehicle ownership, 33–34, 142, 164, *166*
Violence: definition of, 83; nonlethal, 83, 91; rate of violent crimes, *85*
Volunteering, 59–63; by age, *59*; by age, race, ethnic group, and sex, *60*; alternative measurement of, 62–63; hours spent, *60*, *61*; by types of organization, 61, *61*
Voter participation and registration, 56–57, *57*

Walking: as exercise, 72; as transportation, 40. *See also* Pedestrian deaths
West: educational attainment in, 105–6; outmigration from, 28; population growth, 17
Widowers, 8, *9*
Widows, 8, *9*, 12
Women: club or organizational membership of, 58; as crime victims, *85*, 85; educational attainment of, 100, *102*, 102–3, *103*, *104*, 105, 107–8; and elder abuse, 94; hobbies of, 74–75, *76*; in labor force, 182–83, 186–87, *189*; living arrangements of, 10–11; marital status of, 8, *9*; as Social Security beneficiaries, *205*, 205–6, *207*; spectator sports favored by, *72*; sports favored by, 71–73; volunteering of, 59
Work. *See* Employment

About the Authors

Elizabeth Vierck and **Kris Hodges** are the co-authors of *Aging: Demographics, Health, and Health Services* (Greenwood Press, 2003).

Elizabeth Vierck is a well-known information specialist, analyst, and writer on aging, health and related topics. She is a widely published author with sixteen books and numerous other publications to her credit including health education publications, demographic and policy analyses, research reports, public information materials, and newsletters. Vierck is currently Senior Editor/Writer with the Society for Certified Senior Advisors.

Kris Hodges is a market research professional with more than 20 years of experience in survey and secondary data research. Currently, she provides freelance qualitative and quantitative research support for various clients and is a member of the Qualitative Research Consultants Association. Her analytical insights and industry perspective have added to the usability of the information presented in the book, especially in the area of finances, work, retirement, and consumer spending.